Disease and Discrimination

UNIVERSITY PRESS OF FLORIDA

Florida A&M University, Tallahassee
Florida Atlantic University, Boca Raton
Florida Gulf Coast University, Ft. Myers
Florida International University, Miami
Florida State University, Tallahassee
New College of Florida, Sarasota
University of Central Florida, Orlando
University of Florida, Gainesville
University of North Florida, Jacksonville
University of South Florida, Tampa
University of West Florida, Pensacola

Disease and Discrimination

Poverty and Pestilence in Colonial Atlantic America

DALE L. HUTCHINSON

UNIVERSITY PRESS OF FLORIDA

Gainesville / Tallahassee / Tampa / Boca Raton

Pensacola / Orlando / Miami / Jacksonville / Ft. Myers / Sarasota

This book may be available in an electronic edition.

First cloth printing, 2016
First paperback printing, 2019

24 23 22 21 20 19   6 5 4 3 2 1

Library of Congress Cataloging-in-Publication Data
Names: Hutchinson, Dale L., author.
Title: Disease and discrimination : poverty and pestilence in colonial
Atlantic America / Dale L. Hutchinson.
Description: Gainesville : University Press of Florida, [2016] | Includes
bibliographical references and index.
Identifiers: LCCN 2015048925 | ISBN 9780813062693 (cloth) |
ISBN 9780813064345 (pbk.)
Subjects: LCSH: Chronic diseases—United States—Psychological
aspects—History. | Poor—Health and hygiene—United States—History. |
Discrimination against people with disabilities—United States—History. |
Communicable diseases—United States—History. | Poverty—United
States—History. | Public health—United States—History.
Classification: LCC RA644.6 .H88 2016 | DDC 616/.044086942—dc23
LC record available at http://lccn.loc.gov/2015048925

The University Press of Florida is the scholarly publishing agency for the State
University System of Florida, comprising Florida A&M University, Florida
Atlantic University, Florida Gulf Coast University, Florida International
University, Florida State University, New College of Florida, University of
Central Florida, University of Florida, University of North Florida, University
of South Florida, and University of West Florida.

University Press of Florida
2046 NE Waldo Road
Suite 2100
Gainesville, FL 32609
http://upress.ufl.edu

Contents

FIGURES

MAPS

Tables

ACKNOWLEDGMENTS

The origin of most books, I suspect, is not located on a linear path. In fact, there is likely no single point on the path that is origin, but rather several points of a rather wandering journey. This is certainly such a book.

I should definitely thank a few people who have been helpful in my passage through that journey. Foremost, I thank my wife, Lorraine Aragon. In addition to the numerous insights that come daily from her keen intellect, she has consistently tried to divert to my scholarship some of the boldness I exhibit driving in crosstown traffic. Without the companionship I share with Lorraine and our son, Will, and without their guidance, I would certainly be a far less complete person.

Several people read chapters and gave me useful advice, including Anna Agbe-Davies, Amy Anderson, Sophia Dent, Kathleen DuVal, Robbie Ethridge, Van Gosse, Ashley Peles, Eliza Reilly, Mark Sorensen, and Amanda Thompson. Generations of students, first in a course titled Human Health and Disease Ecology at East Carolina University, and then in one titled Global Health at UNC Chapel Hill, have contributed observations, questions, and clarifications that refined my thoughts. As I grew closer to completing the book, I benefited from teaching a seminar course of the same title. Amy Anderson took that course, and later she read, edited, and offered comments on the entire manuscript. It would be a less-accessible book had she not done so. Likewise, Meredith Babb insisted that I "get beyond the box" for this book, and I thank her not only for that, but for her recommendations to read a few people who write less like professors. Two anonymous reviewers for the press identified many less-developed conversations, and I thank them for steering me to correcting those deficiencies. Finally, many of the maps and other illustrations were done by Susan Brannock-Gaul, with whom I've enjoyed many years of collaboration.

Grants to support my research and for many of the studies that led me to write these essays were provided over the years by the University of Illinois, East Carolina University, University of North Carolina, National Science Foundation, Wenner-Gren Foundation for Anthropological Research, and the Margaret-Cullinan Wray Trust Foundation.

Time and funding for writing, and space for thought, were provided by the College of Arts and Sciences, Department of Anthropology, the Research Laboratories of Archaeology, the Institute of Arts and Humanities, and the Center for the Study of the American South, all at the University of North Carolina at Chapel Hill. Other welcoming places to think and write have been the Chapel Hill Tennis Club and Weaver Street Market, both in Carrboro. Our cabin on the Pungo River in North Carolina has long provided a refuge from the hustle and bustle of city life, as well as a constant source of maintenance demands. While I sometimes grumble, repairs to it have often helped divert my attention from less immediately rewarding tasks.

Many of the arguments contained within this book were presented first in a manuscript coauthored with Lorraine Aragon and submitted to the journal *Current Anthropology* several years ago. While their rejection was painful, the arguments are better crafted and situated because of the comments of the reviewers.

Finally, to all of the readers, I thank you for thinking I might have something of interest to say—I hope you enjoy the book.

TIMELINE

Date	Northeast	New England	Chesapeake	Carolina
1500				
1525				
1534	First fur trade Cartier—Chaleur Bay, Nova Scotia			
1550				
1575				
1580	Fishing important industry by now			
1585			Roanoke established	
1599	Trading post at Tadoussac established			
1600				
1607			Jamestown Established	
1608	Quebec established			
1609–10	Dutch Hudson River fur trade begins		Starvation winter, Jamestown	
1614	Dutch Fort Nassau (Orange) established			

continued

Date	Northeast	New England	Chesapeake	Carolina
1616	1615 Recollects arrive		John Rolfe plants first tobacco	
1620		Plymouth established	1620–50 major immigration to Chesapeake	
1621–26			Typhoid epidemics, Jamestown	
1625	New Amsterdam established; Jesuits arrive—Saint Marie established			
1626	Yellow fever epidemic, NY			
1632			Maryland Established	
1634	Trois-Rivières established; measles epidemic	Measles, smallpox epidemics		
1636	Scarlet fever(?) epidemic			
1642	Montreal established			
1644–57	Ordinances issued in New Amsterdam against trash in street			
1650			Health has improved in Virginia	Virginia traders move into Carolina Piedmont
1659			1660–80 tobacco prices fall; land becomes scarce	Westos living by the Savanna River by now
1667			Smallpox epidemic Virginia	
1670				First ships arrive from Barbados; Charleston established

Date	Northeast	New England	Chesapeake	Carolina
1675	British forces capture New Amsterdam			Slavery common
1676	Influenza epidemic			
1691		Yellow fever epidemic, Boston	Slavery common	Rice developed as commodity
1693			Measles epidemic	Yellow fever epidemic, Charleston
1699			Virginia enacts closed deer-hunting season	
1700				
1711–13				Tuscarora War
1712–94	African burial ground, NYC			
1715–17				Yamasee War
1725				
1729–30			Maryland enacts closed deer hunting season	
1738				First record of Tidewater rice
1749			Virginia begins plans to move into Ohio Valley	
1750				Indigo begins; deer becoming scarce (Bartram)
1753	Forts Duquesne, Presque Isle, LeBoeuf, and Machault built in Ohio Valley			

continued

Date	Northeast	New England	Chesapeake	Carolina
1756–63				French and Indian War; Ends with Treaty of Paris that enables deerskin trading with Creeks, Cherokees
1768				NC passes hunting legislation
1772			Virginia enacts four-year deer-hunting ban	
1775				
1777		Washington has Continental Army inoculated for smallpox		
1785				SC fire and night deer-hunting ban
1793		Major yellow fever epidemic, Philadelphia		
1800				
1825				
1832	Cholera epidemic, NYC			
1842	Croton aqueduct—first public water system, NYC			
1850	Underground sewage system, NYC			
1875				
1900				
1918	Influenza epidemic	Influenza epidemic	Influenza epidemic	Influenza epidemic

Prologue

In the year 1348 after the fruitful incarnation of the Son of God, that most beautiful of Italian cities, noble Florence, was attacked by deadly plague. It started in the East either through the influence of the heavenly bodies or because God's just anger with our wicked deeds sent it as a punishment to mortal men; and in a few years killed an innumerable quantity of people. Carelessly passing from place to place, it extended its miserable length over the West. . . . So violent was the malignancy of this plague that it was communicated, not only from one man to another, but from the garments of the sick or dead man to animals of another species, which caught the disease in that way and very quickly died of it. One day among other occasions I saw with my own eyes (as I said just now) the rags left lying in the street of a poor man who had died of the plague; two pigs came along and, as their habit is, turned the clothes over with their snouts and then munched at them, with the result they both fell dead almost at once on the rags, as if they had been poisoned.

Giovanni Boccaccio, *The Decameron*

Plague-stricken Europe is portrayed even more graphically in the 1989 film *The Navigator: A Medieval Oddysey.*[1] Amidst a backdrop of carts filled with bodies of the dead, and roads filled with those who are fleeing cities, Connor returns to the village from the outside world. He brings news of an evil force, and the villagers decide to meet that night and discuss their options. One villager offers up a vision received—a delegation is to go to a distant church seen in the vision and erect a cross on the spire in order to end the epidemic. Connor does not embrace this plan, and he speaks of his experiences in the outside world.

I've seen pilgrims, Martin. I've seen so many bodies, there weren't enough livin' to bury them. I've seen mobs chasin' monks from their abbeys for refusin' last rites to dying. You can trust no one. Children . . . begged me for food. I didn't dare go near 'em. They had black boils under their armpits ready to burst, and still they denied the plague was on them. All the churches are empty, and, still not satisfied, the evil keeps striding forward with each full moon. We've got a month, maybe two, with a scrap of God's grace.

Suddenly, one of the villagers cries out a warning as a small ship filled with refugees from the east attempts a nocturnal landing. The villagers intercede and, pushing the ship away from the shore with long poles, they fire burning arrows into the sails. The pilgrims try to reach shore, but the poles keep pushing—pushing—pushing. Women and children on the ship are desperate, but the poles prevail. Under a full moon, the crowd gathered on the rocks watches the ship far out in the water, completely on fire.

This vision of disease epidemics, capitalizing on rampant death, invincible pathogens, widespread panic, and helpless victimization, is a common one. In only a few short years, the Black Death became the very model of the power of pestilence, a model where pestilence can eradicate nation-states and chisel away at the civilized world. Yet during the Black Death the people of Europe did not vanish. Yes, lots of people died; but European society recovered and went on, albeit somewhat changed.

The central premise in this book is that any depiction of Europe, or the Americas, or anywhere else assaulted by "invincible" pathogens, leaves out many less-apparent details, dramatizing the effects at the expense of understanding the causes. There are many misunderstandings about how people acquire pathogens and become ill. Disease, the actual outcome of infection, is only a small part of the story. Numerous social, political, economic, and ecological influences guide the possibility and the path of infection. *Diseases are processes, not things, and they exist within an ecological and social context.* In order to understand the influence of disease on populations, we must understand the conditions under which infection occurs and endangers health.

PART I

Of Apples and Edens

1

The Transformation of Native America

In respect of us they are a people poor, and for want of skill and judgement in the knowledge of our things, do esteem our trifles before things of greater value: Notwithstanding in their proper manner considering the want of such means as we have, they seeme very ingenious; For although they have no such tools, nor any such crafts, sciences and artes as we; yet in those things they do, they show excellence of wit. And by how much they upon due consideration shall find our manner of knowledges and crafts to exceed theirs in perfection and speed for doing or execution, by so much the more is it probable that they should desire our friendships and love, and have the greater respect for pleasing and obeying us. Whereby may be hoped if means of good judgement be, that they may in short time be brought to civilty, and the embracing of true religion.

Thomas Hariot, *A Briefe and True Report of the New Found Land of Virginia*

On a slightly chilly Sunday, I stood with my family for an hour and a half as we waited to see an exhibit of John White's paintings and drawings on loan from the British Museum. White and a few others brought to Europe the first glimpses of the animals, plants, and people of the Americas at the time of initial contact between two very different worlds. The title "Mysteries of the Lost Colony" had drawn thousands, but I was there to see firsthand the art I know so well.

For those of you who have never seen a John White watercolor, it is an experience somewhat like smelling the first sweet scent of spring flowers, or tasting a perfectly harvested forest mushroom sautéed with slight hints of garlic and beef. His sensual attention to detail, the provocative feathers and fins, makes seeing his art an experience that lasts for years (Figures 1.1–1.5).

My favorite White paintings include the Algonkian village of Secoton

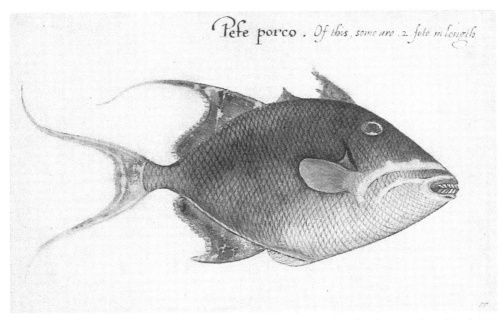

Figure 1.1. *Pefe porco* (Queen Trigger-Fish). Painting by John White and used with permission of the British Museum of Natural History (© The Trustees of the British Museum; Museum number 1906,0509.1.55).

with several small scenes contained within, the palisaded village of Pomeiock (Pomeiooc), a scene of natives fishing with a weir, and the depiction of two insects, so deftly characterized by White. The captions for the last one are "A flye which in the night semeth a flame of fyer" and "A dangerous byting flye." Theodore de Bry, a sixteenth-century Belgian engraver, engraved several of White's drawings from Virginia, as well as those made by Jacques Le Moyne de Morgues, a French Huguenot who was present in the short-lived French settlement of 1562–65 in Florida. DeBry's engravings and White's drawings provide a rich visual image of the people who inhabited the Atlantic coast.[1]

As with all art, though, the early images of America are filtered through the eyes and interpretive lens of the artist. For most artists of the early Americas, almost anything they encountered was novel, and their choice to depict people's appearance, or architecture, or plants, or animals, was partially their personal preference—what caught their eye, so to speak. Imagine walking with your camera while traveling in a new place. It is spring and a particular flower has a wonderful, almost iridescent purple color in the sunlight. It is with five or six similar flowers among an entire field of white daisies. You adjust your focal length so that the purple flow-

Within the image the following inscriptions appear:

Their rype corne

Their greene corne.

Corne newly sproing

Their sitting at meate

prayer

the place of solemne prayer

The house wherin the Tombe of their Herounds standeth.

SECOTON.

A Ceremony in their prayers wt strange iestures and soings dansing abowt postts carued on the topps lyke mens faces.

Figure 1.2. *The Towne of Secoton*. Painting by John White and used with permission of the British Museum of Natural History (© The Trustees of the British Museum; Museum number 1906,0509.1.7).

Figure 1.3. *The Manner of Their Fishing* (Indians Fishing). Painting by John White and used with permission of the British Museum of Natural History (© The Trustees of the British Museum; Museum number 1906.0509.1.6).

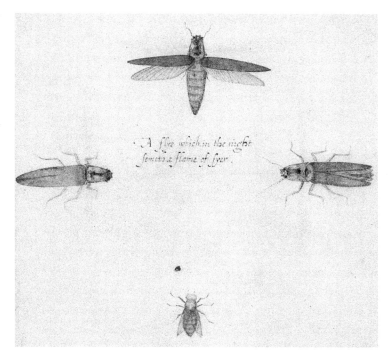

A flye which in the night semeth a flame of fyer.

Figure 1.4. *Fireflies and Gadfly*. Painting by John White and used with permission of the British Museum of Natural History (© The Trustees of the British Museum; Museum number 1906,0509.1.67).

Figure 1.5. *The Towne of Pomeiooc*. Painting by John White and used with permission of the British Museum of Natural History (© The Trustees of the British Museum; Museum number 1906,0509.1.8).

ers are the point of focus, with the other plants slightly out of focus in the background. Another time, or day, the sunlight might be different, or you might choose to set the focus on the surrounding plants, or you might photograph instead an insect on the plants. You assign your prized photograph a caption on social media that says *Spring in Virginia*. At least some viewers will assume it is a common scene, not one that happens to be rather rare. A painting of the scene would allow for even more artistic liberties, such as including plants not actually in the scene being viewed.

We have come to realize that, in much the same way, the early art of the New World contains more than simple images of the people and things encountered by early explorers and colonists. It contains misconceptions, misrepresentations, propaganda, and perhaps even lies.[2] What complicates things is that we want to believe the pictures. Without them we have no images of the early Americas.

Accuracy is always a problem when dealing with representations of the past and, for that matter, of the present. It is often unclear whether the information is witnessed firsthand or comes from another source. Did the author have a stake in the portrayal of the "facts" and outcome reported? How much did the author really know about the subjects and events portrayed? Was a report made shortly after the incidents that occurred, or years later?

Archaeological remains suffer from the same problems of accuracy—usually only a portion of the original materials is preserved, or the remains represent accumulations over long time periods, or the original context has been either accidentally or purposefully altered. No matter what, depictions of the past are probably biased in some fashion. Like the visual art presented through the lens of the artist, historical documents and archaeological remains present only one view of a past situation, one snapshot. The view is not complete, and whether by conscious intent or accidental preservation, only some of the original content and context is present.

The problems of interpretation go even deeper, though. Whether visual art, historical documents, or archaeological remains, those snapshots go through a second translative lens—that of the observer—and the translation occurs in a different time, place, and cultural context. The original context is literally re-created. Consequently, we need to be careful in making our translations. We need to consider as many sources as possible, recognizing that each source offers particular strengths and weaknesses, and that each source represents an incomplete and possibly distorted picture of the events, processes, and details portrayed. We hope the sources complement each other and fill in the gaps that each possesses.

Just prior to the sixteenth century, somewhere between 900,000 and 18,000,000 people inhabited the Americas, north and south. There is a lot of disagreement on how many native people there actually were at the time of European arrival, partly because of the relative absence of written documents, and partly because of the events that occurred later.[3] Despite disagreement about the actual numbers, though, we know that sometime after 1492 a few European explorers and potential colonizers began slowly to drift into the Americas. Their advance was often made from the Caribbean islands, where for the first two decades or so, Spaniards mined for gold and established sugar plantations. In that short period, native populations were decimated, and landscapes changed. Then, Europeans slowly reached the long yardarms of their sails outward from the islands and planned their next territorial advance.

In 1519 Hernan Cortés marched with a substantial army into the Valley of Mexico with the intent of rapidly subduing the native inhabitants there. He was in for a surprise. In one of the largest assaults on the capital city of Tenochtitlan, the famed *Noche Triste* (sad night), the Aztecs sent the conquistadors running. But then something unexpected happened. Another Spaniard, Pánfilo de Narváez, arrived with orders to arrest Cortés and return him to Spain. The king, Philip, was worried about Cortés' defection from the Spanish crown. The story goes that one of Narváez' men had contracted smallpox while in the Caribbean, and thus it was introduced to the natives of Mexico. Smallpox, it is said, became the true conqueror.

Historic accounts by the Spanish are particularly powerful at presenting the impact of smallpox on the Aztecs:

> Those who did survive, having scratched themselves, were left in such a condition that they frightened the others with the many deep pits on their faces, hands and bodies. And then came famine, not because of want of bread, but of meal, for the women do nothing but grind maize between two stones and bake it. The women, then, fell sick of the smallpox, bread failed, and many died of hunger. The corpses stank so horribly that no one would bury them; the streets were filled with them.[4]

Another description of the same epidemic from Cortés' own hand evokes a picture of massive mortality:

> The people of the city had to walk upon their dead while others swam or drowned in the waters of that wide lake where they had their canoes; indeed, so great was their suffering that it was beyond our understanding how they could endure it. . . . And so in those streets where they were we came across such piles of the dead that we were forced to walk upon them.[5]

In the following decades, smallpox and a series of other new diseases accompanied the advance of Spaniards through Central and South America. Some people think they may have spread farther and faster than the conquistadors north and east into North America. A common depiction is that they cut through native populations like a scythe reaping the nonimmune.[6] It is often said that within a hundred years most natives in the Americas had died.

The problems with that depiction are multiple. For one, the limited historic accounts for the first hundred years are based on a mixture of first-hand experience and that which comes from others, often distant in space and time. Think of the childhood game of "telephone," where the details become more distorted with each new relay of information. The second problem is that measuring native population loss is difficult when the original population numbers are actually not known. Some scholars of the native "demise" actually assume a percentage population loss based on estimates of mortality due to new diseases and add it to the estimates for the original population number.[7] Most egregiously, the assumption that new diseases universally affected populations across America projects the same disease transmission rate, population structure, housing design, and so on. It assumes the conditions of disease are the same for everyone, everywhere. And it just ain't so. Just as with the art of de Bry, not all of the details are the same everywhere. Native settlements varied from those with dispersed small structures to those with immense longhouses to those with clustered cliff dwellings. Some populations were relatively sedentary, while others were highly mobile; some lived in coastal regions, some far inland.

This book is a series of narratives about the changing landscapes of America—not only the natural landscapes, but the social, political, and economic landscapes—and how they all contributed to the nutrition and health of natives and newcomers in the Atlantic coastal colonies. The narratives are neither exhaustive nor completely factual representations. Rather, like a painter or photographer, I have chosen what to accentuate. There are omissions that come with such an approach. For instance, I did not include Spanish Florida, because it would involve another colonial empire and its associated histories and strategies of colonization. I have tried to present accurate depictions of how certain processes and events likely influenced health outcomes, by discussing not so much what did happen, but the environmental, political, and social dynamics that put certain subsets of the population at risk for suffering from malnutrition or disease.

As an anthropologist, I tend to see people's lives and the web of relationships in which they are situated from multiple perspectives, and those multiple perspectives require multiple sources of information.[8] I began with the issues raised by the early White paintings and de Bry engravings, because materials reporting on the past always tell only part of a story. The first images of the New World were created within a specific historical, political, social, and economic context. They are based on limited information, because Europeans were unaccustomed to much in this new place. Try to imagine a Joseph Cornell box. Cornell made these wonderful boxes in the early to mid-1900s. They were simple shadow boxes, sides and backs with glass fronts, and in them he would arrange found objects that he felt belonged with each other. To some degree, what is preserved in the art depicting the early Americas is like Cornell boxes, filled with novel New World items and displayed within a European sixteenth-century social and political template.

Thinking about art, about depiction and translation and interpretation, is a very useful exercise. One of my favorite paintings is *The Peaceable Kingdom* by Edward Hicks (Figure 1.6). I have revisited it for years, and I have continued to learn from it. When I was young, I loved to sit and look at the animals. I'd try and understand the relationship of the other animals to the humans, and what the humans and the other animals were doing. At some point it struck me, as I leafed through books from the public library, that the animals and humans kept shifting on the page and recreating the scene with different stances and positions. Details changed in the paintings. In my adolescent years, it was as if the pictures were telling me a story as it unfolded.

It turns out that there are 62 known versions of *The Peaceable Kingdom*, all painted by Edward Hicks. Hicks, who was a Quaker, used the paintings to communicate what he saw as growing disharmony among the Quakers.

Figure 1.6. *The Peaceable Kingdom*, 1834, Edward Hicks. Courtesy National Gallery of Art, Washington.

My favorite version, not the one depicted here, is one attributed to 1846–48 (sometimes called *The Peaceable Kingdom with the Leopard of Serenity*). I find the animals in this one quite vivid. The humans, which in some versions are just other animals on the landscape, take on special symbolic meaning. There is a woman with a dove on one hand, the symbol of peace. Her other hand strokes an eagle, America rising. On the left side, one child covers a hole with her hand. The other child holds a serpent. What I didn't fully appreciate until the other day in any of the versions is the scene to the left that clearly depicts someone, probably William Penn, signing a treaty with the Indians. In some versions, a European landing party offloads supplies at the shore.

I have read that Edward Hicks was deeply troubled by divisions among the Quakers, and that this made him acutely aware of the struggles of many to define their place on earth, and their relationships to other people and beings. Like Hicks, in this respect I am deeply troubled by the picture of native populations in the Americas decimated by invincible pathogens. Such a picture separates germs from the contexts in which they proliferate, become transmitted, and cause disease. It deprives them of their relationships to other organisms, and natural and artificial settings, and events that changed all of those things.

The fact is that most scholars interested in postcontact native population trends agree that native populations reached their lowest point sometime around 1850, not a hundred years after initial contact. The question is: "What happened in those 300 years after initial contact, and how did the events during that time contribute to changes in nutrition and health?"

Instead of focusing on the first century of colonization and the entry of new germs, we must examine the dynamic environmental and social interactions that shaped, altered, and created the Americas that emerged in the twentieth century. The assertion by Jared Diamond in his book *Guns, Germs, and Steel* that "far more Native Americans and other non-Eurasian peoples were killed by Eurasian germs than by Eurasian guns or steel weapons" separates germs from the ecological and behavioral context in which they cause sickness.[9] In fact, one cannot understand the impact of Eurasian germs without understanding how diseases in Europe came to exist as they did and by also considering the concomitant role of Eurasian guns and steel weapons.

2

Of Plagues and Peoples

And I looked, and beheld a pale horse: and his name that sat on him was
Death, and Hell followed with him. And power was given unto them over the
fourth part of the earth, to kill with sword, and with hunger, and with death,
and with the beasts of the earth.

The Holy Bible, King James Version, Revelation 6:8

One cannot understand the changing disease patterns of America without
first understanding the history of health and disease in Eurasia and what
factors contributed to the development of disease patterns there. It is the
place where at least some of the diseases new to the Americas originated.
It probably would be best to start with a short conversation about disease
ecology, which is not so much a discipline as it is a way of looking at things,
of appreciating the relationships between organisms and landscapes.

Disease ecologists speak of landscapes broadly. Natural environments
figure prominently, but so do those modified and created by humans, the
so-called built environments. How humans choose the landscapes they use
and inhabit, how they modify those landscapes, and how and when they use
them all influence the continuity and transmission of infectious diseases, as
well as the prevalence of noninfectious diseases. Transmission is essential
in disease cycles. The use of landscapes by multiple species figures into
those transmission cycles, and the when-where-how of infectious disease
transmission cycles extends beyond people to pets, pests, and pathogens. In
fact, transmission cycles are affected beyond biological organisms to habitats, climates, and inanimate objects; and so one can define landscapes of
disease or epidemiological landscapes (epidemiologists study what causes
disease outbreaks with an orientation toward disease prevention) as the

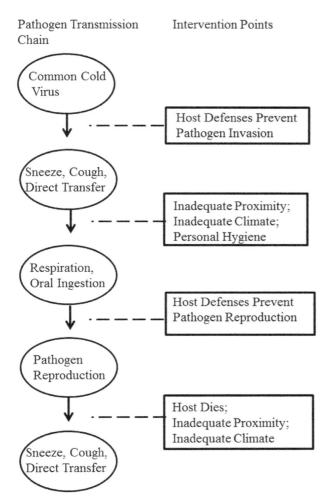

Pathogen Transmission Chain   Intervention Points

Common Cold Virus

→ — — — Host Defenses Prevent Pathogen Invasion

Sneeze, Cough, Direct Transfer

→ — — — Inadequate Proximity; Inadequate Climate; Personal Hygiene

Respiration, Oral Ingestion

→ — — — Host Defenses Prevent Pathogen Reproduction

Pathogen Reproduction

→ — — — Host Dies; Inadequate Proximity; Inadequate Climate

Sneeze, Cough, Direct Transfer

Figure 2.1. Disease transmission cycle for the common cold, a directly transmitted disease. Chart prepared by Dale Hutchinson.

complex overlaps of environments, behaviors, and biological organisms that contribute to disease (Figures 2.1–2.3).

There are many organisms and many ways in which organisms use other organisms. A few terms will facilitate the rest of our discussions. A *parasite* is any living thing that lives in or on another living thing. A *pathogen* is a microorganism that parasitizes an animal or plant (a host) and causes host tissue damage (disease)—*germ* is a common name for a pathogen. *Hosts* are organisms that provide some life-cycle support for parasites. *Vectors* are organisms and devices that facilitate the transfer of

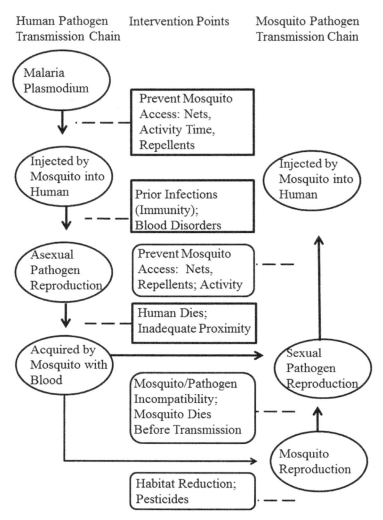

Human Pathogen   Intervention Points   Mosquito Pathogen
Transmission Chain   Transmission Chain

Malaria Plasmodium

Prevent Mosquito Access: Nets, Activity Time, Repellents

Injected by Mosquito into Human

Injected by Mosquito into Human

Prior Infections (Immunity); Blood Disorders

Asexual Pathogen Reproduction

Prevent Mosquito Access: Nets, Repellents; Activity

Human Dies; Inadequate Proximity

Acquired by Mosquito with Blood

Sexual Pathogen Reproduction

Mosquito/Pathogen Incompatibility; Mosquito Dies Before Transmission

Mosquito Reproduction

Habitat Reduction; Pesticides

Figure 2.2. Disease transmission cycle for malaria, a biologically vectored disease. Chart prepared by Dale Hutchinson.

the pathogen from one host to another. There are *biological vectors* that are essential to some part of the pathogen's life cycle (e.g., the *Anopheles* mosquito), and *mechanical vectors*, those that simply carry the pathogen from one place to another (e.g., flies). Rivers, ambulances, and hospital workers can all be mechanical vectors as well. Survival and reproduction are necessary for all those organisms (hosts, vectors, pathogens), and there is a fair amount of interdependence involved. A *zoonosis* is a disease that cycles primarily among nonhuman hosts. *Prevalence* refers to the number

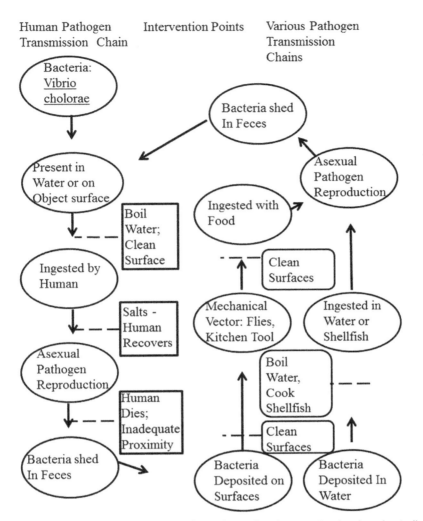

Human Pathogen Transmission Chain

Bacteria: Vibrio cholorae

Present in Water or on Object surface

Ingested by Human

Asexual Pathogen Reproduction

Bacteria shed In Feces

Intervention Points

Boil Water; Clean Surface

Salts - Human Recovers

Human Dies; Inadequate Proximity

Various Pathogen Transmission Chains

Bacteria shed In Feces

Asexual Pathogen Reproduction

Ingested with Food

Clean Surfaces

Mechanical Vector: Flies, Kitchen Tool

Ingested in Water or Shellfish

Boil Water, Cook Shellfish

Clean Surfaces

Bacteria Deposited on Surfaces

Bacteria Deposited In Water

Figure 2.3. Disease transmission cycle for cholera, a directly transmitted and mechanically vectored disease. Chart prepared by Dale Hutchinson.

of cases (people) affected by a disease. An *endemic* disease is one that is constantly present, while an *epidemic* disease occurs at levels beyond those expected. A disease is *pandemic* when it reaches global spread.

In a contemporary example of a disease ecology approach, Edward Michelson and his colleagues examined predisposing factors in the contraction of schistosomiasis among several previously studied populations.[1] Schistosomiasis, also known as bilharzia, is a disease caused by parasitic worms. The worms spend two segments of their life cycle in freshwater snails, and it is through water contact that people are exposed to the infectious parasite. More than 200 million people in the world are affected by schistosomiasis, making it second only to malaria in number of people impacted globally by an infectious disease. The free-swimming larval form of the parasite, the *cercariae*, penetrate the skins of people in the water and then migrate to the liver to mature into adults. There the adults mate, migrate to the bowel and/or rectum, and produce eggs, which are shed back into the water.

The cycle of reproduction thus involves water, temperature, snails, humans, and water contact. Michelson found, in a marvelous unfolding of the factors involved in the disease cycle, that rates of infection differed between men and women, and that the patterns of infection are linked to who spends more time in the water, and when they spend that time. For instance, in the populations in question, there was a marked sexual division of labor. Women tend to do more washing of utensils and clothes, whereas men tend to have water contact through farming, fishing, and basket weaving. Those activities occur at different times of day, which affects how much chance there is for transmission of the parasite. For two species, *Schistosoma mansoni* and *Schistosoma haematobium*, the time when the most *cercariae* are active in the water is between one and three o'clock in the afternoon. For a third, *Schistosoma japonicum*, it is after sunset. This study noted that women tend to wash clothes in the morning, when the cercarial density is low. Cultural restrictions regarding water contact reduces the chances of infection for women. In particular, in Muslim communities ritual ablutions are required of males several times a day, while bathing opportunities for women are severely restricted. Thus, behavior *and* ecology are important factors in schistosomiasis infection.

One of the landmark books that explains the history and context of disease change in Eurasia is William H. McNeill's *Plagues and Peoples*. McNeill carefully outlines how the major trends in agriculture and increasing migration between state-level societies led to disease epidemics. McNeill's perspective takes into account not only the germs that cause disease, but the social, economic, political, and ecological settings in which those germs occur, and it is there that we must turn our attention to appreciate the intricate details.

Agriculture, the production of and increased reliance on domesticated plants and animals, was associated with many changes in behavior and alterations of environment. Agriculture stimulated a trend toward the built environment through landscape alterations such as cleared fields, terraces, raised fields, ridged fields, and irrigation complexes. Fields and irrigation complexes, especially raised fields and wet rice fields, created aquatic habitats for the reproduction of mosquitoes and other insects (arthropod vectors) that transmit germs.

Agriculture was associated as well with permanent (sedentary) residence, larger and more aggregated urban populations, houses, courtyards, public buildings, and plazas for large community gatherings. Those all necessitated paths and roads. Domesticated animals served as labor and transport, in addition to being sources of food and other by-products. They tended to be kept in close proximity to humans, sometimes in separate outbuildings, sometimes under elevated houses.

Agriculture and sedentary residence brought about the first major transition in human health patterns. Quite simply, moving about the landscape periodically as a forager reduces several problems. For one, short-term use of resources such as plants, animals, and water tends to lessen overuse and contamination. Human wastes tend to be more dispersed. Population size is smaller. Once people stop moving around so much, human wastes pile up, and with more people there are more piles. Bring domestic animals into the landscape, and the piles get even bigger. With piles there are often parasites, especially those of intestinal nature—worms and the like.

Larger populations packed into smaller spaces enable the spread of crowd diseases, diseases that are transmitted directly. Crowd diseases need an adequate population level to ensure continuous transmission, as well as a steady supply of those who are not immune to maintain it. They are often diseases of childhood where the infectious stages are brief, and they spread quickly: influenza, smallpox, mumps, measles, and chicken pox. Those diseases exist entirely by rapid transmission from one host to another. They generally cannot survive in small populations and thus are among the so-called diseases of civilization.

From both archaeological excavations and historic texts, we know that agriculture and urbanism began as early as 10,000 B.C. in the Middle East, and that similar trends occurred by 500 B.C. in China, India/Pakistan, and the Mediterranean region.[2] In those four regions agriculture was accompanied by the transition from mobile to sedentary populations. Aggregation, combined with agricultural landscape change, enabled the development of what McNeill termed "civilized disease pools."[3] Each civilized disease pool shared the common characteristics described above for agriculture and permanent villages but retained some unique characters as well.

Among the diseases present in early Egypt were tuberculosis, smallpox, malaria, bilharzia, intestinal tapeworms, and chronic growth arrests. Chinese populations in northern China experienced a dramatic decline in community health after 5,000 B.P., as indicated by stature reduction and increased prevalence of anemia indicators. The same increased prevalence of anemia indicators associated with an increased dietary focus on domesticated plants is present for Neolithic Greek populations. Further, indicators of increased workload and trauma are found during the period from 5,000 to 3,200 B.C. in Greece.[4]

Beginning in the fifth century A.D., those separate civilized disease pools were united through mercantilism, migration, colonial expansion, and warfare. Particularly important was the Silk Road across Asia, which between 100 B.C. and A.D. 1500 transformed previously isolated geographic localities into stepping stones across Eurasia. Running between Jiuquan, China, in the east, and the Roman Empire (Antioch) in the west, the Silk Road brought populations into contact via the caravans that traversed the route. Plague and several other diseases were likely transported beyond their original foci into other areas through the increased traffic that moved hosts, vectors, and pathogens across the vast space of several empires.[5]

It was during intensification of trade with central Asia along the Silk Road that the first major outbreak of plague occurred in the Mediterranean during the Justinian Wars. Known as the Justinian Plague, it ravaged Mediterranean populations from A.D. 541 to 542, and appeared intermittently until A.D. 750. Procopius describes the epidemic with great care and observation:

> Some doctors were at a loss because the symptoms were unfamiliar to them and, believing that the focus of the disease was to be found in the bubos, decided to investigate the bodies of the dead. Cutting into some of the bubos, they found that a kind of malignant carbuncle had developed inside. . . . In cases where the bubos grew very large and discharged pus, the patients overcame the disease and survived, as it was clear that for them the eruption of the carbuncle found relief

in this way; for the most part, this was a sign of health. But in cases where the bubos remained in the same condition, these patients had to endure all of the misfortunes that I just described [madness, quick death].[6]

Procopius also describes the breakdown of normal conditions and the chaos that follows in the wake of epidemic disease:

And when the existing graves were full of dead bodies, at first they dug up all the open sites in the city, one after another, placed the dead in there, each person as he could, and departed. But later those who were digging these ditches could no longer keep up with the number of those dying, and they climbed up the towers of the fortified enclosure, the one in Sykai, tore off the roofs, and tossed the bodies in there in a tangled heap. . . . All of the customs of burial were overlooked at that time. For the dead were neither escorted by a procession in the customary way nor were they accompanied by chanting, as was usual; rather, it was enough if a person carried one of the dead on his shoulders to a place where the city met the sea and throw him down; and there they were thrown down into barges in a pile and taken to who knows where.[7]

The Mongol military campaigns further transected immense spaces of Europe and Asia at fast speed and transformed the political and epidemiological landscape of Eurasia between A.D. 1200 and 1370. The best-known of the early Eurasian epidemics, the Black Death, was connected to the Mongols, but it cannot be understood without considering the context of both the pre-plague years and the behavior of humans during the epidemic.

In the mid-thirteenth century, social and climatic changes in western Europe resulted in crop failures and famine.[8] During the 1290s Europe was struck by another series of famines. Conditions deteriorated even further between A.D. 1300 and 1347 when a succession of crop failures and food shortages continued; they would not come to an end until after the Black Death. From 1316 until 1322 a series of livestock epidemics decimated what remained of Europe's cattle population. The pattern of crop failures continued until bubonic plague began to expand throughout Eurasia.

In 1345 Mongol troops led by Janibeg Khan had besieged Genoese trading merchants at their fortified trading post at Caffa on the Black Sea intermittently for two years. Most information about the set of events that occurred then and followed comes from an account by the Italian Gabriele de' Mussi, written sometime around 1348. De' Mussi's narrative asserts that in 1345 an epidemic of plague broke out in the Mongol troops. Seeing how many casualties the disease took, the Mongol commander decided to use it as a weapon to bring the siege of the city of Caffa to an end. In what some have interpreted as the first act of biological warfare, he began to catapult the diseased corpses over the city walls and waited for the disease to finish the conquest.[9] It did, and from Caffa in 1346 the Black Death spread via Genoese merchants along sea routes to the Mediterranean ports of southern Europe, then north through Spain and France, east into Germany, and across the English Channel to the British Isles. By 1348 most of France and Switzerland was affected by plague, which soon reached the southern coasts of England, Germany, Sweden, Poland, and, later, Russia.

Those affected had black swellings in the armpits and groin that oozed blood and pus, and they died within a few days. The disease has generally been attributed to bubonic plague, and it spread rapidly from village to village, and country to country. The only recourse was flight, especially away from the crowded spaces of urban centers, and that was available only to those of financial means. Reports of fields and streets full of rotting corpses were common.

In the fourteenth century, rats and fleas were not known to be the vehicles of transmission. Earthquakes were blamed instead, as were "foul winds" and the wrath of God. Because so many thought the plague was brought about by the wrath of God, penitents sprang up; they implored mercy, sometimes with ropes around their necks, sometimes beating themselves with whips. Efforts to cope with the plague were many and varied. Smudge pots lined streets and gates into cities—the aromatic substances they effused were thought to purify the air. Bleeding, purgative enemas, compounds of various herbs and powdered minerals were administered, to no avail.

By the time the plague ended in 1352, by one estimate a third of Europe had died: roughly 24 million people.[10] No one really knows how many died, but the Black Death left an enduring vision of epidemics as phantom forces sweeping across vast tracts of land, possessing an urgency of time, and imparting utter certainty that once a village was affected, death could come for anyone, at any moment.

The very foundations of the Middle Ages were torn away by the Black

Death and replaced with new economic and social power for peasants, and loss of power for the church and nobility.[11] Peasants, who undoubtedly suffered the greater loss of population numbers, saw an increased sense of their value, both social and financial, as their relative importance was realized and their wages increased. The nobility suffered less mortality, but since the pattern of inheritance was more important to the nobility than to the peasants, the biological crisis was more severe for nobles. Given the high infant mortality rates during the Middle Ages, it was already difficult to produce an heir. The plague only made the situation worse, and the failure of noble families to produce heirs meant a continual shuffling of power, as old families died out and new ones replaced them.

One response to this tremendous fluidity was a renewed emphasis by the older families on the importance of knightly ritual. Great exhibitions, largely attended by people in ceremonial dress, were held among prestigious knightly orders such as the Golden Fleece. Another response, although less common, was a retreat for the lords toward grace and courtesy. Dozens of books were published on grace and etiquette, and the disdain the nobility felt for the manual laborers and merchants was reflected in these texts. It was essential that the disfranchised, in whatever ways possible, remained so in order that the nobility remain firmly entrenched in the control of economic, social, and political power.

The maintenance and transmission of the plague goes far beyond climatic shifts, crop failure, and human migration, to include host, vector, pathogen, and ecological relationships. A Russian medical geographer, Evgeny Pavlovsky, unraveled the marvelous ecology of plague in the 1930s. Pavlovsky discovered that plague bacteria circulated within a complex web of relationships that Pavlovsky termed a "natural nidus."[12]

The natural nidus for plague exists as follows. Plague is a rodent zoonosis transmitted by fleas. *Yersinia pestis*, the bacterial agent of bubonic plague, circulates continually among rodents living in the Central Asian grasslands, as it has done for centuries. The rodents live in deep burrows with a variety of arthropod inhabitants, such as flies, fleas, and roaches. The rodents show no symptoms and are not bothered by the ancient infection.

The landscape of the rodent communities is influential in their survival. The slope of the land affects flooding during rains, and there must be the right kinds of vegetation for the rats to eat, and a certain mix of predators and competitors to keep the population regulated. Undoubtedly, human foragers would occasionally wander into the nidus and become accidental hosts for the disease, much in the same way that Lyme disease or hantavirus have been accidental human infections.

The ecology of plague in European cities is as complicated as the ecology of plague in its natural setting. Space in medieval cities was at a premium. The streets were narrow and unpaved. Chamber pots were often emptied from upper-story windows. Water supplies were generally polluted, and other beverages such as beer usually took the place of water. Houses were dark, with dirt floors. Food was often stored in or near houses. Not surprisingly, there were several other household inhabitants besides humans, including huge urban black rat (*Rattus rattus*) populations.[13]

Unlike the Russian steppe rodents, black rats are especially susceptible to the bubonic plague, and in plague epidemics they die in great numbers. In fact, rat corpses probably numbered greater than humans, leaving hungry fleas looking for other blood meals. As with many disease vectors, there is a complicated ecology. The vector has to be able not only to move the pathogen from host to host but also in some cases to keep it alive. Any incompatibility results in nontransmission.

Two of the more historically important vectors are the Oriental rat flea, *Xenopsylla cheopis,* and the human flea *Pulex irritans. X. cheopis* is an especially efficient vector, because a bend in its feeding tube, or proventriculus, creates a location for growth of the plague pathogen *Yersinia pestis*, such that the proventriculus becomes blocked, and the flea, unable to swallow a full blood meal, becomes thirsty. Attempting to dislodge the wad of infected material and quench its thirst, the flea desperately infects multiple new mammalian hosts. Other fleas clear the pathogen more quickly. Equally important is vector behavior—both of these flea species will feed on humans, while many other species will not.

Sometime after 1500 a combination of factors brought about a reduction in European plague rates. One factor was that quite simply the rat population changed. The brown rat, *Rattus norwegicus*, also a migrant from Asia, displaced the black rat. Brown rats preferred to live away from humans and inhabited sewers and other places where they and their fleas avoided people. Other factors helped end plague epidemics. Climate improved, contributing to better crop yields and thus better nutrition, and improved housing lessened crowding.

Modern historians and specialists in historical epidemiology have struggled with several inconsistencies in the picture of the Black Death presented in the last few pages. It seemed to spread too quickly for bubonic plague. As a warm-weather disease, its high mortality during the winter months doesn't fit the normal pattern of the disease. Both of those issues have led some to ask if the principal causative agent was *Yersinia pestis* or perhaps either a different disease or multiple diseases. The transmission of the Black Death has often been linked to trade routes, but there is considerable variation in the magnitude of mortality, with some trade cities (e.g., Milan) hardly affected. Oscillations in the temporal and geographic pattern suggest there may have been multiple introductions of infectious disease agents. Other conditions, such as climate, may have been more influential than previously perceived.[14]

Current information suggests a number of revisions to the classic picture of the Black Death of 1346–52. In addition to detailed analysis of historical documents, several medieval cemeteries that are purported to contain victims of the Black Death have been discovered and excavated.[15] Molecular studies conducted over the past couple of decades indicate that people buried in medieval grave sites in the Netherlands, Germany, Italy, France, and England have at least two distinct clades of *Yersinia pestis*.[16] Those molecular studies indicate that there was not a single introduction of the plague. A study of climatic fluctuations also indicates that there was not a single introduction of the plague, but that it was introduced multiple times, and that wild rodent populations were likely impacted by climatic fluctuations and involved in the process.[17] Multiple issues regarding plague transmission mechanisms, including the vectors involved and whether rats could have been intermediate hosts, indicate that there may have been pneumonic as well as bubonic plague.[18] It would seem at the moment that the conditions under which the Black Death of A.D. 1346–52 embraced Europe were extremely varied.

Plague continues to be resident in rodent burrows, where it is maintained through generations of rodents, often as a chronic disease. In fact, the tourist to the southwestern United States often encounters signs warning that rodents in national parks carry the plague. It has broken out several times in epidemics in the past two centuries, always associated with war, deforestation, natural disasters, or other severe ecological disturbances. One recent example, the Vietnam War, serves to remind us that when the cultural–biological interface is disturbed, plague can quickly flare into epidemics. When refugees crowded into Saigon, epidemic plague broke out in the city and the countryside of South Vietnam.[19] Plague serves to remind us that the maintenance and transmission of infectious diseases include many variables other than the pathogens that cause them. Agriculture and urbanism in the Old World, while they enabled the development of civilization, also gave rise to the crowd infections that periodically winnow populations.

Agriculture and urbanism came much later to the Americas, after A.D. 500, although cultivation of some plants was under way by 2500 B.C.[20] Landscape alterations such as raised field complexes (often associated with aquaculture), terraced fields, and deforestation were also made centuries before the arrival of Europeans. Extensive trade networks were present between the Gulf Coast and the interior midwestern United States by at least 300 B.C., as demonstrated by "exotic" items distributed far from their sources, such as whelks from Florida, copper from the Great Lakes, and mica from Georgia. Large urban centers with plazas, public architecture, and aggregated resident populations were present in many regions of the Americas by at least A.D. 1000.

The changes in the New World epidemiological landscape coincident with agriculture and urbanism, however, appear to have been far less dramatic than those that had occurred in Eurasia by A.D. 1500.[21] Infectious diseases and other health issues were undoubtedly common, although documenting them is more challenging in the absence of written records. Human skeletal remains have been a major source of information. Populations inhabiting the Americas between A.D. 800 and 1500 show that in numerous regions the onset of agriculture was accompanied by decreased nutrition and health. Skeletal lesions have been crucial for demonstrating the presence of nonvenereal syphilis, tuberculosis, mycotic (fungal) diseases, and other diseases in the precontact Americas.

Recovery of mummified remains in the Americas has facilitated the documentation of specific diseases such as tuberculosis. In addition to tuberculosis, South American mummies indicate that prior to contact with Europeans, those populations also suffered from treponemal infection (see chapter 3), Bartonellosis, Chagas' disease, and several types of parasites, including hookworms and whipworms, roundworms, pinworms, and fish tapeworms.[22] Mummified individuals from Alaska and the Aleutian Islands provide evidence that coronary artery disease was common, as well as intestinal parasites.

There is little evidence that any of the diseases and other health conditions present in the precolumbian Americas decimated populations through epidemics. The expansive mercantilism and rapid transport across great distances characteristic of Eurasia were not present until the arrival of Europeans. However, in A.D. 1500 indigenous Americans were about to experience economic, social, and natural landscape reformation on a level they could never have imagined.

3

Virginity and Virulence

There was then no sickness; they had no aching bones; they had then no high fever; they had then no smallpox; they had then no burning chest; they had then no abdominal pain; they had then no consumption; they had then no headache. At that time the course of humanity was orderly. The foreigners made it otherwise when they arrived here.

The Book of Chilam Balam of Chumayel

The Maya vision of a disease-free world recorded in the Chilam Balam is probably too idealistic, but it is certainly true that many infectious diseases were unknown to them before Europeans came into their world. Alfred Crosby coined the term "virgin soil epidemics" as "those in which the populations at risk have had no previous contact with the diseases that strike them and are therefore immunologically defenseless."[1] The classic example is measles. Measles is highly contagious, and one generally is afflicted as a child. Prior to modern vaccination, measles affected almost anyone who had not been previously infected, but once a person had measles, he or she usually experienced lifelong immunity.

Virulence is the disease-producing ability, the relative tissue damage, produced by a pathogen. More virulent pathogens are those that cause more acute and serious disease. A classic interpretation of disease evolution goes like this: pathogens new to a population are highly contagious and virulent, but as they circulate among a population in successive generations, they evolve toward more benign (less virulent) forms.[2] And so, virginity and virulence are chained at the wrist and ankle, so to speak.

Syphilis seems an appropriate place to turn to in a discussion of virginity and virulence. Venereal syphilis, which is a sexually transmitted disease, is related to three other skin diseases—pinta, yaws, and bejel—which are not. Each treponemal disease has a propensity for a specific climatic setting. They are called treponemal diseases, or treponemes, and they are caused by corkscrew-shaped bacteria known as spirochetes. The geographic and temporal origin of venereal syphilis has been one of the great medical mysteries, occupying numerous researchers for hundreds of years.

Three of the treponemes cause skeletal lesions: yaws, bejel (also known as endemic syphilis), and venereal syphilis. Those lesions overlap in morphology and distribution across the body such that most researchers do not believe that they alone can be used to delineate which form of treponemal infection afflicted an individual. The four treponemal diseases exhibit substantial cross-immunity; some would argue, in fact, that they are indistinguishable serologically. Thus, the historical question has been "Is it one disease or many?" It seems appropriate, therefore, to refer to the suite of diseases as "treponemal infections or treponemes" and to venereal syphilis as "syphilis."

Humans and a few other primates provide the ideal hosts for the delicate syphilis pathogen, which has rather precise humidity and temperature requirements. It is not viable after exposure to air for more than a few moments, and temperatures in excess of 104 degrees Fahrenheit destroy it. Penicillin is still the antibiotic used for treatment; no resistant strains have been reported. The evolutionary history of the syphilis pathogen is of great interest, and a number of theories have been formulated to explain the relationship between the treponemes. Some stress that they are simply climatic variants, despite having separate pathogen names, while others stress the role of mutations that created different pathogens. Whether they existed and evolved in multiple geographic localities has been one of the most vibrant conversations.

Let's begin with the relationships of the treponemal infections. As mentioned before, skeletal lesions are relatively indistinguishable between the treponemes, with only a few exceptions. One of those is venereal syphilis that is transferred across the placenta from an infected mother to an unborn fetus. Known as congenital syphilis, the infection causes growth and development impacts and does appear to have some rather specific dental and skeletal lesions.[3] It has been molecular information, however, more than anything else that has provided the necessary interpretive closure on the issue.

In 1998 and 1999, researchers reported on the complete genome of the syphilis spirochete as well as on finding differences in one specific region between the pathogen that causes venereal syphilis (*Treponema pallidum pallidum*) and those causing nonvenereal treponemal infections. The pathogens that cause yaws (*Treponema pallidum pertenue*) and endemic syphilis (*Treponema pallidum endemicum*) were reported as essentially identical. One of the interesting things to come out of the recent genome analysis of *Treponema pallidum* (venereal syphilis) is that it is closely related to the spirochete that causes Lyme disease.[4] At present the molecular research on syphilis is as confusing as ever. The current literature reports on many more genetic regions and stresses both the diversity of the pathogens and the close similarity between them.[5]

As for origin, syphilis caught everyone's attention in Europe, or so it seems, shortly after the return of Columbus. It appeared to be one of those newly introduced diseases connected with "the Columbian Exchange." Alfred Crosby coined that term as well, and it refers to an accelerated trade in biological organisms, often unintentional, that occurred during the fifteenth- and sixteenth-century global exploration and colonization efforts of Europeans.[6] It included the transfer not only of humans, but also of other animals, plants, and microbes across vast tracts of geographic and biological space.

One of those organisms involved in the Columbian Exchange may have been the syphilis spirochete, but unlike many biological organisms that were transferred from the Old World to the New World, syphilis may have traveled in the other direction—from the New World to the Old World. Shortly after the return of Columbus, syphilis marched across the European continent, accompanying warfare, rape, and pillage. Historic documents indicate that syphilis caused more severe illness than it does now, and that it caused death more frequently and earlier in the course of the disease. The severity of the disease, combined with its seeming prior absence, has led many to interpret it as a new disease in Europe at this time.

Within a few short years, syphilis gained marked notoriety in Europe (Figure 3.1). With no sure homeland, it was blamed on and named for every European country except the one doing the naming. It was known as the English pox, the Portuguese disease, the Castilian disease, the disease of Naples, the French disease, the Neapolitan disease, the pestilence of Egypt, the disease of the Christians, the great poxe, and the serpentine disease. By 1530 Girolamo Fracastoro, an Italian physician and poet, had composed a three-part tale in which a shepherd boy, named Syphilis, aroused the wrath of Apollo. As punishment, Syphilis was visited by a disease that destroyed him as well as many of the poet's contemporaries. The poem became popular and ended all the name-calling. Perhaps Fracastoro was right.

The novelty of the disease can partially be blamed for its constant appearance in art and literature, as can the mode of transmission. But it is the sheer number of people afflicted that brought syphilis into the spotlight. In fact, to be admitted into some social circles at that time in Europe, you simply *must* have experienced the disease.

The fact that syphilis appeared immediately after Columbus' return has often directed the search for its origins to the Caribbean islands and the Americas. Fracastoro, though, questioned that assumption:

> Some instances in divers lands are shown
> To whom all Indian Traffick is unknown
> Nor could th'infection from the Western Clime
> Seize distant nations at the self same time.

Still, several things support a New World origin. Caribbean natives seemed to have knowledge of the disease. Skeletal lesions resembling those of advanced syphilis predate European arrival in America by thousands of years.[7] Syphilis penetrated rapidly throughout Europe, and with severe consequences, indicating its status as a new disease. And thus most scholarship on the subject attributed the origin of venereal syphilis to the Americas, until recently.

Recent scholarship suggests caution regarding New World origins for syphilis. The first European syphilis epidemic in 1495, and several thereafter, occurred during military campaigns. The rapid spread of the disease may be more linked to the behavior of mercenary soldiers than to being a new disease. Before 1495 syphilis may have been mistaken for leprosy, which causes similar lesions. Skeletal remains from Europe increasingly suggest syphilis was present before New World encounters, but they cur-

Figure 3.1. *Victim of Syphilis*. Woodcut attributed to Albrecht Durer.

rently either lack sufficient diagnostic lesions or are too close in date to 1495. Genetic studies have produced complicated explanations, one of which proposes the origin of *Treponema pallidum* in the Old World as a nonvenereal infection that spread to the New World as yaws. Treponemal strains were then transferred back to the Old World as venereal syphilis.[8] In fact, the origin of venereal syphilis is as unclear now as it ever has been. And thus, syphilis serves well to illustrate the complexities of historical epidemiology.

Historical epidemiology, the field of study that deals with disease history, evolution, and transmission, is fraught with difficulties. Paleopathology, the study of skeletal and dental lesions in past populations, suffers similar problems. For instance, historical descriptions of disease symptoms are often deficient. Variability in disease expression can often make the same disease seem like several different diseases. European accounts of the diseases are often vague and attribute no particular name to the affliction other than "fever" or "ague." Rashes, fevers, and wasting characterize many. Spots are a common skin symptom. Skeletal and dental lesions occur only for some diseases, and usually only in chronic, long-term diseases. Even when lesions do occur, they commonly manifest in a few cases: 5–10 percent of syphilis cases, for instance. And, of course, our perceptions and possibilities for the presence of certain diseases could be misinformed by present symptoms and geographic distributions.

People who reconstruct diseases in the past, much like modern physicians, make differential diagnoses to sort out the overlapping signs and symptoms. Differential diagnosis involves taking all diseases with overlapping clinical symptoms and examining the case in question against those clinical descriptions to make the best possible diagnosis. They assemble all of the information—lesion types, lesion distribution, other symptoms, when contracted, and so on—and list those diseases that fit the information. The differential diagnosis, once the necessary comparisons have been made, indicates the mostly likely disease candidate. When working with past populations, there is always the additional complication that the symptoms of the disease, or the description of those symptoms, might be different than they are for modern clinical cases.

When I think of establishing a disease diagnosis, I often think of my car mechanic: What does it sound like when you start it? Does it sputter after you give it gas or does it run well at that point? Is it better when the engine is warm? How long has it been doing this?

Disease diagnosis has the same trial-and-error approach to it as automotive repair at times. And, if you followed a 2004 case involving a North Carolina hospital, you know there is some chance your scalpel could be treated with lubricating oil before surgery rather than with a more congenial antiseptic. "We've never seen this in a Volvo before" is like the comment "This disease is known only in Eurasia."

My favorite case of diagnostic difficulty in historical epidemiology is tuberculosis (TB), notoriously variable in its expression.[9] Tuberculosis has many names historically: scrofula, phthisis, white swelling, hectic fever, hip-joint disease, consumption, and dropsy of the lungs, to name a few. Numerous diseases with symptoms similar to those of TB have been misdiagnosed over the years. Medical workers still found differential diagnosis difficult even after the isolation of the tuberculosis bacillus in 1882.

TB is well documented in Europe prior to the Columbian Exchange. Irrefutable evidence for TB in the Americas prior to European colonization was not found until recently, and so it remained a hotly debated topic for nearly a century, despite several pieces of evidence. Precolumbian Mexican ceramics depicted people with misshapen backs. Misshapen vertebrae with crater-like lesions resembling TB were found in several precolumbian skeletons (Figure 3.2). Nonetheless, strong personalities and flawed concepts of disease prevailed in tossing the issue of TB out of the pub every time it tried to enter, because of insufficient identification.

One of those strong personalities was Dr. Daniel Morse of Peoria, Illinois. Morse was well suited to take on the debate regarding precolumbian TB. He had an avid interest in ancient disease, a thorough medical knowledge of tuberculosis gained from his medical practice at the Peoria Municipal Tuberculosis Sanitorium, and an avocational background in anthropology. His argument against precolumbian TB, well crafted and extensive, generally rested on the differences between those cases that had been put forth as evidence for precolumbian TB and the patterns of bone lesions that he saw in contemporary cases (Figure 3.3).[10] It is not surprising that Morse saw a difference between the lesions of modern cases and those of prehistoric populations. One could expect some differences in appearance given probable changes in the disease over time, modern medical interventions, such as the sanitorium, and

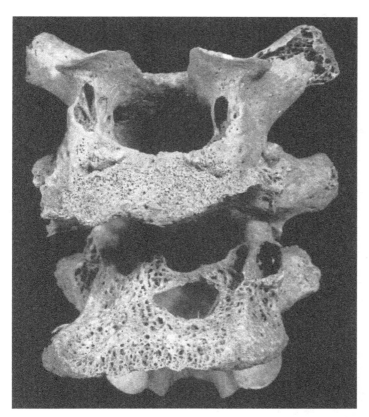

Figure 3.2. Thoracic vertebra with TB erosive lesions from the prehistoric
Norris Farms site in Illinois. Courtesy of George R. Milner.

the biased sampling of prehistoric skeletal remains, often with incomplete
skeletons.

Aidan Cockburn, another strong personality, published a rejection of
precolumbian TB in 1963, one largely based on his evolutionary theories
of disease. Cockburn based his arguments on several assumptions and
criteria that supported his interpretation of TB as a new disease among
Indian populations.[11] Principal among them was that the high rate of tuberculosis, and the magnitude with which it affected native populations
of the Americas, must indicate it was a new or "virgin soil" disease.

Aleš Hrdlička, the famed physical anthropologist, came to the same
conclusion in his classic 1909 volume *Tuberculosis among Certain Indian
Tribes*. In that volume, Hrdlička reviewed the evidence for TB among

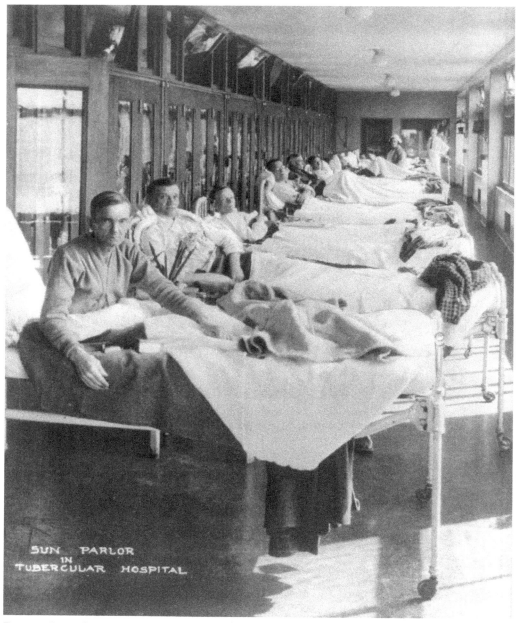

SUN PARLOR
IN
TUBERCULAR HOSPITAL

Figure 3.3. Sun parlor in tubercular hospital in Dayton, Ohio, between 1910 and 1920. Library of Congress Prints and Photographs Division Washington, D.C. 20540 USA, http://hdl.loc.gov/loc.pnp/pp.print.

contemporary Indian tribes and looked at the historic evidence for the disease, and at the skeletal evidence for precolumbian TB. Hrdlička's conclusions that "tuberculosis was rare, if it did exist" in precolumbian America was supported by eight compelling observations.[12] Among those observations were that there was epidemic tuberculosis in virtually every location where Indians had been established on reservations, that convincing prehistoric tissue evidence of TB was not available, and that there were no clear early contact period descriptions of TB among Indians or European explorers.

The conclusions of both Cockburn and Hrdlička regarding tuberculosis rested on two major assumptions about diseases and evolution. First, virgin-soil populations will have higher rates of an infectious disease, and it will be more severe. Second, that diseases (pathogens, really) evolve toward more benign forms the longer they circulate in a population. While these ideas are not inherently flawed, they present an oversimplified view of disease ecology that fails to consider the impacts of human behavior and environment.

At the risk of repetition, a virgin-soil population is conceived as one that has no experience with the disease—therefore, those in the population suffer more cases, often with worse symptoms and higher mortality rates. It is much more a matter of previous exposure during one's lifetime than of genetic predisposition. Some diseases cannot be maintained in small populations, even if there has been prior exposure. For instance, populations of a sufficient size or density to allow for a continuous chain of transmission of measles would not have developed until at least 2500 B.C.[13] Thus, until a population attains the demographic and residential profile necessary to support the seasonal outbreak of diseases like measles, and until it attains a level of transmission that allows the continuous introduction and maintenance of an infectious disease, it will fluctuate between the status of "virgin soil" and "non-virgin soil population."

Part and parcel of the concept of virgin-soil diseases is the concept of obligatory evolution toward less virulent forms. It's a simple premise: the more experience a population has with a pathogen, the less severe the effects of the pathogen. The biologist Paul Ewald investigated pathogens and virulence, and he discovered that these were not the only forces determining virulence; mode of disease transmission has a lot to do with virulence. Two of his classic examples are the common cold and malaria.

Colds are transmitted through nasal secretions either by direct contact (touching an object infected with nasal secretions) or inhaled air. Mobility is an issue in the sense that more uninfected (and presumably susceptible) people become infected if an affected individual (host) is mobile. An immobilized host presumably would have limited contacts and thus would limit the number of people who could keep the virus circulating. Therefore, evolutionary forces favor a less-virulent infection that leaves the host well enough to move about. Malaria, on the other hand, is transmitted by an insect vector, the mosquito. Mobility of the host is not therefore an issue in the disease transmission. In fact, an immobilized host slaps and kills fewer mosquitoes. Thus, when vectors (insect or otherwise) are involved, evolutionary forces favor a more virulent disease.

Virulence is only one of the issues of pathogen evolution. Studies of pathogen evolution continue to demonstrate the complexity of pathogen/host/transmission relationships.[14] Those studies demonstrate the many ways, most previously unappreciated, that survival, reproduction, and transmission of pathogens can and do occur. Pathogens do not always evolve from virulent to benign; their evolutionary pathways are much more complicated.

Neither Aidan Cockburn nor Aleš Hrdlička were privy to contemporary views of disease evolution. What they saw is that tuberculosis was rampant among Plains and Southwestern Indians living on reservations in the late 1800s and early 1900s. For instance, Sioux prisoners of war were moved into army barracks in 1880. Acute tuberculosis soon developed, and the death rate climbed to 10 times that of the worst European epidemic of former centuries. Oglala Sioux living on a reservation had a death rate of 25.3 per 1,000 in 1896. Soon after their confinement began, several hundred Apaches, who were interned at Mt. Vernon Barracks, Alabama, and later moved to Ft. Sill, Oklahoma, displayed a rapid increase in death rate: from 54.6 per 1,000 in 1887–88 to 142.82 per 1,000 in 1890–91. More than half the deaths were attributed to tuberculosis.[15] Undoubtedly, in the minds of Cockburn and Hrdlička, the evidence pointed to a late virgin-soil arrival of TB from Europe. There was plenty of evidence for TB in the Old World prior to 1492, and there seemed to be none in the New World.

Of course, we also now know that there are many people who harbor

A small house of typical construction

A house of average size, with an exceptionally large window

OGLALA LOG HOUSES

Figure 3.4. Oglala homes on reservation. From Hrdlička, *Tuberculosis among Certain Indian Tribes of the United States*, Plate 7.

the tuberculosis bacillus but never develop the disease.[16] The classic precursors of full-blown infection are malnutrition and poor living conditions. But in the early-to-mid-1900s, political and social contributors to disease were overshadowed by deterministic views of disease and disease evolution. Approaches to health from the perspectives of ecology and political economy were virtually nonexistent. It is very easy to blame illness on the germ. It makes it easy for individuals, populations, and governments to place blame elsewhere. The fact of the matter is that germs have to get from here to there in some fashion, and they have to survive long enough to travel. The various ways in which we conduct our lives influence those factors.

Aleš Hrdlička offered numerous observations about contagion, sanitation, and the poverty present on Indian reservations. He failed, however, to recognize that tuberculosis was rampant in Indian populations *because* of their living conditions, not because it was a new disease. Crowded into poor housing and with substandard nutrition, native populations in the 1800s were exactly the kind of population in which tuberculosis thrives (Figure 3.4). It is a matter of disease and discrimination, not of pathogen/host evolution.

There is another twist to the story, though. In 1973 Marvin Allison and coworkers who had been working on mummies from the Nazca plain in Chile were able to document TB in a child dated to A.D. 700. The child had long-standing bone and soft-tissue disease of the lungs, with demonstrable acid-fast bacilli in the tissue that were identified as *Mycobacterium tuberculosis*. DNA evidence has been used since then to add to the number of indisputable cases of precolumbian tuberculosis, and it has added a new chapter to pathogen origin and evolution in the same way as previously discussed for plague and syphilis.[17]

The diagnostic difficulty of precolumbian TB illustrates the trouble with a focus on pathogens and pathogen evolution over social and environmental context. To simply attribute infectious disease and demographic change to new pathogens misrepresents the underlying influence of social, political, economic, and environmental factors associated with changing health in the colonies. Postcolonial native populations are often portrayed as if they were physically and genetically isolated from the majority of Europeans during the colonial process. Nothing could be further from the truth. In fact, they were drawn into many of the same colonial processes experienced by the colonizers. Colonial development created a set of intersecting landscapes that Indians transected in an attempt to find their place in a rapidly changing world. Their disease and depopulation is one chapter in a much larger and longer story.

PART II

Natives and Newcomers

4

MERCHANTS AND MALADIES

The Iroquois used to keep us so closely confined that we did not even dare till the lands that were under the cannons of the forts, much less go any distance to discover all the bounties of a soil which is hardly different from that of France. But now the terror of His Majesty's arms has filled these barbarians with fear and compelled them to seek our friendship, instead of constantly molesting us in bloody war. Thanks to the ensuing calm, we are exploring the riches of this country and finding how much promise it holds for the future.

François Le Mercier, "Relation of 1666–67"

The sixteenth and seventeenth centuries in early America were the times of natives and newcomers.[1] Natives were on their home ground. They knew the landscape, the resources, and the multiple climates—natural, social, political, and economic—into which the newcomers wandered. For their part, the newcomers brought their own notions regarding social, political, and economic standards alongside technologies unfamiliar to the natives. Both natives and newcomers approached each other with mistrust, lack of understanding, and misconceptions during those early interactions. European customs were often viewed by the natives as ridiculous and uninformed. Native customs were often seen as barbaric and, by the European priests, demonic. Nonetheless, newcomers continually acknowledged the skills and knowledge of the natives. Familiarity by both parties was gained slowly.

⦾

It is important when discussing the emerging social and economic fabric of Atlantic America to understand the nature of native social and political relationships in the Northeast just before and during the initial European colonial endeavors. The native societies of the Northeast were divided principally into two groups, the Iroquoians and the Algonkians. The Iroquoians were centrally located and clustered around Lake Ontario, along the St. Lawrence Valley, and the Susquehanna Valley (Map 4.1). They practiced hunting and gathering, supplemented by a rich horticulture that supported large villages. Algonkian-speaking groups occupied the Atlantic seaboard and areas north and west of the Iroquois to Lake Superior and south along the coast from New England to North Carolina. The southern Algonkian groups practiced both farming and foraging, while those to the north did not farm and were more mobile, moving seasonally to harvest wild resources.

Iroquois beliefs about spiritual power were heavily entwined with interpersonal violence, and their perspectives influenced and were shared with many neighboring groups. As part of this spiritual existence, the Iroquois conducted "mourning wars," in which they sought prisoners from their enemies to replace dead warriors. Prisoners were presented by chiefs to grieving matrilineages, where elder women decided whether the fate of the captives would be adoption or death. Captives were initially subjected to torture, and some were "rescued" if adoption was their fate. Those not chosen for adoption were expected to stoically face skilled torture and finally death by their captors. Both captors and captives endeavored to gain spiritual power: the captors through their skill in torture while keeping their captive alive, the captive by facing torture as long as possible without acknowledging pain or yielding to their efforts. When death finally came, the dead were butchered and eaten, ensuring further gain of spiritual power.

Shortly before the arrival of the newcomers, the Iroquois formed the Great League of Peace and Power, an alliance of the Five Nations: from east to west, the Mohawk, Oneida, Onondaga, Cayuga, and Seneca. In a context of long-standing conflicts evident from the archaeological remains of heavily fortified and palisaded villages, the Great League indicates a need for mutual aid against outside aggression from neighboring Indian nations.

Whether Europeans came to this new place to find new lands, to escape religious persecution, or to become rich, they came largely with the anticipation of extracting resources. Even those who came as custodians of the

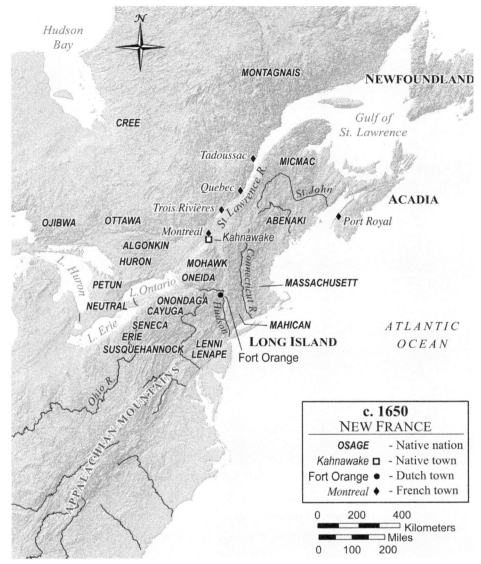

Map 4.1. New France, circa 1650. Drawn by Susan Brannock-Gaul.

church sought to gain the souls of those whom they could convert. They came, however, with a European cognitive map into a land they did not know. Tentative coastal movements led to more aggressive thrusts into the rivers that flowed inland, and soon the newcomers followed ancient trails into the interior. Among the many things they brought with them on their slow infiltration of native North America were merchandise and maladies.

In the early sixteenth century, fishermen from France, Spain, Portugal, and England journeyed into the coastal waters off Newfoundland, the Gulf of St. Lawrence, and Cape Breton south to Maine. They came for numerous species of fish, seals, and whales that formed their bounty, but their principal harvest was cod, which remained a major resource throughout the colonial period.[2] In addition to casting their nets and lines at sea, the fishing expeditions frequented the nearby shores to gather firewood, obtain fresh water, prepare fish for shipping, and repair nets. The first contacts with natives occurred during those forays and led to the first social and economic bonds through gifts or exchanges.

Although the first recorded fur trading occurred between the French explorer Jacques Cartier and Micmac Indians in 1534 at Chaleur Bay, an arm of the Bay of St. Lawrence, the natives at that time appeared to already understand that trade for European items might be a possibility.

> July 7. The next day a party of wild men came in nine boats to the point and the salt bay where we were staying in our ships. As soon as we realized they were coming, we put in our two boats to meet them at the point. When they saw us, they fled, making signs to us that they had come to trade. They showed us the pelts they were wearing, which weren't worth much. We made similar signs that we didn't mean them any harm and sent two of our men ashore with knives and other ironware, as well as a red hat for their captain.[3]

At Tadoussac, the terminus of an important native trade route on the Saguenay River near the mouth of the St. Lawrence, French traders developed alliances after 1550 with northern Algonkian-speaking people, especially the Micmacs, Montagnais, and Algonkin. It rapidly became the principal port of trade. By 1580 the fishing industry in that area employed some 400 vessels and 12,000 people, and the coastal area adjacent to the Saint Lawrence River had become the object of commercial speculation, not only for the rich fishing resources, but also for the trade of furs, which the French dominated during the latter half of the sixteenth century.[4]

Given the cold climate in the northern part of the Atlantic colonies, furs were thick and highly desirable items. Beaver hats were in high fashion in Europe in the second half of the sixteenth century, and the demand for pelts increased. European beaver were nearly extinct, and the furs from the northern climates of the St. Lawrence region were a valuable commodity.

Other luxury furs were marten, otter, ermine, fox, raccoon, and lynx. Hides of moose, caribou, and wapiti were also highly desired.

By the early 1600s, the French had long been trading with Algonkin groups, and they made further trade alliances with the Iroquoian Huron. Samuel de Champlain established a fort in 1608 on high ground where the river narrowed at Quebec; the location was chosen largely to facilitate the French emphasis on fur trading and to secure their place as the primary European colony trading furs. From Quebec the French could defend their territory against interlopers and establish a permanent colony. The place of the French in the fur trade, however, was to be anything but secure.

One cost of the French trade with the Huron was the alienation of the Five Nations Iroquois. The Huron were both populous and prosperous, with an Iroquoian culture. Their trade with the French broke them from their fellow Iroquois. The Dutch were thus able to trade with Iroquois groups and establish their own trade partnerships. In 1610 the Dutch initiated the fur trade on the Hudson River with the Iroquoian Mohawks. They erected a permanent trading post near Albany on the Hudson River in 1614. Initially called Fort Nassau (in 1624 it was renamed Fort Orange), it was the Dutch equivalent of Quebec. By occupying two adjacent river systems, the French and Dutch not only established mercantile battle lines but engaged the economic and social rivalries of their native constituents. Chronic territorial raids and warfare between native populations resulted from competition for access to furs and European trade goods.

The British, meanwhile, were primarily located farther south along the Chesapeake, but British privateers plundered the short-lived North Atlantic coastal trading settlements of Sable Island (1598–1603; south of modern Nova Scotia), St. Croix River (1604–5; between modern Maine and New Brunswick), and Port Royal (1605–7, 1610–13; modern Nova Scotia). An English pirate destroyed Port Royal in 1613 and ended the French coastal enterprise. John Smith explored the Atlantic coast a bit south of Port Royal in 1614 and named it New England, because the topography and climate reminded him of the homeland.

English Puritans, a religious group who broke with the Church of England, colonized New England in 1620 to seek religious reformation through the recovery of the original and pure church of Jesus Christ. With an initial emigration of 102 people, they founded a colony on the south shore of Massachusetts Bay and called it Plymouth. Their strong will and idealism seemed to favor their efforts, and unlike the Chesapeake or New France, which remained demographically stifled for a long time, New England swelled in population. By 1630 about 1,500 English dwelled in the Plymouth colony.[5]

It was in the climate of commercial enterprise that the French, Dutch, and British all competed to establish relationships with native trading partners and build permanent colonial outposts. The northern territories where New France was established were only sparsely peppered with French, mostly traders. Despite their ambitions for success, in 1627 New France still had only 85 colonists, all men and all at Quebec. The Dutch realized that they also needed to protect their trade partnerships and established New Amsterdam (modern New York) at the mouth of the Hudson in 1625. At the same time, they extended their merchant efforts to agriculture in adjacent areas on Long Island into the present-day New Jersey. The mid-Atlantic remained open for English colonization.

War broke out between France and England in 1627, and soon English ships were deployed to move down the St. Lawrence and capture Quebec. Although Champlain resisted, the continual capture and prevention of settlers and goods destined for Quebec left the colonists starving. In 1629 Champlain surrendered the city to the English. A few French remained in the area while working for the English, but most abandoned the area for a few short years, returning after a treaty restored the ruins of their previous settlements in 1632.

For a decade following 1630, a larger Puritan emigration occurred under the leadership of a wealthy Puritan lawyer named John Winthrop. About 14,000 people immigrated via 198 recorded voyages to New England during the "Great Migration." From their initial settlement of Boston, they expanded into the interior and farther up the coast, founding the colonies of New Hampshire, Maine, Connecticut, and New Haven.

The Dutch, meanwhile, continued to encroach on English and French interests through a growing fur trade between the Dutch and the Iroquois, successful agricultural colonies in the lower Hudson, and an active shipping commerce. They especially irritated the English by charging 33 percent less than their English competitors for shipping tobacco and sugar. The English reacted to a growing Dutch oceanic trade by creating a series of Navigation Acts that prohibited trade of English merchandise with any other nation. Three wars that followed between the Dutch and English finally climaxed with the surrender of New Netherland to England in 1667 and 1674.

The French, for their own part, realized that their failure to sustain a colony or to hold on to Quebec necessitated changes in their colonial strategies. As one of the reforms following the return of Quebec in 1632, Champlain insisted that the Huron accept the involvement of Jesuit priests in their villages, which was no small feat. Missionaries of the Recollect Order began to evangelize the Indians in 1615, but their relationships with both natives and their fellow newcomers were regularly strained. They viewed the native way of life as savage and without moral standards, lacking discipline and governance.

The Recollects were very harsh with the Indians, insisting they in essence give up all of their prior cultural patterns, learn the French language, become more sedentary, and essentially "become French." Although the Recollects traveled into Indian territory, they focused their major conversion attempts on having young Indian boys live among them. Their hope was that the youths would eventually go back and act as missionaries among their own people, some perhaps even becoming priests.

Many of these goals were in conflict with those of the traders, and bitter opposition marked the missionary and trader relationships. The missionaries felt that the traders subverted their attempts to bring moral behavior to the natives through such practices as traders maintaining sexual relationships and marriages. Over a ten-year period, the Recollect efforts yielded almost no converts.

The Jesuits took a new tactic when they arrived in 1625 by learning native languages and recognizing that change must occur slowly, with coercion and patience. Known to the Indians as Black Robes because of their attire, they moved farther west into Huron territory. The Jesuits were very good record keepers, and so we know a fair amount about native customs and historic events from their *Jesuit Relations*.[6] They established houses in many Indian villages and traveled with the Indians as they moved on their seasonal rounds. Their journeys were often arduous, as priest Paul Le Jeune discusses on a winter hunt.

From the twelfth of November of the year 1633, when we entered these vast forests, to the twenty-second of April of this year 1634, when we returned to the banks of the great river St. Lawrence, we camped at twenty-three different places. . . . To paint for you the hardships of the journey, I have neither pen nor brush equal to the task. You would have to see them to understand, as this is a meal that must be tasted to be appreciated. We did nothing but go up and go down. Frequently we had to bend over double to pass under partly fallen trees, and step over others lying upon the ground whose branches sometimes knocked us over, gently enough to be sure, but always coldly, for we fell upon the snow. . . . When we reached the place where we were to camp, the women went to cut the poles for the cabin, and the men to clear away the snow. Now a person had to work at this building, or shiver with cold for three long hours upon the snow waiting until it is finished.[7]

Many of the customs of the Jesuits were suspect to the Indians—their avoidance of undressing in public, their self-flagellation, their insistence that baptism would send the dead to heaven and not to the native burial grounds all caused concern. The Jesuits did not help matters by threatening to employ their control of supernatural forces. It suggested to the natives that they were sorcerers.

A typical event occurred in 1628, a year of drought in the Huron country. One of the famous shamans in the region, Tehorenhaegnon, failed to make rain and announced that the red-painted cross in front of priest Jean de Brébeuf's cabin was frightening the thunderbird and causing the rain clouds to divide before they reached the village of Toanché. When the headmen of the village asked Father Brébeuf to take down the cross or hide it, he refused and further threatened the Huron with supernatural punishment should they take it down themselves. He did agree to paint it white but announced that if rain did not soon come, Tehorenhaegnon should be denounced as an impostor. After several days of continued drought, the cross was painted red again, and Brébeuf implored the local people to join him in kissing the cross and offering corn, which he redistributed among the village. Rain came shortly thereafter, but the emphasis on supernatural powers contributed more to the notion of the authority of the priests and their magical powers than to Christian conversion.

Sadly, the time of the Jesuits coincided with a series of epidemics that reduced native populations in the Northeast by approximately 50 percent within six years (Table 4.1). The elevated mortality and suffering of the natives was often blamed on the Jesuits, especially by the shamans or sorcer-

Table 4.1. Seventeenth-century disease epidemics

Date	Location/Population	Disease	Source
1616–24	Southeastern New England	Viral hepatitis	Spiess and Spiess 1987
1633	Plymouth, Connecticut River	Measles?	Bradford 1908: 302–3
1634–35	Upper Connecticut, Huron	Smallpox	Bradford 1908: 312–13
1634–35	Northern Iroquois	Measles	*Jesuit Relations* 7: 221; 8: 43, 87–89; 12: 265
1635	Huron	Measles	*Jesuit Relations* 8: 87–89
1636–37	Mohawk, Huron, Jesuits	Contagion, scarlet fever?	*Jesuit Relations* 14: 51
1639	Quebec	Smallpox	*Jesuit Relations* 18: 91
1646–47	New England (Indians and Europeans)	Fever, influenza?	Winthrop 1908, 2: 326
1658	Long Island	Smallpox	Ruttenberg 1872
1662	Iroquois	Smallpox	*Jesuit Relations* 47: 193; 50: 63
1664	Massachusetts	Smallpox	Potter 1835
1668	Montagnais and Algonquin; Seneca	Smallpox or measles	*Jesuit Relations* 53: 123–24; 54: 79–81
1669–70	New France; Mohawk	High fever, dementia	*Jesuit Relations* 53: 71–81; 57: 81–83
1675–76	Colonies, then Huron	Influenza	*Jesuit Relations* 60: 175
1678	Iroquois	Smallpox	*Jesuit Relations* 63: 205
1679–80	Iroquois	Smallpox	Dankers and Sluyter 1867: 277
1682	Huron	Measles or smallpox	*Jesuit Relations* 62: 145
1697–98	New England	Influenza	Marshall 152; Mather 1681–1708, 1689–1711: 247. Both in Duffy, *Epidemics in Colonial America*, 189.

Source: All references are from Snow, "Disease and Population Decline in the Northeast," unless otherwise noted. See Snow, "Disease and Population Decline in the Northeast," and Duffy, *Epidemics in Colonial America*, for further discussion.

ers, who had cast shadows on the practices of the priests long before the epidemics began. When the epidemics came and the Jesuits could do little to prevent death except insist on baptism, it was no wonder that the priests were held suspect. Their continued health during many of the epidemics only contributed further to attribution of sorcery, and opposition between them and the local sorcerers only heightened.

Smallpox broke out as early as 1633, but definitely during the winter of 1634–35 in a British fort on the upper Connecticut. Over 900 of the 1,000 Indians resident there became ill, and half of them died.[8] The smallpox epidemic also struck the Plymouth trading house on the lower Connecticut and then moved throughout the New York region. One of the traders, van den Bogaert, described the malady in his journal in 1634–35.

> None of the chiefs was at home, except for the most principal one called Adriochten, who was living one quarter mile from the fort in a small cabin because many Indians here in the castle had died of small-pox. . . . After we had gone a mile or a mile and a half past great tracts of flatland, we entered a castle at about two hours in the evening. I could see nothing else but graves. This castle is called Canagere and is situated on a hill without palisades or any defense."[9]

Father Jérôme Lalemont describes a smallpox epidemic among the Hurons in 1640.

> It was when the Hurons returned from their journey to Quebec that [smallpox] entered the country, our Hurons having thoughtlessly mingled with some Algonquins whom they met on the way up here, most of whom were infected with [it]. The first Huron who introduced it came ashore just beside our house, newly built on the edge of a lake, and from there he carried it to his own village, about a league distant from us, and then promptly died. It would take no great prophet to predict that the illness would soon be spread abroad through all these regions, for the Hurons, regardless of any plague or contagion, live in the midst of their sick, sharing and mingling with them as if they were in perfect health. And indeed, within a few days, almost everyone in the cabin of the deceased was infected, and then the disease spread

from house to house, from town to town, and eventually affected the entire country.[10]

Smallpox was once among the most deadly diseases in the world.[11] It infects as many as 90 percent of those at risk and has no gender, age, or population discrimination. While closely related to monkeypox and cowpox, smallpox appears to have always been an entirely human infection. It is primarily transmitted by respiration, and thus close proximity to infected individuals is the most common method of contracting the disease. Survivors of smallpox are immune for the rest of their lives, and thus a pool of susceptible individuals is necessary to maintain an active, endemic disease.

Because the scabs remain infective for lengthy periods, smallpox can be transmitted through direct contact with the scabs of smallpox victims. It was not uncommon in the past for laundry workers to become infected by contracting the disease from clothing and bedding of smallpox patients. There are suggestions historically that the deliberate distribution of smallpox-infected textiles was a military strategy used against populations with limited prior experience with smallpox. But deliberate or not, transmission of smallpox was facilitated by close contact.

Measles probably struck the Northeast around Plymouth on the Connecticut River in the summer of 1633 and proceeded later into the Iroquoian communities around 1634–35.[12] Jesuit records indicate that measles definitely reached the Huron in 1635. Until recently, measles ranked with smallpox as one of the most infectious diseases of childhood, and one of the most infectious of diseases in general. Measles is a viral disease spread by close contact. Like smallpox, respiratory transmission is the primary route of infection. The clinical symptoms are sneezing, watery discharge from the nose, cough, fever, thirst, headache, and the characteristic spots of the skin grouped in small patches. German measles (rubella) is especially virulent. Bad hygienic conditions or an abundance of susceptible hosts can result in tremendous mortality from measles.[13] Few children escaped the disease prior to the introduction of a vaccine in 1963. Survival of measles usually confers lifelong immunity, as does vaccination.

Because lifelong immunity is conferred once an individual survives smallpox and measles, the diseases must be brought into new groups from elsewhere. It works like this. The more individuals in a population that have immunity, the harder it is to maintain an infection. It is called *herd immunity*, and the two best ways to have an immune herd are through vaccination and acquired immunity. Prior to vaccination, new susceptible individuals were always present in the young. It is why smallpox and measles are childhood diseases; the fact that they are highly contagious is why everyone succumbed to them before the introduction of vaccines.

Measles and smallpox were not the only new infections to reach native populations in the middle and northern latitudes of seventeenth-century North America. In 1636 a new epidemic made its way to the Mohawk and spread into the Huron region. The Jesuits also fell ill with the contagion, which spread throughout the mission system. The disease was characterized by a high fever that came and went episodically over the course of one or two weeks. The patient became flushed during these episodes, and the worst of them were serious enough to cause death. It may have been scarlet fever.[14] Sometimes called scarlatina, scarlet fever has clinical symptoms of sore throat and fever, a violent red rash on the skin, and the characteristic strawberry color of the throat and tongue. It is caused by a streptococcal bacterium and is spread by respiration of the airborne pathogen or through contaminated milk. In severe forms the throat becomes ulcerated as in diphtheria (see discussion in chapter 9), and the death rate is high. The most serious forms of scarlet fever have virtually disappeared.

Influenza appeared with certainty among the Huron in 1676; it may have appeared as early as 1637. According to Jesuit accounts, it affected the priests as well. "He [Father Chastellain] was harassed by a burning fever, which made him very restless and which possessed him until the seventh of October."[15] Just exactly how long influenza has affected human populations is unknown, but it is certainly one of the most contagious and personally challenging diseases. Several species are affected by influenza; these include humans, pigs, horses, other mammals, and several species of birds.

Among humans it is a respiratory infection that has a sudden onset and symptoms of sore throat, headache, fever, chills, runny nose, and muscle and joint pain. Most of us have experienced the flu season and know well the rapidity and thoroughness with which students and coworkers are removed from circulation. The winter of 2005 saw the passage of a particularly contagious strain of flu in North Carolina—my global health course of 60 had approximately 15 people present for the final examination.

Known also as "flu," "grip," and "grippe," influenza is a disease caused by three myxoviruses: influenza viruses A, B, and C. The most common type is A, and it exists in a number of subtypes that are genetically unstable and do not provide cross-immunity. Thus, any fall/winter flu season is characterized by unpredictability—despite the availability of flu shots in contemporary times, their effectiveness in any particular season is challenged by multiple flu strains that are repeatedly changing.

Influenza viruses are spread by respiration in human populations via airborne droplets, or by contamination of surfaces with droplets. Nonhuman populations have additional routes of transmission that include the fecal-oral route. Mortality can be low, with recovery in about seven to ten days following the onset of symptoms. Influenza is a more serious disease for the very young and the very old, or those with compromised immune systems. Complications such as pneumonia and bronchitis can also be fatal. There have been several historically documented pandemics of especially virulent flu—one of the best known occurred in 1918–19 during World War I (see Epilogue).

There is probably no single factor responsible for the repetitious cycles of disease epidemics in the seventeenth century. Certainly, large populations of susceptible hosts contributed to the maintenance and severity of infections that would be childhood diseases in Europe. As native populations were affected substantially by epidemic diseases, their numbers were reduced. It is clear that they were not annihilated, and it is clear that new pathogens were not the only reason for the epidemics. Increased ship traffic, increased colonial outposts, increased mobility of both natives and newcomers—all facilitated the transmission of the pathogens. Among native populations, colonization of the Atlantic coast pushed forward the shadow of death.

What we know about the epidemics that ravaged native populations in the seventeenth century comes almost entirely from historical accounts written by the colonists. The diseases most often recorded are those that occurred at or near settlements that included Europeans and were the diseases that were familiar to Europeans. One can be sure that illness traveled far away from the eyes and ears of those Europeans maintaining historical memory, and so the magnitude of population loss is not really known. Lots of people have made estimates, and those for the Huron and Iroquois seem to center around 50 percent population loss in those early years. Others have made even higher estimates.[16]

Several people have attempted to use archaeological evidence to assess the impact of epidemics on native populations, but it is not as easy as it would seem to recognize the "signature" of epidemic disease in a mortuary setting.[17] Mass graves would seem to be the most obvious indication of epidemic disease, but mass death is caused by numerous initiators, such as mass disaster and warfare. There have been few excavations of mortuary spaces that are known to have originated from epidemic disease, among them Black Death plague cemeteries in England, France, and Germany.

Unfortunately, burial rituals that do not derive from accelerated mortality can yield burial spaces that resemble those from mass death; there is one described for the Huron village of Ossossané, where many who died over a long period of time were re-interred simultaneously.[18] The account describes the ritual burial of individuals in an ossuary, which is a mass grave, mostly of individuals who have decomposed and whose skeletons have become disarticulated. They are usually constructed, and the ritual conducted, about every 10–20 years and often involve entire communities.[19]

There are ossuaries in the Northeast that might indicate mass burial due to epidemics, but the evidence is far from conclusive. Two Ontario ossuaries dating between 1630–50, an Iroquoian one at Ossossané (modern central Ontario) and a Neutral one at Grimsby (southern Ontario), have extremely high juvenile mortality rates, which might be taken as indicative of an epidemic. Ossossané, for instance, has a low survivorship of 40 percent to age 15. In neither of those ossuaries, however, are there conclusive indications of infectious disease ravaging the populations. Only one adult male from Grimsby dating 1640–50 has any skeletal signs that might indicate epidemic disease—lesions characteristic of inflammatory responses at the elbow, one of the pathological outcomes associated with smallpox.[20]

The problem is that most acute infectious diseases, those which cause death quickly, usually don't leave their mark on the skeleton. Either skeletal involvement is not part of the disease process, or people die too quickly for skeletal responses to develop. As discussed in chapters 2 and 3, we are getting better at obtaining molecular signatures of disease from skeletal remains, and scientists have now been able to discuss syphilis, tuberculosis, plague, and leprosy with certainty using that evidence. We have to be a little cautious interpreting it, though, as indicators of infection do not necessarily indicate death due to the disease, or even that the person developed full-blown infections, only that they were exposed to the disease.

Skeletal and dental lesions *have* told us a great deal about human health in the past, as discussed in numerous other places in this book, but acute infectious disease is a more problematic area on which those lesions can speak. Again, it is why a combination of informative sources always yields a richer interpretation. Historic documents have their own weaknesses, and one of those is that people can describe and assess only those things for which they have prior knowledge and understanding. Diseases that were unknown to the European chroniclers would not have been detected or described.

Amidst massive epidemics that swept through the Northeast, and despite the missionary activities, French attention remained centered on the fur trade in the seventeenth century. To protect that trade, they extended their forti-fied trading posts westward up the St. Lawrence, founding Trois-Rivières in 1634 and Montreal in 1642. Still, the country remained largely uninhabited by French colonists save those involved in the fur trade in the 1650s. Fearing another loss of the colony, the French crown ordered the Company of New France to bring more people into the colonial effort. This was done with the assistance of *seigneurs*, men of means who were granted titles and immense estates in exchange for recruiting shiploads of new colonists.

Slowly, with the arrival of the first farm families, New France began to grow, from 700 colonists in 1650 to 3,000 by 1663.[21] Most who immigrated arrived in servitude, as either soldiers or indentured servants. Most were male and from urban settings, where they had learned little about farming in their earlier lives. Most returned to France after their three-year term of servitude was over. Population growth thus occurred only through natu-ral increase, especially after 1673, when for monetary reasons the French government ceased to support immigration. The failure of the French to organize colonial strategies that went beyond the fur trade and fishing, combined with the short growing season that far north, stifled France's bid for colonial success in the Northeast. It was further stifled by the fact that most of the colonists left New France after only a few years.

France's colonial effort was very different from the colonial efforts of the English. Almost immediately after the Puritan settlement of New England in 1630, the colonists began "improving" the lands to create farms. They cut clearings in the forest and used the timber to build barns, houses, and fences. A typical farm consisted of crops of wheat, rye, maize, potatoes, beans, and garden plants, with a modest herd of livestock—a few cattle, a horse or two, a couple sheep, and a few pigs. None of these crops was particularly profitable for shipping to England, but they allowed the New England farmers to subsist on their own produce, trade some of the rest for goods or services, and remain outside of the boom-and-bust cycle experienced by other colonies. By 1660 the English had 58,000 colonists in New England and the Chesapeake; by 1700 English colonies held 265,000, while New France held 15,000.

5

COMMERCE AND CONSEQUENCE

The Beaver is taken in several ways. The Indians say that it is the animal well beloved by the French, English, and Basques: in a word, by the Europeans. I heard my host say one day jokingly, Missi picoutau amiscou, "The beaver knows how to make all things to perfection: It makes kettles, hatchets, swords, knives, bread; in short, it makes everything." He was making sport of our Europeans, who have such a fondness for the skin of this animal and who fight to see who will give the most to these barbarians to get it. They carry this to such an extent that my host said to me one day, showing me a very beautiful knife, "The English have no sense; they give us twenty knives like this for one beaver skin."

Paul Le Jeune, "Relation of 1634"

Enticing native populations into an incipient market economy entailed several consequences. Furs were principally traded for items of European manufacture, and an enormous volume of French trade goods went into New France in the early 1600s (Figure 5.1). Guillaume de Caën, who held the trading monopoly with the Huron, sent two ships to Tadoussac each year with freight that Charles Lalemant describes as including cloaks, blankets, shirts, hatchets, iron arrowheads, swords, knives, kettles, prunes, peas, crackers, and tobacco.[1] There are debates about how much trade items changed the lives of the Indians—many feel that in the earliest years items of European manufacture were simply utilized in the same ways as those of native manufacture.

However, for many Indians of the Maritimes, trade in furs brought about a dramatic shift in their subsistence patterns. Previously, they had passed much of the year harvesting resources on the coast, while hunting in the

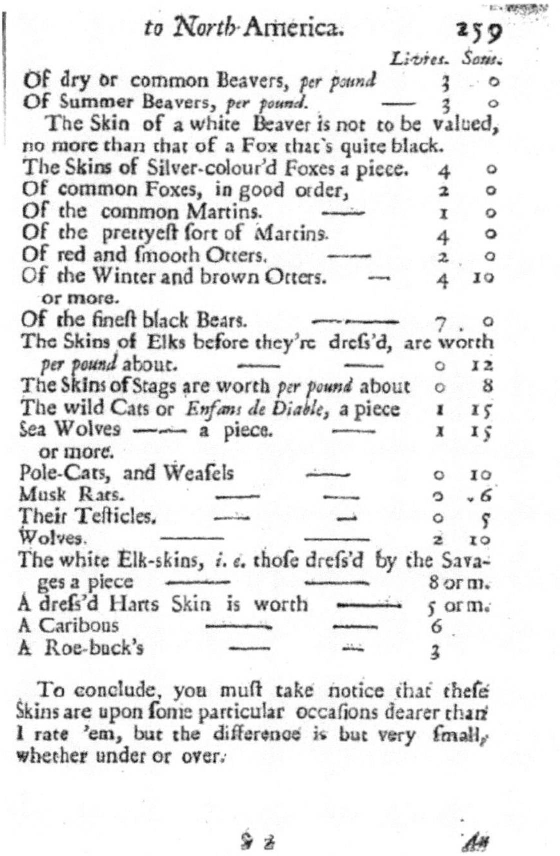

Livres. Sous.

Of dry or common Beavers, *per pound*   3   0
Of Summer Beavers, *per pound.*   —   3   0
    The Skin of a white Beaver is not to be valued, no more than that of a Fox that's quite black.
The Skins of Silver-colour'd Foxes a piece.   4   0
Of common Foxes, in good order,   2   0
Of the common Martins.   ——   1   0
Of the prettyest sort of Martins.   4   0
Of red and smooth Otters.   ——   2   0
Of the Winter and brown Otters.   —   4 10
  or more.
Of the finest black Bears.   ———   7   0
The Skins of Elks before they're dress'd, are worth
    per pound about.   ——   0 12
The Skins of Stags are worth *per pound* about   0   8
The wild Cats or *Enfans de Diable,* a piece   1 15
Sea Wolves ——— a piece.   ——   1 15
  or more.
Pole-Cats, and Weasels   ——   0 10
Musk Rats.   ——   ——   0   6
Their Testicles.   ——   —   0   5
Wolves.   ——   2 10
The white Elk-skins, *i. e.* those dress'd by the Savages a piece   ——   8 or m.
A dress'd Harts Skin is worth   ——   5 or m.
A Caribous   ——   ——   6
A Roe-buck's   ——   ——   3

    To conclude, you must take notice that these Skins are upon some particular occasions dearer than I rate 'em, but the difference is but very small, whether under or over.

Figure 5.1. The prices of furs. Lahontan, Baron Louis-Armand de Lom d'Ares, 1666–1715, *New Voyages to North-America, vol. 1.* Thwaites, Reuben Gold, ed. Chicago: A. C. McClurg, 1905, 379.

interior only in the winter. Their immersion in a trade economy focused on hunting and trapping meant that they spent more time in the forested interior and less time harvesting coastal resources. The shift in activity patterns meant that they had to supplement their diet with biscuits, dried peas, and other preserved food purchased from the French.[2]

    Hunting furs for a market represented a cognitive shift from a mind-set of hunting animals for food and clothing to one of hunting them for economic gain and exploitation. Anthropologists have seen the same cycle in numerous situations. The seduction of nontraditional goods draws people from subsistence economies to those involving market exchange. Among the Miskito Indians in Central America, for instance, the cash crop was turtle meat. Traditionally, the turtles were hunted for the Miskito's own needs and divided among friends and relatives in the way that anthropologists have seen food sharing in other hunting-gathering groups. But when the Miskito Indians were drawn into a cash economy, they had to catch many more turtles for sale to the merchants. Turtle meat became a commodity in the villages and was weighed and sold to fellow kinsmen rather than redistributed. The turtle population was eventually so reduced that it became threatened, and it meant that the Miskito had to expend far more time obtaining turtles. Fishermen had to journey farther out to sea to catch turtles, and deaths due to oceanic accidents increased.[3] They became, in essence, culturally and economically impoverished.

In the Northeast the fur trade brought Indians from an economy focused on multiple, diverse resources obtained through seasonal rounds to one focused on a few resources. Indians undoubtedly grew to some degree to think of landscapes as Europeans did, as commodities. In the words of William Cronon, "Seeing landscapes in terms of commodities meant something else as well: it treated members of an ecosystem as isolated and extractable units."[4]

There is ample evidence that entire areas of the Atlantic colonies were denuded of fur-bearing animals within decades.[5] In his *Histoire du Canada*, Father Sagard writes that by 1630 the Huron had overhunted the beaver within their territory, and they were not able to find any more. In a 1635 report, Paul Le Jeune notes that beaver had been exterminated by the Huron and that they had to obtain furs from other Indians for trade purposes. While it is difficult to come up with numbers of beaver pelts taken in the course of the fur trade, Charles Lalemant writes that in 1626 12,000–15,000 furs were being traded per year through Tadoussac. Even more left New France in 1627, described by Henry Biggar as the best year for the fur trade within the past few years. By 1650 reports indicate that there was a dramatic decline in beaver populations in the Northeast. Trader John Pynchon procured 9,000 beaver pelts between 1652 and 1658, a time when beaver were already declining (Figure 5.2). Beavers farther south persisted longer, partially because the warmer weather did not result in the thick, rich coats found in the colder north, and they were thus less desirable.

Competition for furs and trading partners fueled already tense native rivalries. The sheer magnitude of population movement in the latter half of the seventeenth century was likely unsurpassed during any prior time in native history. The fur trade necessitated movement beyond territories

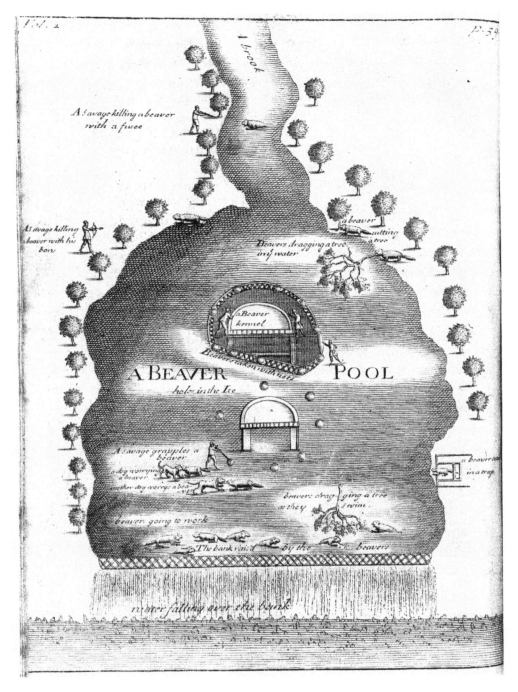

Figure 5.2. A beaver pool and methods for hunting beaver. From Lahontan, Baron Louis-Armand de Lom d'Ares, 1666–1715, *New Voyages to North-America, vol. 2*. 1905. Thwaites, Reuben Gold, ed. Chicago: A. C. McClurg, 556.

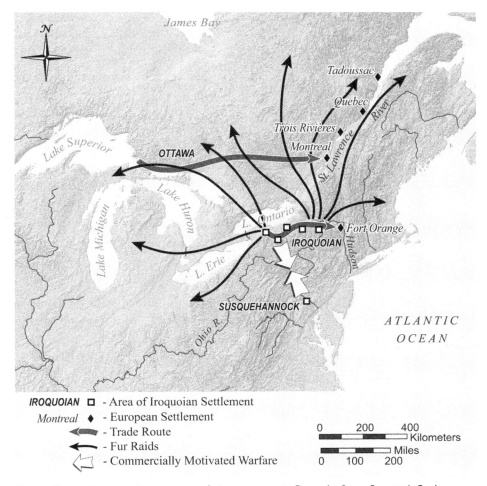

IROQUOIAN ☐ - Area of Iroquoian Settlement
Montreal ◆ - European Settlement
⬅ - Trade Route
⬅ - Fur Raids
⬅ - Commercially Motivated Warfare

0   200   400
     Kilometers
     Miles
0   100   200

Map 5.1. Sixteenth-century Iroquoian population movements. Drawn by Susan Brannock-Gaul.

where furs became scarce. Conflict, often about access to trading partners, displaced populations who moved into other territories, and they in turn often displaced other populations.

The Iroquois had already displaced the Mahicans in the Northeast Atlantic region, as well as the Huron and their allies—the Petun, Neutral, Wenroes, and Erie (Map 5.1).[6] The Great Lakes region saw resettlement from some of these groups, and they forced local groups there, such as the Sioux, to flee west. Other groups moved south into the mid-Atlantic. The Seneca, Susquehannocks, and other northern groups displaced by the Iroquois were pushed southward into the Chesapeake region. They in turn impacted the Chesapeake Bay Indians and other groups in present-day Virginia and Maryland. Slave raids by the Iroquois in the Ohio and Mississippi valleys, and perhaps farther south, displaced even more populations. To say the native world was in chaos hardly captures the moment.

Paul Ragueneau captures the time well in his description of the capture of villages of the Mission of St. Ignace in March 1649.

> The Iroquois, enemies of the Hurons, arrived by night at the frontier of this country. They numbered about a thousand men, well furnished with weapons, most of them carrying firearms obtained from their allies, the Dutch. We had no knowledge of their approach, although they had started from their country in the autumn, hunting in the forests throughout the winter, and had made a difficult journey of nearly two hundred leagues over the snow in order to take us by surprise. By night, they had reconnoitered the condition of the first place upon which they had designs. It was surrounded by a pine stockade fifteen or sixteen feet in height, and a deep ditch with which nature had strongly fortified this place on three sides. There remained only a small space that was weaker than the others.
>
> It was at this weak point that the enemy made a breach at daybreak, but so secretly and promptly that he was master of the place before anyone could mount a defense. All were then sleeping deeply, and they had no time to recognize the danger. Thus this village was taken, almost without striking a blow and with only ten Iroquois killed. Part of the Hurons—men, women, and children—were massacred then and there, while the others were made captives and were reserved for cruelties more terrible than death.[7]

A number of things recovered from archaeological excavations indicate that the mid- to late sixteenth century was a time of population displacement and conflict. Palisades were common at sites such as the Adams site in New York, dated to A.D. 1565–75, and at two slightly later Seneca sites, Tram (A.D. 1595–1610) and Cameron (A.D. 1600–1610). Even more interesting is that some of the women buried at Adams appear to be from other populations and are thought to be either captives or refugees from the region west of the contemporary Seneca territory.[8]

Trade in furs and skins came later to the Southeast, perhaps as late as the mid- to late 1600s.[9] Deerskins were by far the most desired and often-traded skins in the Southeast. With the establishment of Charleston in 1670, South Carolina became firmly established as the major gateway for the deerskin industry. Between 1717 and 1719, 17,000–24,000 deerskins were being exported from Charleston annually. This figure rose to more than 60,000 by 1725. A decade later, in the mid-1730s, 80,000 deerskins were leaving Charleston per year, a number that reached 100,000–150,000 deerskins by 1750.[10]

Such large-scale hunting by the Indians obviously took its toll on the deer population. Colonists placed additional stresses on the dwindling number of deer. Deer were an important source of meat, both for personal consumption and for the provisioning of servants and slaves. Faced with constant hunting from both colonists and Indians, the deer populations inevitably became stressed, and by the turn of the seventeenth century, it became necessary to enact formal sanctions on hunting.

In 1699 Virginia enacted a season closed to hunting from February 1 until July 31. Maryland enacted similar closed-season laws in 1729 and 1730. Indians were exempted from the laws but could not kill deer for sale. In Catawba and Cherokee country (Carolinas), deer were becoming scarce by 1750. William Bartram, the surveyor and traveler, reported the Creeks were having trouble finding deer after 1760. To stem movement of hunters from territories that were overhunted and overtrapped into new, more plentiful ones, North Carolina passed legislation in 1768 that required hunters to prove they had planted within the county where they hunted.[11] South Carolina followed a year later with a regulation that hunters could not hunt more than seven miles from their homes. In 1772 Virginia put a four-year moratorium on commercial deer hunting. Other animals, such as beaver and muskrat, also began to suffer population reductions. In South Carolina night hunting was forbidden in 1785.

Many of the consequences of the Southeastern fur trade were the same as those for Indian populations located farther north—increased time away from other economic tasks and, as furs were trapped out, further excursions into the territories of other tribes. Increased movement into other territories was certain to create political friction and result in conflicts that yielded captives, as it did with the fur trade in the Northeast. Part and parcel of the time was the development of militaristic slaving societies.[12]

Indian slaves were a highly desired commodity, and the British supported their sale, particularly through Charleston. One of these slaving societies was the Westo, who raided populations from the present-day areas of Georgia, North and South Carolina, Florida, and perhaps west as far as Alabama.

The Westos were an Iroquoian-speaking nation who originally lived on Lake Erie. After suffering defeat by the Five Nations, who were allied with the Dutch, they moved into Virginia. There they established trading relationships with the British, principally for Indian captives and deerskins. By 1659 they had moved farther south and were living by the Savannah River. There they conducted massive military campaigns across a broad area, principally for the capture of Indian slaves. Their campaigns, in turn, kept other groups on the move. By the late 1600s, nearly all of eastern North America was a fabric of oscillating displacement and resettlement.

Unlike in the Northeast, where the Iroquois took slaves to replace the deceased, slavery in the Southeast was entirely a commercial venture. In the Southeast militaristic slaving societies organized the capture of other Indians for sale in a rapidly emerging market for human labor to feed European economic activities. Trade in munitions played a large role in the slave trade. Initially against the law, trading of guns and ammunition was common by 1650. Guns not only made the capture of other natives easier but fueled the fires of trade. Guns required bullets and powder, and so further trade was required. Guns enabled the taking of more deer than did bows and arrows, and facilitated the trade of deerskins for more ammunition. Guns were the cutting edge of new technology—their burst of fire and thunderous sound, their immediate destruction, and the quick death they caused gave guns a desirability surpassed by few other trade items.

Virginia's slave traders began to move into the Carolina Piedmont by about 1650, and within a decade their commercial links extended as far south as the Savannah River. Native captives ended up on plantations in Carolina or Virginia, while others were shipped farther north or to the West Indies sugar plantations. No one really knows how many Indians suffered this fate. Until 1682 keeping Indians as slaves was illegal in Virginia, and so purchases of Indian captives went unrecorded. Historic documents indicate, however, that Indians were often found on plantations. Alan Gallay estimates that between 1670 and 1715 as many as 30,000 to 50,000 Indians were either captured by the British or sold to the British and enslaved.[13] What is even more surprising is that those estimates indicate that there were more Indian slaves exported from Carolina before 1714 than there were African slaves who entered it.

With the settlement of Carolina after 1670, traders expanded deep into the interior, and English trade in deerskins reached a volume hitherto unseen. Along with knives, beads, tobacco, cloth, and other items, the native slave trade dramatically increased in the second half of the seventeenth century. The combination of these trading endeavors meant that traders, slave raiders, slaves, and refugees moved through the landscape in larger numbers than ever before. The intense violence associated with the slave trade induced famine, crowding, and exhaustion.

Between the fur trade and the Indian slave trade, movements between the coast and the interior became much more frequent. The Iroquois had moved westward by the second half of the seventeenth century, into the Ohio Valley and Illinois, as well as farther south into the Southeast along the Atlantic (see Map 5.1). Their movements displaced other groups who moved into Illinois and Ohio, as well as south to Chesapeake Bay. Groups in the Southeast were displaced by movement from the north as well as by the interior movement of European colonial populations.

It was into this environment of famine, displacement, and increased population movement that smallpox made a dramatic entry. One of the first smallpox epidemics documented on the South Atlantic coast was in 1667, but in 1696 English colonialism connected native communities with one another in a perhaps unprecedented fashion. A massive smallpox epidemic began in 1696, likely in Virginia, and it ravaged Indians, Africans, and British populations there before moving into Carolina. Historic evidence suggests that the epidemic reached as far as the Mississippi Valley and the Gulf Coast during a four-year period ending in 1700. In those four years, smallpox decimated many native populations of the Southeast.

It is hard to come up with population mortality estimates, but historic documents indicate that mortality rates of 50–60 percent in native villages were not uncommon. Epidemics of smallpox, usually lasting three to five years, ravaged Southeastern native populations in 1696–1700, 1729–33, 1738–39, 1755–60, and 1779–83 (Map 5.2).[14] Measles epidemics were frequent in the Southeast as well, occurring in 1693, 1717, 1747, 1759, and 1772.

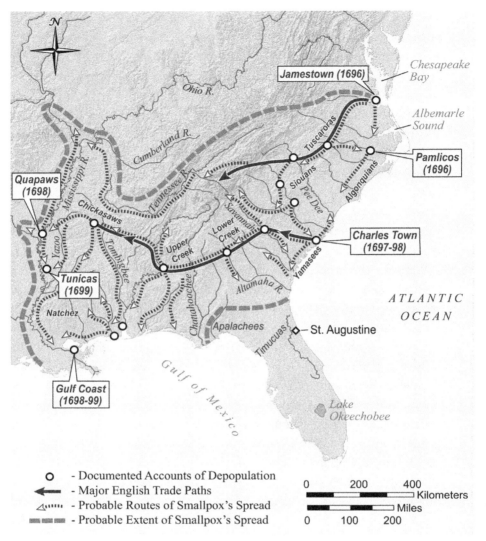

Map 5.2. The great southeastern smallpox epidemic of 1696–1700. Drawn by Susan Brannock-Gaul based on Kelton, *Epidemics and Enslavement*, 151.

Those individuals that survived the epidemics frequently joined coalescent communities such as the Lower and Upper Creeks, the Catawba, and the Chickasaws in order to have large enough populations for survival and defense against the many forces of colonialism and slavery.[15]

The mechanisms of coalescence varied and are only now becoming clear to scholars of the Mississippian shatter zone. Robbie Ethridge provides a concise discussion:

[Ned] Jenkins, in delineating the origins of the Creek Confederacy, shows that migration and coalescence into plural societies were common mechanisms for dealing with political upheavals. These mechanisms were most likely put to a new use in the Mississippian shatter zone in order to merge the polities in central Alabama and into the Creek Confederacy and to take in refugee groups. In the case of the Creeks all of the various groups retained their political and social identities. The Chickasaws too put an old social institution to a new use in the Mississippian shatter zone but with different results. The Chickasaws absorbed people through the *fanimingo* institution wherein an outside group was ritually adopted. The Chakchiumas and others were completely absorbed in the Chickasaw order, and, as far as we can tell, they became Chickasaws.[16]

Indeed, the chaos that emerged from new economic strategies, epidemic diseases, and massive social and political upheaval redefined the native landscape.

The fur and deerskin trade is a time when humans made frequent and distant migrations, a time when overhunting, processing of furs, and "improvement" of the landscape severely altered local ecology. Human relationships with nonhuman mammal populations took a distinct departure from prior patterns, and there were undoubtedly shifts in the epidemiological landscape. Those shifts may well have involved tick-vectored diseases.

In the past three decades or so, we have only begun to appreciate the complexity of tick-vectored diseases, not only in terms of their "emergence," but also of their antiquity and diversity. Along the Atlantic coast, there are at least three tick-vectored diseases newly discovered in the past 20–30 years.[17] Southern tick-associated rash illness (STARI) occurs in the Southeast and was first recognized as a distinct disease in the late 1990s. Ehrlichiosis was first recognized as a distinct disease in the United States in the late 1980s but did not become a reportable disease until 1999. *Rickettsia parkeri* was first described in 2004 when a serviceman in Tidewater Virginia was diagnosed with a disease that was like tick-borne spotted fever diseases (for example, Rocky Mountain spotted fever). All three "new" tick diseases are likely to have much greater antiquity and were just not recognized as human diseases.

A fourth tick-vectored disease, Lyme disease, was first reported in Connecticut in the late 1970s. By now most of us know about Lyme disease, but at the time it was thought to be a newly emerging infectious disease. It turns out to be a disease not only of much longer duration, but of much greater geographic dispersal, and it is an epidemic moving outward both west and south of its original point of discovery.[18] Much of the transmission cycle of Lyme disease is tied to a few simple factors: nonhuman mammalian hosts, mast years for oak acorns, and ecological disturbance bringing tick-bearing deer and humans into increased contact.

Lyme disease is a bacterial disease caused by a corkscrew-shaped bacterium known as a spirochete, *Borrelia bergdorferi*. Interestingly, on a molecular level it is closely related to the spirochete that causes syphilis, genus *Treponema* (see chapter 3). Lyme is carried by the *Ixodes scapularis* (deer) tick. It is but one of many tick-carried diseases that include Rocky Mountain spotted fever and Babesiosis. Tick-vectored diseases are not uniform in their transmission cycle, and that variance impacts the size of the nonhuman host population needed to maintain an infection. Ticks, like all arthropods, have a complicated life cycle that includes four stages of development: egg, larval, nymph, and adult. During all of them, a blood meal is necessary to reproduce and advance into the next stage.

Larval ticks hatch from eggs in midsummer and seek a host, generally a small mammal such as a mouse or a bird. They feed for two or three days, and then within a month molt and emerge as nymphs about the size of a poppyseed. They remain in that state all winter and late in the spring or summer of the following year feed again. About three months later the final molt occurs, and the ticks emerge as adults. The peak season for adult activity is mid-autumn. The adult tick feeds and mates on its preferred host, the white-tailed deer (*Odecoileus virginianus*), or on other potential hosts such as humans and dogs.

Not all ticks need to acquire an infection in the first nymph stage in order to become infectious, however, and that is what makes some of the tick-vectored diseases unique. Some, like Rocky Mountain spotted fever, are transmitted as *transovarial* infections from adult to offspring, so larvae hatch already carrying the disease. The implications of transovarial infections are immense. For one, it means that there does not need to be a large number of infected hosts in order to maintain a transmission cycle of disease.

Lyme disease is not transmitted transovarially, and the pathogenic bacteria need to be obtained from infected hosts, so a larger infected host population translates into a greater chance of acquiring an infection. Common hosts for Lyme disease include humans, dogs, mice (especially white-footed mice, *Peromyscus leucopus*), and birds. In areas with endemic Lyme disease, about 25–35 percent of tick nymphs and about 50–70 percent of adults are infected. Richard Ostfeld, of the Cary Institute of Ecosystem Studies, has been studying Lyme disease for a couple of decades. He says that the number of nymphs is generally a good predictor of human infections. The nymphs are smaller than adults, less detectable on clothing, and feed during a time of year when people are active outside, at least in modern times. Ostfeld and his coworkers found a number of years ago that one of the most powerful predictors of the number of nymphs in an area is the number of acorns.[19]

White-tailed deer feed on forest browse during much of the year. When acorns are available, though, deer prefer those to other foods, and so during years of high acorn production, so-called mast years, white-tailed deer populations congregate in oak forests. Traditional knowledge would argue that it is the presence of deer that makes for higher rates of Lyme disease. To some degree that is true, but Ostfeld and colleagues have added a twist to our knowledge of the transmission cycle.

Deer are not the only mammals with a preference for acorns; white-footed mice also consume them. In winters following a mast year, mouse populations experience higher survivorship, and immensely higher reproduction levels. The mice have lots of food, survivorship is high, and the number of offspring is even higher. And so, the following summer there are lots more white-footed mice. Simply put, years when there are more acorns are good predictors for higher levels of Lyme disease two years later, the time it takes a nymph to emerge.

Lyme disease probably still hasn't fully moved out of the category of "emerging infectious diseases," given that it is still enlarging its infectivity zone by leaps and bounds. It is a perfect example of an emerging infection. Most are emerging only in the sense that they have cycled primarily among nonhuman populations as zoonoses for millennia, and only through the intersection of nonhumans, humans, and the correct biozone have they crossed into human populations (or in many cases humans have crossed over into a new epidemiological landscape). As in Pavlovsky's nidal zones of plague, described in chapter 2, those intersections, sometimes brought about as well at times by climatic disturbance, have resulted in epidemics. Lyme has probably been cycling among indigenous populations in North America for centuries, and native populations may well have made some connection between local ecology and cycles of disease. It wouldn't be the first time that at least some aspect or aspects of transmission chains were detected without the use of modern technology.

Here is an example. Several hemorrhagic fevers are among the diseases called "emerging infections." One such disease is the Four Corners virus. In May 1993, two members of the same family living near the Four Corners region in New Mexico died of an acute respiratory disease within five days of each other. Public health workers sent samples of their lung tissue to the Centers for Disease Control, where it was determined that the cause of their deaths was a virus belonging to a group called hantaviruses. Widespread in Asia and Europe, hantaviruses are responsible for diseases that cause hemorrhaging in the kidneys.[20] With further detective work, the scientists determined that the disease had circulated for some time in rodents in the area, particularly among the white-footed deer mouse, *Peromyscus maniculatus.* Local ecological conditions contributed to the 1993 infection. The Four Corners had been in a drought for several years, but in 1993 much more rain and snowfall facilitated mouse survival and reproduction. With so many mice, more mouse/human interactions were unavoidable. When CDC workers interviewed the local Navajo, neither the disease nor its non-human hosts were news at all. The Navajo had a long-standing tradition that includes mice as agents of disease who should be avoided.

I think we can safely assume that in the sixteenth through eighteenth centuries in eastern North America—a time of increased human intrusion into nonhuman mammalian habitats, a time of increased animal harvests, a time of immense reformation of the natural landscape, a time of unprecedented human migration—increased transmission of vectored zoonotic diseases occurred. The activity that was likely most closely linked to Lyme emergence is forest habitat destruction. It would have simplified the species diversity, which has been identified as a primary factor in rising Lyme disease prevalence. I think tick-carried fevers undoubtedly impacted native and newcomer populations but remained, as those diseases often have, epidemiological oscillations under the radar of detection.

The Europeans who wrote the history of the time were probably unfamiliar with zoonotic diseases and attributed illness caused by them to other infectious diseases or causes. Arthropod vectors and disease transmission chains that included those vectors were simply not concepts. Despite the fact that zoonotic infections were present in the Old World—the plague for instance—I think it has been a long time since those descended from Rome appreciated the natural world in a way that allowed them to make the subtle observations that were made by the Navajo.

6

CONTESTED COLONIES

It was a feature peculiar to the colonial wars of North America, that the toils and dangers of the wilderness were to be encountered before the adverse hosts could meet. A wide and apparently an impervious boundary of forests severed the possessions of the hostile provinces of France and England. The hardy colonist, and the trained European who fought at his side, frequently expended months in struggling against the rapids of the streams, or in effecting the rugged passes of the mountains, in quest of an opportunity to exhibit their courage in a more martial conflict. But, emulating the patience and self-denial of the practised native warriors, they learned to overcome every difficulty; and it would seem that, in time, there was no recess of the woods so dark, nor any secret place so lovely, that it might claim exemption from the inroads of those who had pledged their blood to satiate their vengeance, or to uphold the cold and selfish policy of the distant monarchs of Europe.

James Fenimore Cooper, *The Last of the Mohicans: A Narrative of 1757*

During the earliest colonial years, when Europeans pressed into the un-known wilderness of the Americas, conflicts were largely waged between those who had lived there for centuries and those who had not. Skirmishes were fought by natives to protect their kin, their provisions, and their ter-ritories. Europeans fought to gain entry to new lands and to acquire new resources. But through time the yardarms of ships from distant lands more frequently advanced.

These American conflicts were distinct from the conflicts of the old or-der. Whereas Europeans had for centuries amassed legions in open plains to fight in armed combat, or laid siege to fortified cities, or hauled massive war machines across well-mapped terrain, conflicts in the Americas offered no opportunity for those known strategies. On the frontier, maps were embryonic at best, and roads consisted of trails through the wilderness. Indian allies were involved on each side of every conflict. Europeans were further accustomed to marching toward the enemy and standing ground in the face of the approaching armies. No Indian would stand and take such casualties. Indians fought from cover, a novel approach to Europeans, and they aimed at specific targets, a dramatic departure from the European practice of loosing massed volleys into enemy troops.

Although the native slave trade endured a fairly lengthy period of prosperity from at least 1650 until 1715, by the turn of the century the commercial partnerships between Europeans and Indians were well on their way to fraying. The smallpox epidemic of 1696–1700 did little to stabilize native populations, and several epidemics that followed for the next decade—measles, influenza, yellow fever, and typhus—continued to impose suffering and high mortality. Disputes over trade abuses, insults, land encroachments, hunting rights, and of course, slaving, dominated relations between Europeans and Indians. Finally, frustration and anger led to two great wars between Indians and colonists, and when the second war was over, the Indian slave trade would for all intents and purposes be over.

The Tuscarora War, the first of these, was fought between 1711 and 1713. Ostensibly, it was about land encroachments by the British along the Trent and Neuse Rivers in eastern North Carolina, but lots of other discontents factored into the general hostilities. Allied with the Tuscarora were Algonkians, and with the British were Yamasee, Apalachee, Yuchi, and Siouan. After a series of military engagements in 1711, a Port Royal (South Carolina) planter named John Barnwell led colonial forces against the Tuscarora. From January to March they campaigned against the Tuscarora, until in early March they came finally to the main Tuscarora fort on Contentnea Creek in North Carolina, named Hancock's Town after the Tuscarora leader.

The town had a well-conceived defensive structure consisting of a palisade-and-trench system, and the Tuscarora withstood British attempts to breach their fortifications for several weeks. Famine certainly added to the problems of the Tuscarora during the siege, but illness also must have reduced their strength. A "pestilential distemper" circulated through North Carolina in December of 1711, and it likely struck the Tuscarora and Algonkian sometime just before the siege. When the victorious British forces entered Hancock's Town in April, they found that there were "a good number of sick and wounded and a very great mortality which with their nastiness produced such stink."[1]

Despite a treaty after the capture of Hancock's Town in April of 1712, by August of the same year, war had erupted again. This time, the Tuscarora and their allies retreated to Fort Neoheroka (Nohoroco), located on Contentnea Creek in Greene County, North Carolina. Within the palisade at Neoheroka, the Indians sequestered themselves and battled from there. Following a three-week siege led by commander James Moore, on March 22, 1713, British forces set fire to the fort, and about 200 Indian men, women, and children were burned inside. Another 900–1,000 were either killed outside the fort or captured and sold into slavery in South Carolina. All told, about 1,200 Tuscarora and their allies either perished on that day or were taken and sold into slavery.[2] The Neoheroka battle decisively ended Tuscarora resistance.

In the 1990s archaeologists from East Carolina University, directed by David Phelps, located and excavated Fort Neoheroka over a period of four years. They uncovered most of the east wall of the fort and about ten houses within the walls. The houses were actually pits in the ground covered with timbers, then reed or cane mats, then a layer of bark, and finally a top layer of earth. They served as bunkers during the siege. Among the artifacts the archaeologists recovered was a personal bundle, "found with a portion of its storage sack. It contained European trade beads, two smoking pipes, an archer's wrist guard, a copper bracelet, a brass spoon, some decorative copper disks, a pair of brass shoe buckles, buckshot, and a handful of squash and melon seed probably intended for planting when the battle was over."[3] Other artifacts include a burned musket with the trigger guard and butt plate, brass buttons from a long woolen coat, musket balls, metal farm tools, wine and rum bottles, beads, glass arrowheads, and shrapnel from cannon balls. There were also charred food remains and traditional Tuscarora pottery. The archaeological remains provide a testament to the clash of cultures.

The Yamasee War was fought on the heels of the Tuscarora War, between 1715 and 1717, primarily in South Carolina. Many of the same reasons could be cited for its origins, most in some way having to do with discontent on both sides over Indian and colonist relations. The specific charge of the Yamasee against the British was encroachment on their lands without payment, but fear of slavery was also contained in their complaints. Both were serious issues. In 1707 the colony had taken steps to prevent encroachments and had prohibited colonists from settling between the Savannah and Combahee Rivers, and Port Royal Sound, all Yamasee lands in South Carolina. This kept many colonists—those at Port Royal—for instance, limited to the sea islands, but it was a prohibition out of tune with the economic development and support of the colony. With the growing economic importance of rice, the Yamasee lands became more and more desirable. Rice production could not be adequately practiced on the sea islands, but the mainland Yamasee lands, with their many tidal creeks and freshwater rivers, were perfect for rice agriculture. Inward drift and landed invasion began.

In addition, Indian disputes with British traders escalated between 1710 and 1715, almost all involving illegal capture of slaves. It seems from records kept by the Commissioners of the Indian Trade, a body created by the South Carolina House of Commons to hear abuses and to regulate trade with Indians, that a number of cases of British interference and downright illegal slave capture had occurred in the years between 1710 and 1715.[4] Among the charges were several that included the kidnapping of individuals who had been adopted and become kinsmen. The Yamasee and other groups felt, perhaps rightly so, that soon such illegal actions would lead to their own capture and enslavement. The census of 1715 only bolstered their fears; it was seen by some as a first step in documenting their numbers that would lead to their enslavement.[5]

Beyond trader abuses and land encroachment, some also point to rising debt of the Yamasee to the British as a factor in growing discontent. Debt, through credit obtained at the company store, is a hallmark of economic conversion. The prices for items obtained on credit are often very high, given limited availability and the cost of credit. Before long, the goods and services of those in debt serve only to pay past debt, and extraction of the indebted from the trading relationship at that point becomes impossible. The Yamasee and others, with declining deer and human populations to trade, were essentially bankrupt.[6] Finally, in addition to all of the other reasons for discontent, the alliance during the Tuscarora War probably did little to bring the Yamasee and the British closer to each other.

The Yamasee War began on April 15, 1715, as a revolt of the Yamasee against South Carolina, but it soon spiraled into a multitribal war. After killing Carolina traders and others, the Yamasee raided the area around Port Royal and captured 300 British settlers and African slaves. A short while later more traders were killed. The Cherokees and Piedmont groups, as well as the Creek, joined the rebellion and killed traders in the mountains. The war proceeded in a similar fashion, not so much with large battles as with stealth, as traders and others were killed in periodic raids.

After some months of such skirmishes, a realignment of alliances took place between the British and Cherokee. The Yamasee War ended in 1717 after the British made treaties with most of the Indian groups. The Yamasee went south to Florida following the war; some say they were driven southward, some that they retreated of their own accord. The mortality for the British in the war had reached 7 percent or more, and an entire generation of traders was rubbed out. Mortality was likely as high or higher for the Indians, but the rebellion served to end the trade of Indian slaves. With no traders to enlist native groups into war against each other, and with Indians' complete disgust for the British colonial powers, the era of native slavery slowly ground to a halt.

The repercussions of the Yamasee War were large. With severe population losses on both sides, work forces were affected. Food stores were depleted, and food production lagged. Political realignments and social restructuring were necessary. Indian groups moved from spaces previously inhabited, and many Indians living in or around Carolina migrated out. Some of the coastal Indians went inland and joined the Creek or Catawba. As one might expect, as far as Indian groups were concerned, the star of the French and Spanish rose in comparison to that of the British. As for the British, Carolina had begun as a proprietors enterprise, but following the war it was turned officially into a royal colony in 1729. By 1730, after years of rebuilding from the Yamasee War, Carolina entered into markets that centered on production, especially rice production with supplementary involvement in cattle, food, and wood production.

Between 1689 and 1763 four major conflicts erupted in the colonies, largely as a product of the competing appetites of European nations (Table 6.1). The earliest two, King William's War and Queen Anne's War, as their names suggest, were largely about rivalries in the European homeland. But as time went on, those rivalries were further fueled by a struggle to control colonial markets and raw materials. King George's War and the French and Indian War were stimulated by economic interests in America. Britain and France were always on opposite sides, no matter how many other European powers were involved in each conflict.

Table 6.1. Major conflicts, 1689–1763

Dates	European Name	American Name	Major Allies
1689–97	War of the League of Augsburg	King William's War	Britain, Holland, Spain, their colonies, and Native American allies against France, its colonies and Native American allies
1702–13	War of the Spanish Succession	Queen Anne's War	Britain, Holland, their colonies, and Native American allies against France, Spain, their colonies, and Native American allies
1743–48	War of the Austrian Succession	King George's War	Britain, its colonies, its Native American allies, and Austria against France, Spain, their Native American allies, and Prussia
1756–63	Seven Years War	French and Indian War	Britain, its colonies, and Native American allies against France, its colonies, and Native American allies

Source: Breen and Hall, *Colonial America in an Atlantic World*, 166.

The French and Indian War, also known as the Seven Years War, was the last of those conflicts. It was generated by centuries-old rivalries between France and Britain, but the conflict was ultimately over economic resources and territory in the Ohio Valley. In the early 1700s the Ohio Valley was largely unclaimed, a vast territory of potential riches that lay adjacent to both French and the English territorial claims. British land claims lay largely east of the Ohio Valley, while those of the French were situated north, south, and west of the Ohio Country.

Friction caused by territorial disputes and competition for resources was further driven by the entry of the French into the southeastern fur trade. Situated in Louisiana from 1699 until 1763, the French offered a significant trade outlet for deerskins. Their relationships with native groups, especially the Choctaw, their main allies in the region, were more oriented around gift-giving than were those of the British. Each year they lavished gifts that were worth the value of thousands of deerskins.[7] The participation of the French in the deerskin trade allowed groups such as the Choctaws and the Creeks to negotiate between the two European trade alliances.

The prospect of a French empire stretching uninterrupted from Canada to Louisiana was unbearable to the British (Map 6.1). The riches that would flow in both directions could threaten the entire British Empire, and so British expansion westward across the Appalachian Mountains seemed critical to British security and prosperity. The desirability of the Ohio Valley was about far more than land, though. In the early 1700s the Ohio Country was one of the richest hunting grounds in northeastern North America. White-tail deer and several fur-bearing species, including beaver, were abundant in the region.

If the contestations between the British and French were complicated, those of the Indian populations located in the Ohio Valley were even more so. A diverse group of Indians had immigrated into the region from more eastern locales, including the Lenape, Munsee, and Shawnee from the Delaware region, Nanticoke from the Chesapeake, Mahican from the Hudson Valley, Wyandot from near Detroit, and the Iroquois from the St. Lawrence and a bit beyond. The dominant power in the region was the Iroquois Confederacy (see chapters 4 and 5), a union of five nations—later, the Tuscarora joined them, forming the Six Nations.

It was largely the involvement of the Iroquois in the trapping and sales of furs from the Ohio Country after about 1730 that stimulated tremendous interest amongst European traders, and they swarmed into the area. The Iroquois, although wooed by both the French and English, remained neutral in their trading alliances. They resisted attempts by either European nation to maneuver them into solitary trade agreements. Both European powers had commercial designs beyond furs in the Ohio Country, and they made plans to establish enterprises there.

In terms of sheer population, the British had a definite edge. In 1750 New France had a population of 80,000, while that of British America boasted 1,460,000, of which 300,000 were African slaves.[8] Despite lower population numbers, though, France had proven its ability to explore and claim new lands—the amount of land claimed by France was far larger than the territory under British claims.

In the spring of 1749, the governor of New France, the Marquis de la Galissonière, dispatched Pierre Joseph Céloron, a French commander, to reassert French claims to the Ohio territory. But even as Céloron was burying a

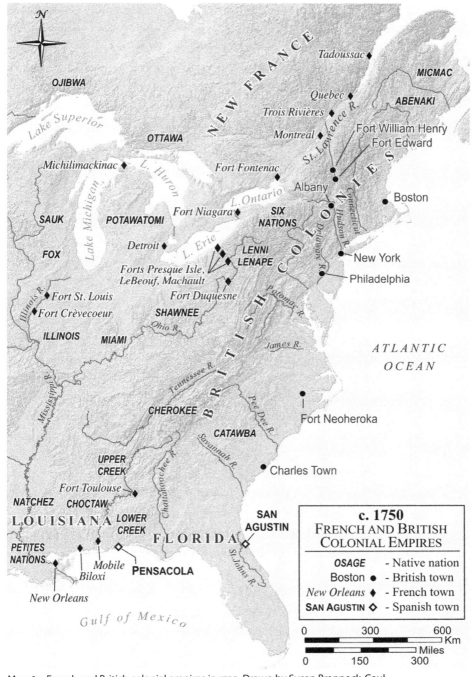

Map 6.1. French and British colonial empires in 1750. Drawn by Susan Brannock-Gaul.

series of six lead plates along the Ohio River that asserted French territorial claims, Virginia was granting land claims to the Ohio Company, a group of 20 or so land speculators from Virginia. In 1749, with a grant from King George II, they began plans to move 100 families into the Ohio Country and to establish a fort. The Ohio Company quickly moved into the Ohio Valley with a surveyor, Christopher Gist, to find the best lands for settlement, deciding on the upper Ohio Valley. Between 1750 and 1754 the British strengthened their presence in the region, but constant disagreements between New York, Pennsylvania, and Virginia over which colony should negotiate with the Six Nations hindered their progress.

The French, well aware of the British incursions, mounted their own movements. In 1753 the new governor, the Marquis de Duquesne, initiated a program to build a series of forts on the upper Ohio River that would strengthen France's frontier. These included Fort Duquesne, Fort Presque Isle, Fort LeBoeuf, and Fort Machault. Fort Duquesne was to be the linchpin of French claims to the Ohio Valley lands. Located at the confluence of the Monongahela and Allegheny Rivers, where the Ohio River originates, it was situated to control all access to the Ohio River and adjacent lands.

While the French were busy establishing forts, the lieutenant governor of Virginia, Robert Dinwiddie, was urging the crown to build its own chain of forts in the region. Dinwiddie made the case that the French establishment of forts, particularly at the forks of the Ohio River, was a threat to future British interests. His emphatic plea was undoubtedly due in no small part to the fact that he was a shareholder in the Ohio Company, which, as previously stated, had land speculation schemes in the Ohio region. In 1753 Dinwiddie directed a young lieutenant colonel, George Washington, to proceed to Fort LeBoeuf and instruct the French to leave. Washington delivered a letter from Dinwiddie that was received and considered by the French commander, Captain Jacques Legardeur de Saint Pierre, and followed by a letter back to Virginia. The French, it seems, were not inclined to leave. Some form of war, commercial or of another nature, was a foregone conclusion. It became formal, more or less, in early 1754 after Washington, through a series of bungled maneuvers, began military action against the French.

The French and Indian War began as one of frontiers. The principal places of battle were either fortifications that guarded important frontier locations, or the forest areas that lay in between those fortifications. But conflicts, like infectious disease, tend to spread far beyond the boundaries of the initial outbreak. The French and Indian War was no exception—by 1761 it had spread to the Caribbean, India, and West Africa, becoming truly a world war. The comparison with disease is more than just simple analogy. Throughout the journals, letters, and other documents reporting on the French and Indian War famine, poor sanitation, trauma, and disease are common references.[9]

Both disease and starvation characterize conflict situations, and the connection between famine and disease is not a new one. The New Testament of the Christian Bible describes four beings that emerge during the apocalypse on horses—they are usually seen as symbolizing conquest, war, famine, and death.[10] What cannot be fully appreciated from the biblical presentation is the true synergism between them—malnutrition, especially protein deficiency, frequently leads to suppressed immunity and infection, while infection interferes with nutrient absorption and increases the need for some nutrients.[11]

Famine is almost always associated in some way with epidemic disease. Famine-driven epidemics are an undeniable example of the synergism between nutrition and disease—undernourished populations are exposed to disease pathogens that successfully mount the immune system due to impaired response; portions of the population are removed from production; the body system requires further nutrients to combat infection; and everything is lacking. Although the argument could be made that large-scale deaths could cause famine, this is not often the case, with one of the exceptions being high mortality in virgin-soil epidemics, where much of the production force is lost very fast. Generally, however, epidemic disease follows on the heels of mass starvation and famine.

A variety of conditions during conflict conspire to cause famine. One is the simple elimination of available food through territorial destruction. Either as an unplanned consequence of bombing and burning, or as a deliberate strategy practiced to hamper the enemy, the destruction of crops and stored foods leads to starvation. A second cause of famine is the depletion of local food stores, either with or without permission, to feed defense or invasion forces. Prevention of food transport is a third common consequence of conflict—it is simply impossible to get foods through blockades and other barriers. A fourth issue is the actual absence of food producers.

Conflicts remove both active military participants and the impacted public from the agricultural workforce. Combine those impacted directly by conflict with those suffering from increased illness, and there aren't enough producers to feed the entire population.

Starvation and malnutrition were commonplace during the French and Indian War. Native populations, so long the source of agricultural products, were often active participants in the conflict. Their removal from agricultural and hunting endeavors left a shortage of food resources for both natives and colonists. Accounts of the French and Indian War contain numerous reports of starvation affecting the militia and civilians during the war. What follows is but one example. In the winter of 1757–58, the French suffered tremendous famine. Wheat harvests failed in 1757 for the second year in a row, and bread became a scarce and expensive resource. In December of 1757, the French colonial government cut the beef ration from a pound a day to a pound and a half a week. Beef was supplemented by horse meat and cod. Throughout the winter of 1757–58, food supplies continued to dwindle, and only a convoy of ships that arrived from France on May 22 averted actual starvation in Quebec.[12]

Production was only one of the one of the issues that resulted in the 1757–58 famine in Quebec. During any war year, food had to be provided for an immense military force that included 15,000 regular soldiers, as well as Indian warriors and other militia on regular assignment. The available local food supplies could not feed such an immense population, and additional food supplies brought in from elsewhere were necessary to supplement food available locally. Supplementary food, however, was difficult to obtain. By the fall of 1757, British naval forces had established effective blockades at Gibraltar, along the Channel coast, and in the Gulf of St. Lawrence. Corruption in the government of New France further affected the distribution of food supplies, through inflation as well as supply and demand. And, finally, the famine occurred exactly at a time when the attention of the king and ministers of France was directed toward pressing political campaigns closer to home.

British forces suffered similar bouts of famine during the war. One of those led to the surrender of Fort Loudoun (Monroe County, Tennessee) in 1760, after a French siege designed to starve the defenders out. Starvation at Fort Loudoun was a slow process that began with reductions in the corn allotments and led to the consumption of the horses. Finally, when there was no more available food, Captain Paul Demere surrendered the fort and its contents to the Cherokee in return for safe passage to Fort Prince George.[13]

One generally thinks of food shortages in the extreme, with the end result being famine and starvation. In the less extreme, shortage of food resources can result in malnutrition. The shortages tend to be of foods containing essential nutrients, and they can be influential in the stamina and cognitive acuity of the troops. They are often fresh foods such as fruits and vegetables. For example, scurvy is caused by a deficiency of vitamin C. Humans are one of the few animals who have lost the ability to synthesize this vitamin and must obtain it from consistent dietary sources. The arms and legs of those affected by scurvy show bruised, purplish markings caused by bleeding beneath the skin. Gums are often seriously distressed, and cartilaginous involvement results in a loosening and subsequent loss of teeth. Other symptoms include general fatigue as well as swelling of the joints and pain with movement. It is associated historically with times that reliance on stored provisions meant that fresh fruit was not available, such as war, long sea voyages, and economic crises.

Scurvy was a problem in the French and Indian War as it has been in many wars before and after. John Knox, a British captain, writes that an infusion of spruce was used as a curative:

The visible effects of the spruss, or hemlock-spruce, which has been given, for some time, to the scorbutic men in the hospitals, put it beyond doubt, that it must also be the best preservative against the scurvy; and, as the lives of brave soldiers are ever to be regarded with the utmost attention, it is ordered that the regiments be provided with a sufficient quantity of that particular spruce, which each corps must send for occasionally; and it is to be made into a liquor, according to the method with which the Surgeons are already acquainted; and Commanding Officers must be answerable that their men drink of this liquor, at least twice every day, mixed with their allowance of rum.[14]

There were less mainstream methods to cure scurvy as well:

This morning I was an eye-witness to the ceremony of burying a sailor alive, *mirabile dictu*, for the cure of the sea scurvy. To explain this matter it must be observed, that a pit was made in the ground, and the patient stood in it, with his head only above the level of the earth; then the mold was thrown in loose about him, and there he remained for some hours: this I am told is to be repeated every day, until his recovery is perfected.[15]

In the Western world the diseases most disposed to reach epidemic proportions during famines have been typhus, smallpox, dysentery, tuberculosis, bubonic plague, influenza, and pneumonia. Two factors, often working together, facilitate the occurrence of epidemics under famine conditions. The first is loss of individual immune competence, and the second is loss of community resistance to the spread of infection. Loss of community resistance to infection can be accounted for in several ways: population dislocations due to migrating, displaced segments of the population; overcrowding of public facilities, which destroys spatial barriers to infectious disease; and fatigue, which undermines domestic hygiene and public sanitation.

Among the diseases commonplace in military encampments were smallpox and typhus. Smallpox, as discussed before and like many diseases, is primarily transmitted by respiration. The pathogen is carried on droplets that are exhaled from the lungs, and thus close proximity to infected individuals is necessary. Throughout history, smallpox has always been one of the consequences of conflict. Smallpox epidemics occur often outside of conflict situations, but smallpox burns brightly in the flames of human aggression. In the centuries that smallpox cycled in human populations, conflicts in Egypt, Rome, Greece, North Africa, and China are but a few marked by smallpox epidemics. It is thus not surprising that folks figured out early on at least some of the ways that one became infected with the disease, and some of the treatment options.

At about the turn of the ninth century, a Baghdad physician, Rhazes, wrote *Treatise on the Smallpox and Measles*. In it, he clearly differentiated the two diseases and revealed smallpox to be the childhood disease that was commonly found in Southwest Asia at his time.[16] No one knows specifically when infections were first intentionally introduced into the healthy, but the practice has considerable history. Known as variolation, the idea was that rubbing a small amount of the material from a smallpox pustule into an open wound of a healthy person generally produced milder cases than smallpox acquired through natural means, but which would leave lifelong immunity. Variolation is not the same thing as vaccination (see below), and the distinction is important. Variolation is the injection of virulent human pathogen into someone, which represented both a significant risk of death and a source of infection that could spread to someone else.

Variolation had been introduced into Constantinople (Turkey) around 1672, having arrived from China or Persia. In China, Joseph Lister, a trader for the East India Company, reported in 1700 the practice of blowing smallpox scabs up the nostril. In other Old World locations, fluids from active smallpox pustules were scratched into the skin of nonimmune individuals, those who had not previously had smallpox. The practice, which was popular among European rural peasants, was known as "buying the smallpox." In the Americas, Cotton Mather, a minister in the Massachusetts Bay colony, learned of the practice of variolation in 1706 from his African slave.

The method was popularized in England by Lady Mary Wortley Montague. Lady Montague was no stranger to smallpox—she suffered facial disfiguration from the disease, following the death of her young brother from smallpox. Consequently, when she was exposed to the practice of variolation in Turkey, where her husband was British ambassador to Turkey, she immediately recognized its importance and potential life-saving properties. In a now-famous letter dated April 1, 1717, she wrote to her friend Sarah Chiswell in London:

> *Apropos* of distempers, I am going to tell you a thing that will make you wish yourself here. The small-pox, so fatal, and so general amongst us, is here entirely harmless, by the invention of *ingrafting*, which is the term they give it. There is a set of old women, who make it their business to perform the operation, every autumn in the month of September, when the great heat is abated.
>
> People send to one another to know if any of their family has a mind to have the small-pox: they make parties for this purpose, and when they are met (commonly fifteen or sixteen together), the old woman comes with a nut-shell full of the matter of the best sort of small-pox, and asks what vein you please to have opened.
>
> She immediately rips open that you offer her, with a large needle (which gives you no more pain than a common scratch) and puts into the vein, as much matter as can lie upon the head of her needle, and after that binds up the little wound with a hollow bit of shell; and in this manner opens four or five veins.[17]

Lady Montague had her young son variolated in Constantinople in 1718.

When she returned to England in 1721, Lady Montague had her daughter variolated, the first professional variolation in England. She invited people to witness the impact of variolation on her daughter, among them Sir Hans Sloane, the physician who attended Lady Montague when she was ill with smallpox. Sir Sloane was then the president of the Royal Society and the king's physician, and it was he who stirred interest among the royal family in the practice of variolation. Over the next few years, several of the royal family were variolated, and those royal variolations began the establishment of an acceptable medical practice in England, but her news was not able to save her friend Sarah Chiswell. She died of smallpox in 1726.

Angela Thompson, a historian, relates a particularly interesting case of variolation.[18] When smallpox threatened to devastate the province of Guanajuato, Mexico, in October of 1797, the intendant of Guanajuato, Juan de Riaño, instituted a program of variolation to protect the children. He recognized that there would be resistance to his plan, and so he performed the protective measure first on his own six children. Through the campaign which followed, approximately 78 percent of the children of Guanajuato province were variolated, a measure that undoubtedly decreased mortality rates by a significant amount—mortality for those variolated was 1 percent, compared with 28 percent for those who did not receive the treatment.[19]

About the same time as Riaño's campaign in Mexico, in 1796 the British physician Edward Jenner noticed that people who had previously contracted a mild pox disease, usually from cattle, failed to produce any smallpox symptoms upon variolation. He injected cowpox into several people, including his son, and found that when he later injected them with smallpox, they failed to develop pustules or exhibit other smallpox symptoms. He termed his protective injection of cowpox *vaccination* (from the Latin *vacca*, for "cow").

Vaccination offered several improvements over variolation. The bovine virus was more benign than smallpox. His vaccine also did not require individuals infected with smallpox to be present in order to provide protective measures. Jenner published his findings in 1798 as *An Inquiry into the Causes and Effects of Variolae Vaccinae, a Disease, Discovered in some of the Western Counties of England, particularly Gloucestershire, and known by the Name of Cow Pox.* By 1801 it had been translated into several languages, including German, French, Spanish, Dutch, Italian, and Latin.

There were, however, still obstacles and practical limitations to the implementation of vaccination. For one, there was a general distrust among folks regarding the injection of bovine material—a popular cartoon depicted vaccination subjects with cow parts emerging from various anatomical structures (Figure 6.1).[20] Another obstacle was distribution—access to the vaccine still required either infected cattle or humans infected with cowpox.

Guanajuato again comes into the story, because it was here (among other places) that an industrious Spanish physician, Francisco Xavier de Balmis, began a series of vaccination campaigns in 1804 that were financed by the Spanish monarchy.[21] Because cattle infected with smallpox aren't to be found everywhere, and undoubtedly also transporting enough cattle entailed additional considerations, Balmis used children as his transport mechanism. At the onset of the voyage from Spain, he administered the

Figure 6.1. *The Cow-Pock—or—the Wonderful Effects of the New Inoculation!*—vide. the Publications of ye Anti-Vaccine Society. Print (color engraving) published June 12, 1802, by H. Humphrey, St. James's Street. Artist James Gillray. Library of Congress, Prints & Photographs Division, LC-USZC4-3147 (color film copy transparency), archival TIFF version (4 MB), converted to JPEG with the GIMP 2.4.5, image quality 88.

cowpox vaccine into the arm of a child, and after about nine days a pustule had formed from which additional vaccine could be derived and administered to a second child. Repeating the process ensured that there would always be vaccine available during the voyage, as long as there were enough susceptible children. Balmis calculated how many children he would need for the first part of the journey from Spain to Cuba and left Spain with 22 boys from ages three to eight.

After several stops along the way to replenish his supply of susceptible children, Balmis arrived in Guanajuato on November 20, 1804, and immediately began training local health officials in the administration of the vaccine. Following his campaign in Mexico, he continued around the world from 1804 through 1806, vaccinating folks in the Philippines, China, and St. Helena. It was but one of many such campaigns conducted throughout the world in the following century and a half.

Smallpox epidemics are reported in numerous historic accounts of the French and Indian War. Archaeological remains of hospitals connected to the forts, as well as their associated cemeteries, provide further documentation of the large numbers of people who succumbed to smallpox and other diseases during the campaigns. In the 1750s the general strategy for combating the disease was quarantine. Smallpox hospitals provided a place where the sick could be isolated and were provided some caregiving, and where they waited to die.

On May 31, 1757, Jabez Fitch, a soldier living on Rogers Island in the Hudson River, wrote in his diary that he was ordered to build a smallpox hospital.[22] The island was the location of Fort Edward, and the principal base camp for Rogers' Rangers, the provincial guerilla fighters of much popular acclaim. The year 1757 was a time of smallpox at Fort Edward. Another soldier, Luke Gridley, reports in his diary that between June and July nearly 120 cases of smallpox had occurred. The hospital was excavated by archaeologists in 1994, although only a few artifacts were found.

Smallpox and other diseases also ravaged the soldiers stationed at Fort William Henry on Lake George in upstate New York. The fort was erected to prevent French militia from moving south out of Canada and was the front line of British defenses. In 1952 the site of Fort William Henry was purchased for development as a tourist attraction, and it was excavated under the direction of Stanley Gifford between 1953 and 1954. Gifford established finding the military cemetery as one of his main goals. The cemetery was located outside the walls of the fort, and Gifford probably located it during grading operations on the south side. He found a number of oblong stains, which revealed human skeletons when he excavated 10 of them further. It seems he discovered one corner of the cemetery, but he made no further excavations.

The people, as interpreted by Gifford, were buried hastily, and generally without coffins. One skeleton had a musket ball embedded near the right elbow. Another had fractures of the skull. One still had traces of a bandage around its neck, held by a hospital pin. Others had limbs missing, presumably from amputation. In 1995 Maria Liston and Brenda Baker, two forensic anthropologists and bioarchaeologists, excavated another portion of the cemetery, uncovering an additional eight graves, which demonstrated that the human burials included men, women, and at least one child. Although historians estimate the death toll at the fort between 1755 and 1757 to have been somewhere between 800 and 1,000, Gifford estimated the cemetery included at most 200–300 people. We can guess that most of the individuals buried in the cemetery probably died of diseases, most likely smallpox and dysentery, and from trauma sustained during various skirmishes.

British soldiers and civilians were not the only victims of smallpox at Lake George. Native people carried smallpox from the fort back to their villages, and whether the exposure of native groups to smallpox was done with intent or not, it was a disease introduced into the indigenous American populations on multiple occasions. The purposeful dissemination of biological agents into a population constitutes another kind of warfare, biological warfare, and there is much conjecture on the earliest instance of biological warfare. As discussed in chapter 2, one of the first instances of biological warfare may have been the launching of corpses from a plague epidemic over the Caffa city wall, and from which followed the Black Death of Eurasia in 1346. By the time of the French and Indian War, the intentional introduction of biological agents into susceptible populations had undoubtedly occurred on more than a few occasions.

Some say that biological warfare during the French and Indian War occurred, specifically involving smallpox. The individual most often mentioned is James Amherst, an officer in the British militia. There are several suggestions in letters written by Amherst in 1763 that the passage of smallpox-infected blankets would reduce the population of treacherous participants in Pontiac's War.[23] It has been further suggested that this strategy was employed a few months earlier during the siege of Fort Pitt, site of the later Pittsburgh. During a parley requested by two Delaware native leaders, Captain Simeon Ecuyer of the Royal American Regiment, so it is said, concluded the meeting with the presentation of provisions, liquor, and other small gifts, including blankets and a handkerchief. Two of the blankets and the handkerchief came from the hospital where smallpox had recently broken out.[24]

Intent and purpose are less an issue than it would seem for smallpox—biological warfare was not a requirement for smallpox to decimate populations during the French and Indian War, or any other conflict, for that matter. The aggregation of soldiers into the cramped spaces of battlegrounds, forts, and ships facilitated transmission. Migration meant that new stocks of susceptible individuals were in relatively constant supply. New recruits served to bring smallpox into susceptible militia populations. Immune responses were stifled by the combination of fatigue and malnutrition.

Smallpox was not the only disease facilitated by the combination of starvation and poor hygiene in the French and Indian War. Typhus is associated with poor sanitation, and thus its many names refer to situations of poverty and sanitation—jail distemper, ship fever, military fever, hospital fever, camp fever, and famine fever. Typhus is also referred to as "spotted fever," which refers to the widespread rash on the trunk and limbs that accompanies the infection. Other symptoms include fever, headache, loss of appetite, and body aches. Historical accounts of typhus epidemics during conflicts are numerous. During the French siege of Naples in 1528, typhus claimed the lives of 30,000 French soldiers. Napoleon's 1812 campaign in Russia was constantly hindered by typhus.[25] From the European revolutions of 1848 through World War I, typhus continued to exact heavy losses.

Typhus is a perfect example of a famine-driven epidemic. Normally confined to isolated pockets of stark poverty, typhus often broke out over vast areas of Europe during starvation winters when massive numbers of people, lacking energy and wrapped in thick layers of clothing to combat hypothermia, found it increasingly difficult to bathe or wash their clothes. This lapse opened the way to heavy louse infestations. Because typhus is spread through entry of the louse feces into the human body through scratches, eye contact, or respiration, the desiccated louse feces clinging to unwashed garments caused rapid spread by casual contact with famished wanderers. During the Irish famine of 1845–52 (the Great Hunger), typhus and relapsing fever caused the death of 193,000 people, as compared to 20,000 by starvation.[26]

Shortly after the turn of the twentieth century, the cause (a bacteria, *Rickettsia prowazekii*) and the vector (the human body louse, *Pediculus humanus humanus*) were discovered. Unfortunately, Charles Nicolle, Howard Ricketts, and Stanislaus von Prowazek, all of whom were instrumental in those discoveries, died of typhus. We now know that the typhus rickettsia are expelled in feces, which are mechanically transmitted to a new human host, usually by the process of scratching them into open skin abrasions. Typhus is most common in unsanitary situations where people crowd together and wear the same garments constantly. Thus, it is often found in cold climates.

Typhus certainly took its toll on both soldiers and civilians during the French and Indian War. In a letter from brigadier general James Murray to William Pitt dated May 25, 1760, Murray reported that soldiers at Quebec had been reduced from 7,000 to 4,000 over the winter. By April, typhus, typhoid, dysentery, scurvy, frostbite, and hypothermia had killed a thousand men, and "above two thousand of what remained, totally unfit for any Service."[27] While there are other mentions of fevers, most are too general to specifically refer to typhus. A scant few years in the future, though, typhus is mentioned during the Revolutionary War. Typhus and smallpox cut through the Continental Army throughout the Revolutionary War; often a shortage of clothing and blankets meant that those who died passed on those items to the living, surely passing on as well the two diseases. In 1777 George Washington ordered the entire Continental Army to be inoculated against smallpox.[28]

There is another side to conflict more immediate and apparent than disease and nutritional deficiency, and that is trauma. Wounds of a variety of types, deep or shallow, debilitating or fatal, are the consequence and commerce of conflict. Although the skeletal signatures of trauma can persist for decades, serving as a pathological memorandum of flesh wounds long past, they can also indicate the physical interruption of life, the final cessation of life on this earth. Acute insults from other causes, disease for instance, generally leave no skeletal signatures at all. Almost all diseases require a lengthy time of infection to leave signatures on bone. Smallpox, in the 9–14 days of infection, can scarcely have time to influence the distribution of bone. A gunshot to the head, however, can leave a very recognizable signature of the cause of death in the twinkle of an eye, so to speak. Trauma requires barely a moment. When it comes to trauma, bones are usually quite revealing.

A case in point is Fort William Henry on the southern shore of Lake George in New York, the site of a legendary siege and massacre. The accuracy of the various accounts of the massacre is somewhat in question, but there seem to be several overlapping themes. Probably the most famous of these accounts occurs in James Fenimore Cooper's novel *The Last of the Mohicans*, published in 1826. The story goes like this: Fort William Henry was under siege in August 1757 by French and Indian forces led by the French commander Marquis de Montcalm. Inside, the British and colonial militia, led by Lieutenant-Colonel George Monro, were severely outnumbered, surrounded, and sickly. They waited, hopeful that a message sent to Major General Daniel Webb would result in his sending reinforcements from Fort Edward, located only 15 miles away. During the several-day siege, the French forces dug trenches closer and closer to the fort and eventually got their large guns close enough to "pound us to dust."[29] Finally, during an offer of surrender, Montcalm delivered a captured letter intended for Monro—Webb was unwilling to risk the remainder of his forces; he urged their surrender.

As part of the terms of the surrender of Fort Henry to the French, the British garrison was to retreat with its arms and possessions to Fort Edward. Both contemporary and fictionalized accounts depict the massacre of the retreating British troops a short distance from the fort. Some accounts include another massacre, that one of wounded soldiers who were left behind in the fort because they could not travel. A French Jesuit priest, Père Pierre Rouboud, who entered the fort with the French forces, described the massacre of about five individuals, one of whom was beheaded.[30]

A grave at Fort William Henry that included five individuals was found in 1957 beneath a floor in one of the east barracks. Known as the burials within "the crypt," they were on display until 1993, when sensitivity to the public display of human remains led to their reburial. According to Liston and Baker, the five individuals appear to be among the diseased and injured who were left behind at the fort after the surrender. All of the individuals buried within the crypt exhibit active skeletal signs of trauma that occurred prior to their deaths. One had a severe fracture of the leg, and another had suffered an amputation of the leg. Three of them have lesions consistent with musket ball wounds. All of these wounds and the surgery were probably made just before or during the siege and prevented the individuals from making the trip to Fort Edward. Unfortunately, leaving them at the fort was not in their best interest.

The five individuals all exhibited other wounds that appear to have occurred during the massacre described by Père Rouboud. One individual had been beheaded and suffered multiple sharp weapon wounds to the thorax and abdomen. The other four individuals also suffered sharp weapon wounds in the chest region. Several of the individuals appear to have been shot during the massacre as well. The pattern and location of the wounds suggests mutilation and trophy taking. One individual was clearly scalped, while another suffered multiple cuts to the pubic region. Cuts in the chest cavity likely involved either wholesale disembowelment or the removal of the heart.

The French and Indian War ended in 1763 with the Treaty of Paris. The French conceded Canada and all lands east of the Mississippi, including the Ohio Valley. In many ways the end of the war, particularly through the transfer to the British of the territories of major economic importance, brought about a decline in the competitive merchant environment between the French and British. The British, meanwhile, were poised to gain control of the Atlantic colonial markets.

PART III

Planters and Pestilence

LANDSCAPES AND LIABILITIES

... this country is such that it causeth much sickness, as the scurvy and the bloody flux and diverse other diseases, which maketh the body very poor, and weak. And when we are sick there is nothing to comfort us; for since I came out of the ship I never ate anything but peas, and loblollie (that is, water gruel). As for deer or venison I never saw any since I came into this land. There is indeed some fowl, but we are not allowed to go and get it, but must work hard both early and late for a mess of water gruel, and a mouthful of bread and beef.

Richard Frethorne, letter to his father and mother, March 20, April 2 & 3, 1623. In *The Records of the Virginia Company of London*, edited by Susan Kingsbury, 1906–35, volume 4:58–62. Washington, D.C.: U.S. Government Printing Office

Richard Frethorne was not happy with the conditions he found awaiting him in Virginia. He arrived from England as an indentured servant, having survived a voyage during which two-thirds of his fellow passengers died. At Jamestown he found disease and deprivation. In a letter to his parents dated March 20, 1623, he pleaded his case to them after only three months in Virginia, hoping they would buy out his indenture. His hope for an improved life had not been met.

England during the late sixteenth and early seventeenth centuries was foundering economically, especially for the poorer classes. The population had swelled from three million in 1500 to five million by 1650. Aristocrats replaced common lands used by peasants with fenced lands, through a process known as "enclosure." As a consequence, peasants were displaced from lands where they formerly lived, pastured livestock, gathered fuel, and raised crops; between 1530 and 1630 about half the peasantry lost their lands. They were known as "sturdy beggars," to differentiate them from those poor due to ailment or injury, and they roved the countryside in great numbers, looking for work or charity. Most eventually gravitated to the larger cities and seaports, especially London and Bristol. Amidst rising crime, vagrancy, and poverty, the colonial enterprise in the New World offered hope for both the poor and those of the middling class in England.[1]

Three-quarters of the immigrants to the Chesapeake during the seventeenth century 90,000 of the 120,000 total—were indentured servants. Those lucky enough to afford their own passage to either Virginia or Maryland between 1610 and 1650, less than one-quarter of the immigrants, were immediately granted 50 acres of land for themselves, and 50 acres for every servant and family member whose passage they paid. Those who were indentured began new lives serving four to seven years in servitude to pay

for their passage. The majority were 19 years old or younger. In addition to their passage, they were promised "freedom dues," consisting of a new set of clothes, food, tools, and 50 acres of land per household at the end of their term.[2] The only requirement was that they survive that long.

Such was the life of those who first tamed the wild Chesapeake lands for farming, a process the eighteenth-century Virginia historian Robert Beverley called "improving the lands."[3] Perhaps nowhere during the first century of British colonization was the transformation of the lands as evident as in the southern "planter colonies" of the Atlantic.[4] Formed of Virginia, Maryland, the Carolinas, and the sugar islands of the Caribbean, the planter colonies soon enabled England to gain vast wealth and resources.

Figure 7.1. *The Cornell Farm*, 1848, Edward Hicks. Courtesy National Gallery of Art, Washington.

Early settlers removed timber in massive quantities to provide for the already deforested Caribbean empires. Cattle thrived in the mild climates and brought about an early focus on ranching. The Indian trade in furs and deerskins supplied a growing market for those items in Europe. But it was the agrarian transformation of the physical landscape, beyond all else, that would bring wealth to later generations of the colonial southern Atlantic, disproportionately distributed as that wealth was (Figure 7.1).

Landscape transformation was not immediate, nor was there an organized plan in the earliest years. It was characterized rather by the necessity of subsistence farming, and by the somewhat chaotic and wholesale extraction of natural resources like timber, tar, and turpentine. These fueled the construction of buildings and ships and kept the fires lit in the homeland and on the Caribbean islands where the conversion of sugar cane to sugar took place.

Humans have been extracting natural resources in a wholesale fashion and rebuilding landscapes for millennia, often without exploring the consequences. The problem is that there are always consequences. Landscape transformation is a costly venture, and it is in some ways, as Forrest Gump once said, "like a box of chocolates—you never know what you're going to get." With all landscapes there are liabilities. Two of the British planter colonies, Tidewater Virginia and the South Carolina lowlands, serve well to illustrate this point.

The first successful transplantation of Europeans to Virginia, as with many of the colonies, came after one or more unsuccessful attempts. In 1585 Sir Walter Raleigh sent about 100 male colonists to settle on a small island called Roanoke, then part of Virginia and now in northern North Carolina. The venture lasted less than a year, due to insufficient supplies. It was followed by a second attempt in 1587 with an eye to the more fertile lands of Chesapeake Bay, but the possible engagement of Spanish ships led the British mariners to dump the colonists on Roanoke Island.

The colony soon ran short of supplies, and their leader, John White (artist of the famed watercolor drawings discussed in chapter 1), returned to England to procure supplies. He was not to make the swift return he predicted, as the Spanish Armada occupied many of the English shipping routes during 1588 and 1589. When White finally returned to Roanoke in

August of 1590, the colony was abandoned, and the only clue to their fate was the word *Croatoan*, the name of a neighboring island, carved into a tree.[5]

It was not until 1607 that the British finally returned to conduct a major occupation. This time it was situated on the Chesapeake Bay, with its numerous waterways, many of them navigable for a hundred miles. As with all of the earliest Atlantic settlements, transportation and defensibility were important factors in selecting the location of the settlement. Four Chesapeake rivers were especially attractive as settlement locations because of their width and depth, and the English named them the James, York, Rappahannock, and Potomac. About 60 miles up the James River, which was broad and navigable, and with deep harbors, the British began their first sustained colonial effort, on Jamestown Island on May 17, 1607 (Map 7.1). One of the early colonists and a leader of the group, George Percy, kept a journal of the voyage and the early years of Jamestown. He describes their arrival that day in May with happiness and hope.

> The twelfth day we went back to our ships, and discovered a point of land, called Archer's Hope, which was sufficient, with a little labor, to defend ourselves against any enemy. The soil was good and fruitful, with excellent good timber. There are also great store of vines in bigness of a man's thigh, running up to the tops of the trees in great abundance. We also did see many squirrels, conies [rabbits], black birds with crimson wings, and diverse other fowls and birds of diverse and sundry colors.[6]

Jamestown was located on a broad swamp that provided refuge from Spanish ships. On the first landing day, John Smith, a leader of the colony, reported that the colonists began to cut down trees, pitch tents, provide clapboard to refurbish the ships, and make gardens for planting and nets for fishing, and that they would cast together the boughs of trees in the form of a half moon for protection.[7] The latter activity was specifically forbidden by the Virginia Company, who perceived that building a defensive structure might upset the local Powhatan Indians.

Within the first month of the landing, some 200 natives attacked the settlers, and work was shifted to building a triangular palisade. The enclosed stockade was completed in 19 days with a bulwark in every corner of the triangular fort outfitted with three to five pieces of mounted artillery. The

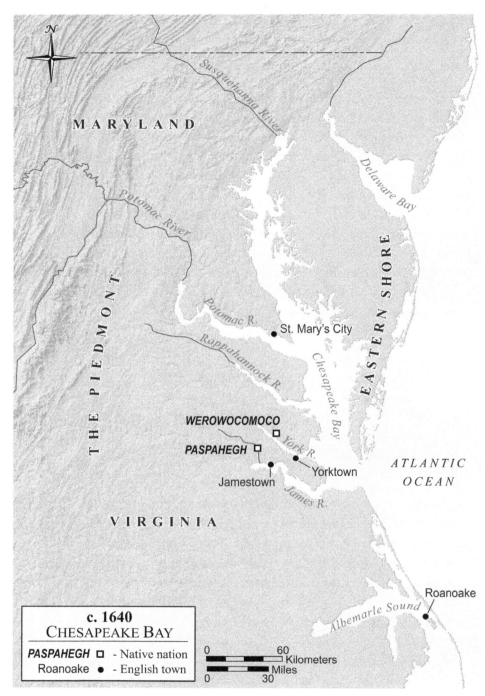

Map 7.1. The Chesapeake Bay region, circa 1640. Drawn by Susan Brannock-Gaul.

first summer proved to be very hard on the settlers. One of them, George Percy, chronicled their hardships:

> The four and twentieth day [of August], died Edward Harington and George Walker, and were buried the same day. The six and twentieth day, died Kenelme Throgmortine. The seven and twentieth day died William Roods. The eight and twentieth day died Thomas Stoodie, Cape Merchant [supply officer]. . . . Our men were destroyed with cruel diseases as swellings, fluxes, burning fevers, and by wars, and some departed suddenly, but for the most part they died of mere famine. There were never Englishmen left in a foreign country in such misery as we were in this new discovered Virginia. . . . Our food was but a small can of barley sod in water to five men a day; our drink cold water taken out of the river, which was at a flood very salty, at a low tide full of slime and filth, which was the destruction of many of our men.[8]

Within nine months of arrival, only 38 of the original 104 colonists were alive. The following few years continued to be hard on the Jamestown settlers. One of the worst times was during the starvation winter of 1609–10. John Smith records that only 60 of 215 settlers survived that winter. George Percy provides an even more detailed account:

> Now all of us at Jamestown beginning to feel that sharp prick of hunger, which no man truly describe but he which hath tasted the bitterness thereof. A world of miseries ensued, as the sequel will express unto you, in so much that some to satisfy their hunger have robbed the store, for the which I caused them to be executed. Then, having fed upon horses and other beasts as long as they lasted, we were glad to make shift with vermin, as dogs, cats, rats, and mice. All was fish that came to net to satisfy cruel hunger, as to eat boots, shoes, or any other leather some could come by. And those being spent and devoured, some were enforced to search the woods and to feed upon serpents and snakes, and to dig the earth for wild and unknown roots, where many of our men were cut off and slain by the savages. And now, famine beginning to look ghastly and pale in every face . . . nothing was spared to maintain life and to do those things which seem incredible, as to dig up dead corpses out of graves and to eat them,

and some have licked up the blood which hath fallen from their weak fellows. And amongst the rest, this was the most lamentable: that one of our colony murdered his wife, ripped the child out of her womb, and threw it into the river, and after, chopped the mother in pieces and salted her for his food.[9]

Archaeological finds corroborate the historical documents regarding the short and painful days that the Jamestown colonists endured between 1607 and 1610. Twenty-one burials recovered from beneath the largest row house at Fort James are probably from those who died during the summer of 1607. One had an arrow embedded in his leg and injuries to his shoulders that were apparently made during an Indian attack. Even more individuals were buried at the site of the Jamestown Statehouse. Seventy-two individuals were removed from 63 graves that probably date between 1610 and 1630, given the artifacts buried with them. The graves appear to be hastily made, were shallow, with the bodies placed in various orientations, sometimes more than one to a grave. One hypothesis is that they are individuals who died during the starvation winter of 1609–10.[10] An analysis of 50 of the statehouse graves shows that almost half of the folks interred in them died in their twenties; 14 percent died before age two.

The most telling evidence is the case of a female individual discovered in 2010. She was found in a cellar pit inside James Fort. Her skull and a section of her leg were buried with pottery, discarded weapons, and other items. She was named Jane by the archaeologists who found her, and she was about 14 years old when she died. Douglas Owsley of the Smithsonian Institution, the osteologist who studied her skeletal remains, encountered a grisly truth. She had been butchered and cannibalized. Chop marks and cut marks indicative of butchery with an axe and knife reveal that she was a victim of the starvation winter of 1609.[11] George Percy's account contained more than a little truth.

Starvation was not the only hardship of those first years in Jamestown. As Percy records, water quality in Jamestown was a major issue. Adequate water quality is crucial because it is an essential resource for biological organisms. Life began in water and evolved there for three billion years before spreading onto land. Most terrestrial life is still heavily bound to water; 70–95 percent of most cells is water. The adult human body consists of some 37 million cells, with water both constituting these cells and acting as a means of transport between them. In a sense, each of us is a vast, mobile pond of human cells, in addition to a variety of microorganisms that live within us.

Water quality and the close proximity to the brackish, lowland swamps were among the most important sources of health problems in seventeenth-century Virginia. At Jamestown the confluence of freshwater with salt water created a zone where permeation of sewage was not possible. Saltwater, because of its higher mineral content, is denser and has a higher water pressure. Through a process called saltwater intrusion, it can push inland underneath freshwater and thus prevent sewage from permeating below the drinking water supply. The Jamestown residents literally drank, bathed, and cooked in their own biological wastes. Famed writer William Strachey observed in 1610 of the Jamestown water supply: "a well sixe or seven fathom deepe, fed by the brackish River oozing into it" was one of the chief causes "of many diseases and sicknesses which have happened to our people, who are indeede strangely afflicted with Fluxes."[12]

Known as the "flux" or "bloody flux," dysentery is a disease of insufficient sanitation, usually due to crowding, unstable conditions, or ecological constraints. It is caused by both bacteria (*Shigella*) and amoebas (*Entamoeba histolytica*).[13] Both forms are spread through what is known as the fecal-oral route; infection is made through fecal contamination of food and water, with flies and other insects sometimes acting as mechanical vectors. Whatever route leads to contamination, the disease is rare when sanitation is good.

General symptoms of dysentery include fever, diarrhea, cramps, and bloody mucus evacuation. Death is more common from bacterial dysentery—about 1 percent of people afflicted in modern developing areas die. The more likely consequences of infection are loss of body fluids and painful intestines. Unfortunately, it can be recurrent. Dysentery may have been confused at times in the early historic records with cholera and typhoid fever, as all share overlapping symptoms and occur in similar conditions.

There was a sense in the seventeenth century that if one lived through the first couple bouts of any particular disease that further infections were not as serious—this process was called "seasoning." Sir Francis Wyatt, governor of Jamestown between 1621 and 1626, indicated in a letter that few escaped the "seasonings" of typhoid:

But certain it is new comers seldome passe July and August without a burning fever, which thorough intemperate drinking of water often drawes after it the fluxe or dropsy, and where many are sick together, is infectious: This requires a skilful Phisitian, convenient diett and lodging with diligent attendance, few dying of the first brunt of sickness, but upon relapses for want of strengthening diett and good drinke, to repaire the loss of that bloud, which is taken from them.[14]

Typhoid fever is caused by the bacterium *Salmonella typhi* and is accompanied by the slow onset of a sustained fever, headache, cough, digestive disturbances, and weakness. It kills about 10 percent of its victims and leaves 2 percent as permanent carriers.[15] Shedding of the bacterium can occur for weeks or months following infection. It is usually an infection of the summer months, and, like dysentery, it is a disease of unsanitary conditions spread through the contamination of water and food. Unlike dysentery, though, typhoid seems to confer some degree of relative immunity once an infection occurs. The average course of the disease ranges from a few hours to days, largely depending on individual factors such as age, health, and nutrition. There are known occurrences where people maintain the infection without symptoms for years; the most famous case is that of Typhoid Mary. I will briefly outline her case below, but the interested reader can find numerous engaging accounts of her exploits.[16]

Mary Mallon was an Irish immigrant who worked as a cook in New York state in the early 1900s. She infected several households with typhoid before it was discovered that she was the source of the infections. Eventually the New York Department of Health confined her for three years to hospitals while they monitored the bacterial count in her stools. Partially due to public outcry over her confinement, in February of 1910 she was released, with the condition she not seek employment as a cook. It is likely around this time that she began to be known as "Typhoid Mary." A few months passed, with bitter complaints from her that the health department had taken away her only source of income, and then she disappeared. She was traced to a few locations, each time under a false name, where further infections occurred, until she was finally taken from a Long Island house where police were forced to climb in through a second-story window to retrieve her. This time her confinement was for good, and she passed the rest of her life in confined solitude. She died of a stroke in 1938. Estimates of the number of people she infected are in the hundreds.

Undoubtedly, dysentery and typhoid fever made the lives of the colonists miserable for the short time that many had before they perished in the early seventeenth century. Food shortages and starvation compounded the problems of infectious diseases. Despite continuous shipping of reinforcements to Jamestown, deaths kept the population low. Between 1607 and 1622 the Virginia Company transported about 10,000 people to Jamestown; only 2,000 were still there in 1622.

Slowly, though, the colonists learned how to keep their health. Certainly, expanding settlements away from the swampy lowlands of Jamestown was a move in the right direction. That move was facilitated when John Rolfe successfully planted tobacco in Virginia. Tobacco had long grown in the West Indies and was popular in England. The numerous harbors and extensive river systems of the Chesapeake enabled Virginia to surge beyond the West Indies as the major supplier of tobacco in England. With long, hot, and humid growing seasons, Virginia had the perfect climate to cultivate the plant. The Chesapeake farmers increased tobacco shipping from 200,000 pounds in 1624 to 3,000,000 pounds in 1638.

By 1648 health in colonial Virginia had dramatically improved. One Virginia writer noted that only one in nine immigrants died during their first year as compared to one in four in the preceding generation. There were probably several reasons for the improvement. After a 1646 displacement of the Powhatan Indians, land became more available to freed servants, and farms moved farther up the Chesapeake, taking them into areas with freshwater and away from the lowland swamps. Planters established apple orchards that provided healthier drink. And more people survived the earliest bouts of illness as they became "seasoned," acquiring a higher level of immunity.

Less mortality in the Chesapeake meant more survivors to inhabit land parcels, and by 1670 lands in the Chesapeake had become crowded. The newer colony of Carolina offered the chance to expand beyond the Chesapeake and acquire vast territories.[17] Comprising present-day North and South Carolina and Georgia, Carolina was largely not settled by new English emigrants, but rather by European settlers previously located in either Barbados or the Chesapeake colonies. In 1670 three ships transported 200 colonists from Barbados to the Ashley River, where they founded Charles Town. Settlement was swift for a couple of reasons. For one, Carolina was far closer to Spanish Florida than to the Chesapeake, and there was substantial pressure to populate the colony quickly for defensive purposes.

Another was the availability of rich, fertile land (Map 7.2). Far larger land grants were given in Carolina than in Virginia—150 acres for the individual and each dependent, and 100 acres for freed servants having completed indentured servitude. It meant that land accumulation could occur rapidly.

The Carolinians knew that they needed to develop a stable agrarian economy. Carolina was too far north to grow sugar, the predominant crop in Barbados, and by 1670 English laws governing the distribution of tobacco made producing it unattractive (as discussed further in chapter 8). Thus, the early Carolina colonists focused on harvesting lumber from the vast pine forests and on cattle ranching. Both required little capital to begin and were ideal enterprises for a newly established colony. Carolinians also produced tar from the pines, a highly desired sealant for shipbuilding, and by 1717 Carolina was the leading producer of tar. It was two other crops, however, rice and indigo (a plant that yields a blue dye), that would propel the economic status of Carolina beyond the other colonies.

Carolina farmers learned how to grow rice from West Africans, who had been farming rice for a long time. Lumber harvesting resulted in major landscape shifts, but rice farming required a reconfiguration of the land far beyond that needed for tobacco in the Chesapeake, including significant management of wetlands. It is unclear exactly when rice agriculture began in Carolina, but in 1690 a plantation manager named John Stewart claims to have successfully planted rice in 22 different locations.[18] Certainly in the 1690s rice fields graced several plantations along the river systems in Carolina.

Annual rice exports reached 400,000 pounds by 1700 and rose to 43 million pounds in 1740. Indigo farming was developed in the 1750s, with an annual production of 63,000 pounds in 1750, rising to 500,000 pounds by 1760.[19] Rice quickly transitioned from a subsistence crop to one of exportation; with rice exportation rising from 400 tons exported in 1700 to 43 million in 1740, rice emerged as the colony's leading trade item and made up over 60 percent of exports as measured by value.

Of course, such intensive agriculture required an extensive workforce that could work under harsh conditions. Most of that labor was drawn from the African individuals who were the custodians of rice agriculture knowledge. Carolina had a large proportion of Africans from the beginning, because of its colonial roots in Barbados, but the development of

Map 7.2. The Carolinas, circa 1740. Drawn by Susan Brannock-Gaul.

rice necessitated increasingly larger numbers of African slaves. A typical rice planter needed 65 laborers per 160 acres of cultivated land, and the workers had to be able to endure the beating sun, the long hours, and the physical labor. And so, from 1,500 Africans in 1690, the African population of Carolina grew to 4,100 in 1710. By 1730 enslaved Africans outnumbered free Carolinians by two to one: 20,000 to 10,000. The majority of Africans were settled in the hot, humid, lowland marshes of the rice-growing coastal plain—there they outnumbered European whites by nine to one. They were, as the historian Peter Wood has said, "the Black Majority."[20]

Most rice plantations were located on the four rivers adjacent to Charlestown: Ashley, Cooper, Santee, and Edisto. Because of the mix of uplands and lowlands, as well as the extensive size of many plantations, rice plantations were generally made up of several types of land. They were a patchwork of banks, canals, floodgates, roads, and drains, which capitalized on the natural topography while extensively modifying it for water control (Figure 7.2).

Rice was first cultivated in inland fields adjacent to the river systems and was largely dependent on natural rainfall at least two months of the year. A system of banks was built to control water flow, protecting the rice fields from salt water and retaining the required level of freshwater. Water control was accomplished through floodgates known as "trunks," and by the mid-1720s rice farmers had learned how to control water availability (Figure 7.3). Bank construction was an extensive process:

> The large banks outside, that is along the canals, rivers, or creeks, were kept a foot or two above the highest spring tides to prevent overflows. The cross banks, dividing the different fields, were kept above the highest point of the fields, so that the entire field could be covered with water without over-topping the enclosing banks. The plantation was divided into separate fields according to the trend of the land, putting into each, as nearly as possible, sections of like level, thus securing an even flow of water over each section during the growing season of the Rice.
>
> Large ditches of four or five feet and of like depth were cut around the entire field, leaving a margin of ten or fifteen feet next to the enclosing banks. Leading from these main ditches, small drains were run across the fields. These were usually about two feet wide and of the same depth, and divided the land into beds of from fifty to seventy feet wide.[21]

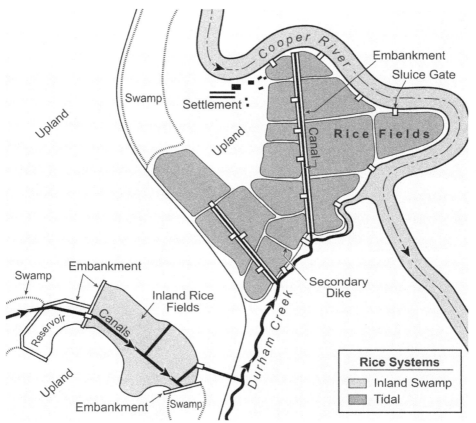

Figure 7.2. Inland and tidal river system, western branch of the Cooper River, South Carolina. Drawn by Susan Brannock-Gaul based on Carney, *Black Rice*: Figure 3.2.

Naturally inundated fields had higher yields but were scarce, and those wishing larger holdings were required to conduct more extensive landscape modification on lands that bordered the salt-water marsh.

One of the earliest references to rice grown along the tidewater is in a notice of land sale by William Swinton of Winyah Bay in 1738.[22] While it is unclear exactly what inspired tidewater rice plantations, within a few years it was clear that the yield was far greater than on those plantations located inland. Tidewater rice was very similar to the African practice of growing rice in mangrove swamps, and Africans provided the knowledge that drove the "huge hydraulic machine" consisting of "floodgates, trunks, canals, banks, and ditches."[23] Tidewater rice required even more extensive bank and floodgate systems. Rice planters often employed a system of dual

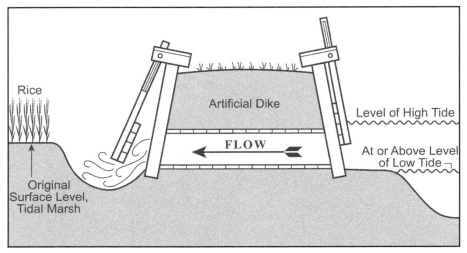

Figure 7.3. Sketch of a hanging trunk. Drawn by Susan Brannock-Gaul based on Carney, *Black Rice*: Figure 3.4.

gates known as "hanging gates" that admitted water at high tide, when freshwater ("sweet water") floated on top, and another gate that could be used to evacuate water from the fields at low tide:

> First, slaves constructed levees, or rice banks, around regular-shaped plots on the mudflats. The rice field was embanked at sufficient height to prevent tidal spillover, with banks often reaching six feet in height. Earth removed in the process resulted in an adjacent canal, while openings in the rice bank admitted the inflow of tidal water onto the field. The next step involved dividing the area into quarter sections (of ten to thirty acres), with river water delivered through secondary ditches. This elaborate system of water control enabled the adjustment of land units to labor demands and allowed slaves to sow rice directly along the floodplain. Sluices built into the embankment and field sections operated as valves for flooding and drainage. When opened at high tide, the tide flooded the field. Closed at low tide, the water remained on the crop. Opened again at ebb tide, excess water was drained from the plot.[24]

In Carolina, as with Virginia, the location of settlements adjacent to the lowlands facilitated the transmission of infectious diseases like typhoid and dysentery, with the added burden of malaria. Quite a different disease from dysentery and typhoid fever, malaria is neither a disease of sanitation nor transmitted directly. Human malaria is a disease caused by four species of a parasitic protozoan of the genus *Plasmodium*. These parasites are spread from one human host to the next by infected mosquitoes, primarily of the genus *Anopheles*.

Several things suggest that malaria was not present in the Americas prior to the arrival of colonial populations. First, malaria probably could not have survived the arctic land bridge crossing traveled by the first human immigrants to North America. Second, very few nonhuman primates carry plasmodia in the Americas, whereas lots of Old World primates and other mammals do carry plasmodia. Third, native populations in the Americas had no immunity to malaria.[25]

Two forms of malaria were introduced into colonial Atlantic America. *Plasmodium vivax* was brought by Europeans. It was common during the sixteenth century in England, Holland, Spain, and Italy, all active colonialist nations. *P. vivax* has an episodic cycle that lasts about 48 hours, causing fever on days one and three, and is therefore known as a *tertian* malaria. While mortality rates can reach 5 percent, mortality is usually lower. There is some dispute about the time when *P. vivax* arrived in America, but it was probably before 1700 in the middle and northern Atlantic colonies.[26]

This letter written by a French Huguenot refugee living in Boston in 1687 aptly describes Carolina in the late seventeenth century, prior to the major modifications of rice fields:

Two young men have just arrived from Carolina, who give some account of the country. In the first place, they have never seen so miserable a country, nor an atmosphere so unhealthy. Fevers prevail all the year, from which those who are attacked seldom recover, and if some escape, their complexion becomes tawny, like that of the two who have arrived here, and who are pitiable to behold. Moreover, the heat is so intense as to be almost unendurable, and as to infect the water, consequently producing sickness as they have no other beverage. They bring us also tidings that before their departure a ship had arrived from London, with one hundred and thirty persons on board, including the crew; of whom one hundred and fifteen died as soon as they landed, all from malignant fevers which spread among them.[27]

There is some debate about the presence or absence of malaria in Virginia in the seventeenth century, but the timing of its arrival is more of an issue than is simple presence or absence of the disease. Several historians have produced convincing evidence that malaria was endemic in the Chesapeake in the eighteenth century, and that it was certainly present by 1680, if not before. For instance, William Fitzhugh wrote that his sister, newly arrived in 1687 "has had two or three small fits of fever and ague, which now has left her, and so consequently has had her seasoning."[28] There is no doubt it affected people in Virginia in the later seventeenth century, as indicated by descriptions of the ague, fever and ague, country fevers, autumnal fever, or the seasonings.

The typical malarial infection manifests itself as episodes of fever and chills followed by intense sweating, subsiding fever, and eventually the relief of sleep. The cycles vary in length from 48 to 72 hours and can go on for several days to weeks.[29] A person may reach some equilibrium with the parasite in the sense that while bouts of fever are not active, red blood cell destruction still leaves them anemic, weak, and tired. Because malarial episodes consist of intermittent fevers interspersed with chills, it was classified early on as an "intermittent fever" recognizably different from the continuous fever of such diseases as typhoid.

It is often not the chills and fever of malaria that cause death, but complications arising from high densities of parasites and ruptured blood cells in small arteries, the brain, and kidneys. In endemic areas it is primarily those below age five that suffer the worst attacks and the highest mortality rates. Repeated exposure appears to yield some immunity to the malaria parasite, or at least the ability to tolerate infection and function in life's tasks, and thus in endemic areas the disease is harder on the very young.

In a transmission cycle generally lacking a vector, such as dysentery or typhoid, the important variables for disease transmission include survival and reproduction of the parasite (which rely in turn upon environmental conditions conducive to survival and replication), the survival of infected human hosts (long enough for the pathogen to replicate), and human behavior that leads to successful pathogen transmission. The addition of an insect vector greatly complicates the transmission cycle, because the life cycle requirements of the vector (in this case a mosquito) must also be met for the disease to exist.

There are several important variables in mosquito ecology and disease transmission. Mosquitoes need water to reproduce, shade to preserve their limited bound water, and a blood source. Beyond that, a myriad of variations makes them successful and efficient vectors of a number of parasites that cause disease. Only a few species of mosquito transmit multiple parasites, though, and species specificity between vector and parasite marks long-term adaptive relationships. In fact, generalizing about mosquitoes undermines the complexity of their differences. Their water requirements differ—some need brackish water, some freshwater; they differ in their preference for standing, slow-moving, or fast-moving currents, in whether they like the water sunlit or shaded, with or without vegetation. Feeding preferences vary—some prefer humans, some prefer nonhumans, some aren't choosy. Flight distance, height, and time of feeding all affect who is a target, as does their resting time and preferred resting environment. All mosquitoes rest, but some prefer to rest indoors, while some do not.

While there were several species of *Anopheles* mosquitoes in America, *A. quadrimaculatus* was probably one of the most significant vectors of malaria.[30] It has often been said that *A. quadrimaculatus* is not choosy and will feed on anyone and anything, beast or human. That said, there is contrary evidence that *A. quadrimaculatus* prefers to feed on animals other than humans, particularly cattle.[31] It may be that as cattle ranching in the planter colonies was replaced by agriculture, malaria rates increased. If that is the case, it would not be the first instance where the removal of a preferred host results in increased feeding on an alternate host. For instance, in Thailand the shift to mechanized plows from traditional plows powered by water buffalo resulted in spiraling rates of human cases of the virus *Culex tritaeniorhynchus*, Japanese encephalitis.[32] Thai mosquitoes turned toward humans once their preferred host, water buffalo, was no longer available.

Plasmodium falciparum was brought by Africans into South Carolina in the 1680s. *P. falciparum* is a far more virulent malaria than *P. vivax*. Parasite densities in the host are high, and the spleen and liver become enlarged. Invasion of the brain and kidneys leads to loss of blood flow in essential areas and can cause coma. Mortality rates range from 20 to 40 percent and are especially high for individuals who have not previously been infected and therefore have no acquired immunity, especially children.[33] Consequently, while Europeans had some immunity to *P. vivax*, they had never been exposed to *P. falciparum*, and it was a deadly form of malaria for them.

In contrast, African populations in Carolina had several forms of malaria immunity. Because they were from an area with endemic *P. falciparum*, they had some acquired immunity to that disease, at least in the generation who came from West Africa. They also had some partial or full immunity due to evolutionary adaptations of their red blood cells. One of these was the sickle-cell trait. Sickle-cell trait is caused by a point mutation that replaces the amino acid glutamine with valine. That single change results in hemoglobin that is inefficient in acquiring or releasing oxygen, which reduces the flexibility of the cells and causes impeded red blood cell movement and aggregation. Individuals with this recessive condition, having inherited the gene for the sickle-cell trait from both parents, suffer numerous health impacts and usually die prior to the age of reproduction. In such a situation, one would expect that the abnormal hemoglobin variant would disappear eventually.

In 1953–54 Tony Allison examined the sickle-trait distribution and found higher-than-normal frequencies in populations of tropical Africa, southern Arabia, and the Mediterranean. He compared the distribution of the sickle-cell trait to that of *P. falciparum* and began to make sense of the evolutionary relationships of the two conditions. It works like this: individuals who have the recessive sickle-cell condition die early in life due to medical complications. Those with normal hemoglobin cells also suffer increased mortality in a malarial region. It is those with a mixture of "normal" and "abnormal" hemoglobin who fare best in a malarial environment, because the same characteristics of the sickle cells that cause problems in oxygen transport also impede the reproduction of the malaria parasite.

Thus, individuals living in areas of Africa with endemic *Plasmodium falciparum* are shielded from the worst effects of malaria if they are heterozygous for sickle-cell hemoglobin. Sickle-cell anemia is a disease caused by the homozygous recessive hemoglobin where red blood cells are sickle-shaped and carry insufficient amounts of oxygen. In heterozygous individuals only some of the cells are sickle-shaped, enough to cause anemia only in some low oxygen states (air travel, high altitudes) but also enough to thwart malaria parasites. The maintenance of a trait, such as this one, that should otherwise disappear is called a *balanced polymorphism*.[34] Eventually, a population reaches a stable distribution in which there is the retention of both the normal and the mutated allele, and therefore the retention of both heterozygotes and homozygotes with sickle-cell anemia. Thus, individuals who came to America from Africa were relatively protected from both forms of malaria. Native American populations, on the other hand, seemed to have no immunity to either form of malaria, suggesting that malaria was not present in the Americas prior to colonization.

Mosquitoes were probably always a nuisance in the lowlands of the Atlantic coast, but the extensive modification of the Carolina landscape, specifically with the creation of wet agricultural fields and nearby houses and outbuildings, surely enhanced their reproductive and resting spaces. What the colonists did not understand is that tidewater swamps, reengineered to keep out salt water and to periodically flood the fields with freshwater to irrigate the crop during the summer, had become a landscape that couldn't have favored mosquito reproduction any better than if it had been designed by the mosquito.[35] The furrows and other pockets in the fields hold water long enough for the development of mosquito larvae and radically increase the number of mosquitoes hatched.

By 1800 people had begun to piece together the conditions that resulted in malarial sickness. Most people attribute the name of the disease to the Italians, who at least by the seventeenth century applied "mal aria" (meaning "bad air") to refer to putrid gases ("miasmas") that rose from swampy areas and caused intermittent fevers. The Italian name comes from the Latin "malus aria," which described bad air and its association with disease, but not any particular disease. It was more often known in the colonies as "ague," "fever and ague," "country fever," or "autumnal fever." Regardless of the name used, it was one of the most recognizable of the fevers, given the alternating cycles of chills and fever. People knew that swamps, lowlands, and other wet landscapes were those where people were most likely to get sick. They knew that summer and autumn were the prime times for malaria attacks.

Even in populations where malaria has not been endemic for several generations, high mortality is not the major issue. Rather it is the seasonally chronic illness that lasts for several months and leaves an individual debilitated, malnourished, and vulnerable to other infections. In epidemics, substantial portions of the labor force can be removed from service, contributing to shortages of food and personnel for medical care. It is not immediate death that characterizes malaria, but the chronic wasting of populations season by season and the eventual slippage into death through a combination of forces, slowly and painfully.

While typhoid and dysentery were among the most prevalent diseases in the first century of the planter colonies, malaria was among the most feared of the colonial experiences—virtually no one in Carolina escaped the seasoning. Colonists to the Atlantic coast could hardly have made the job of a parasite-bearing mosquito easier. Agricultural fields and nearby houses and outbuildings surely enhanced their reproductive and resting spaces. Early colonial settlements were all placed so that ships, the major source of transport, could reach them easily. Locations easily accessible along the coast, natural harbors, and deep rivers were choice landing sites and refuges from storms. Throughout the first two or three centuries of the colonies, regular deliveries of susceptible and infected humans, mosquitoes, and parasites ensured repetitive cycles of illness.

8

POVERTY AND PESTILENCE BEYOND THE BIG HOUSE

The rations are good, plain victuals, and there are plenty of them, and about twice a week there was something for a treat. The master sure is particular about feeding, especially for the children in the nursery. You see, there is a nursery for children's care while their mothers are working.

John Finnely, Fort Worth, Texas.
In *When I Was a Slave: Memoirs from the Slave Narrative Collection*

We didn't know what it was to get biscuits for breakfast every morning. It was corn bread except on Sundays, then we'd get four biscuits apiece. We got fatback most every morning. Sometimes we might get chicken for dinner on a Sunday or some holiday like Christmas. It was mighty seldom we got anything like that, though. We liked possums and rabbits but they didn't come until winter when some of the men would run across one in the field. They never had a chance to get out and hunt.

Narrative of Mary Ella Grandberry, Sheffield, Alabama.
In *When I Was a Slave: Memoirs from the Slave Narrative Collection*

On a midsummer day in June, I visited Hampton Plantation, located on a tributary of the Santee River in South Carolina. Like many of the rice and indigo plantations, it was located some distance from the main road and very close to the river. In the eighteenth and nineteenth centuries, when plantations were established in Carolina, rivers were the primary routes for human travel and for the transport of mercantile products. At about 95 degrees and 95 percent humidity, it was a fairly tolerable day in coastal South Carolina. Yet, as I trekked the half mile down a trail to the old rice fields, I gained considerable appreciation for the tribulations of the field laborers who'd had little choice in their servitude in the sun. I actually never made it to the remnants of the rice fields myself and instead worked up ample perspiration while jogging back to my car in retreat from biting flies and mosquitoes. I suffered substantial blood loss during my brief investigation of life on the plantation.

Plantation owners quickly learned the same lessons, and during the summer months they generally retreated from the lowlands to locations either farther north, farther inland, or on the coast. Any of those offered fewer mosquitoes and surely more healthy environments. Charleston was known for being fairly malaria free and was thus a popular summer retreat. There are numerous documents that mention the more healthy environment of Charleston and of the retreat of plantation owners during "the sickly time."[1] The common laborer, on the other hand, was left to suffer the brutal working conditions and the disease-ridden environments of the coastal lowlands (Figure 8.1).

Unfortunately, most historic narratives of the early colonial years come from letters or journals of large plantation owners, not the laborers. They do not come from the perspective of those laboring in the fields, but from those living in the big house. Virtually no Indians or Africans could read or write—the customs and rules of the times prohibited education for those folks. Mary Anderson reports, "But they would not teach any of us to read and write. Books and papers were forbidden."[2] Robert Glenn echoes a similar story: "The food was generally common. Hog meat and corn bread most all the time. Slaves got biscuits on Sunday morning. Our clothes were poor and I worked barefooted most of the time, winter and summer. No books, papers, or anything concerning education was allowed the slaves by his rules and the customs of these times."[3]

Consequently, stratification brought about a class separation beyond housing and working conditions—it distilled the presentation of the facts, of written memory, through the filter of the privileged and educated. Most owners of large estates were not privy to many of the experiences of common laborers, nor were they inclined to tell of those experiences they did know.

One of the ways that we can bridge the gap between documents and drudgery is by examining the skeletons and teeth of folks who lived then. Analysis of the bones of indentured servants and slaves from plantations provides a lot of information about their quality of life, and about the health issues colonial folks faced. Their skeletons help to verify the historic records, or clarify them, and they help to fill in the gaps when there are no historic records. Most indicate that physical stresses were common for both men and women. Muscle and tendon attachment sites that are excessively large (hypertrophic) suggest that most laborers, men and women, experienced muscle stress on a daily basis. Arthritis of the bones and cartilage (osteoarthritis) was generally common among laborers, and it occurred at quite a young age, certainly by the 20- to 30-year age range. Undoubtedly, the common laborer worked hard and put much physical stress on his or her body.

Many of them suffered from infections, sometimes combined with dietary deficiencies. Both of these ailments leave visible markers on bone if the individual survives long enough. Sometimes the lesions are specific to certain diseases, or their patterning is indicative of a particular disease. Though we can't always tell what specific infection caused the lesions, we can, at the very least, tell that a person was ill or suffered trauma due to excess bone growth stimulated by inflammation or hemorrhage. Teeth and adjacent jaws tell us about dental care and sometimes about the habitual uses of teeth, such as holding objects, like clay pipes. Dietary deficiencies can also leave indicative lesions, and chemical signatures in bones and teeth can tell us what people ate and where they lived. The fields of study dedicated to those kinds of analyses are paleopathology and bioarchaeology.

Another source of information is that found through the archaeological excavation of the built landscapes of the colonies. Houses, fields, gardens, privies, walls, and wells are all good sources of artifacts and features left through the day-to-day movements of the early colonists.[4] Archaeological remains contribute information about past lives in a few ways. For one, they correct those misrepresentations in the historic record that are due to social and economic class. The passage of time tends to favor the larger, more grandiose, and often better-built structures. Large plantation houses, the big houses, tended to be built of brick, which endures the ravages of time and decay longer. However, few houses in the colonies were built of anything but wood or thatch. In the ground, though, are often preserved the stains of posts from wooden structures, the pits used for storage, and, most important, the discarded and forgotten material items used by "common" folks who lived there. Food remains are also often found in pits in the form of seeds or charred remnants—chenopodium and peach pits are examples.

Those food remains are garbage, and garbage is much of what archaeologists excavate and analyze. A number of years ago, an archaeologist in Arizona named Bill Rathje recognized the importance of garbage as a test of truth. He decided to use modern-day trash to investigate the subtle (or maybe not-so-subtle) differences between what people reported on their

Figure 8.1. *The Plantation*, c. 1825. Artist unknown. Courtesy of the Metropolitan Museum of Art, Gift of Edgar William and Bernice Chrysler Garbisch, 1963.

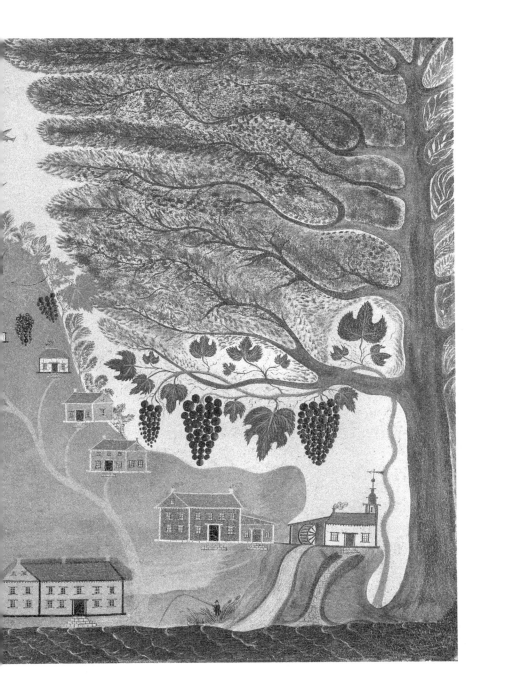

use of things and what actually ended up in the garbage. Not surprisingly, his project became affectionately known as "the garbage project." The project went on for years and had several different stages of research. In one of them Rathje asked his informants to report what they consumed, and how much of it. He also asked their permission to search through their garbage to verify their reported discards. Again, not surprisingly, his team found quite a few things out.

First, people don't actually know how much they consume of many items. Most of us aren't tabulating how much milk our household of six uses in a week. It probably varies. So, instead of the gallon of milk a week you reported, actually it might be three gallons. Second, people aren't necessarily going to report accurately those things seen as vices. Routinely, tobacco, alcohol, and pornography went either unreported or attested in substantially smaller quantities than the reality.

Some of what Rathje's research revealed what we already knew. Those of us who have excavated privies (yes, for some of us garbage is a step up) know that you tend to find in them lots of things people want hidden, such as liquor bottles. Broken dishes, shoes, and hardware are often recovered. Sometimes dead bodies, or even parts of bodies, are found in privies.[5]

In short, self-reported information is often unreliable. It is one reason that anthropologists regularly use participant research—we go and watch people and ask them questions about what they are doing, and why they are doing it. We frequently find out, by the way, that people may think they do something a particular way for a particular reason, but that there are other ways to interpret the stimuli for their actions.

Back to Rathje's study, what really shines through is how much we can actually learn from garbage, the discards of day-to-day living. Garbage doesn't lie. And so the garbage of the early colonists contributes to rounding out the picture of their lives.

Garbage in Virginia around 1600 indicates that people experienced less class difference in the early years. The initial years of settlement were marked by a fairly egalitarian status—almost everyone was an indentured servant, and almost everyone would be dead soon. Though egalitarian, it wasn't terribly comforting.[6] Even without the shackles of servitude during the initial years in Virginia, the Chesapeake offered few rewards and numerous obstacles for early settlers. Workdays were long and disease was common. Fewer than half of the immigrants would live to see their children reach adulthood, because they perished from the physical challenges of colonial life.[7]

Yet those that lived amassed land and were able to secure a fairly good living. They were thus afforded a chance to ascend the ladder of social and economic standing. Most early Chesapeake settlers during the early colonial years were able to build rudimentary houses, grow enough food to eat, and secure healthy profits on their tobacco. The houses in the early seventeenth century were hastily built of clapboards on a timber frame with a shingle roof. Many had only one room, with a fireplace at one end. Another common design was to have one end subdivided into two additional rooms. The floors were dirt, and if there were windows, they were small. Houses were usually smaller than 16 by 20 feet. More successful planters had houses with two rooms—one for cooking and one that was general purpose—and a sleeping loft upstairs. These "ordinary beginners" houses were of earthfast construction, otherwise known as post-in-ground construction (Figure 8.2).[8] They were generally not built with permanence in mind, but rather to "usually endure ten years without repair."[9] It was the goal of most planters to build a larger, more elaborate, and permanent house after becoming established, but the impoverished had to wait much longer.

By 1665 the social mobility afforded freedmen in the Chesapeake a few decades earlier had ended. A major force of increased stratification was Virginia governor William Berkeley, who did everything in his power to create further social and economic distance through heavy taxes and biased land grants. The best tobacco-producing lands along the rivers were occupied by the more wealthy land owners, and new freedmen were forced to move farther into the interior. So much tobacco was produced that it lowered the prices in England below the cost of production. England passed new laws requiring that tobacco from the colony be shipped to England on English ships, an act designed to eliminate the Dutch from a growing Dutch tobacco market. The resulting economic collapse allowed the wealthier planters to buy up even more land. Higher levels of production were the only route to increased income, but few had the means to provide more labor. Thus, life between 1650 and 1680 was a trade-off for most planters; on the one hand, health in the Chesapeake improved; but on the other, times got financially harder.

That precarious balance between wealth and health may be reflected at

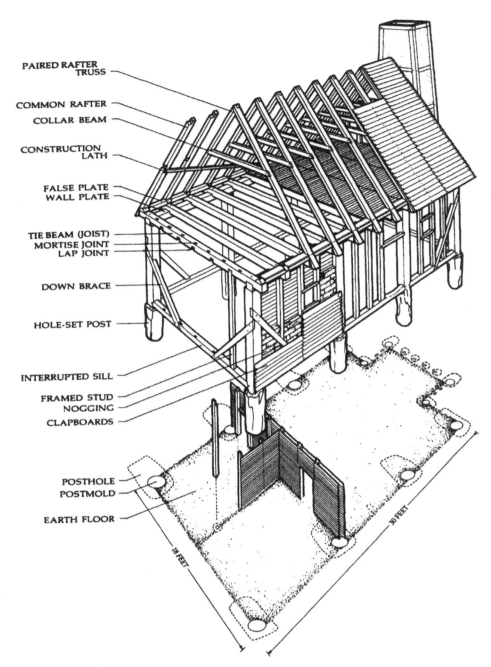

PAIRED RAFTER TRUSS

COMMON RAFTER

COLLAR BEAM

CONSTRUCTION LATH

FALSE PLATE
WALL PLATE

TIE BEAM (JOIST)
MORTISE JOINT
LAP JOINT

DOWN BRACE

HOLE-SET POST

INTERRUPTED SILL

FRAMED STUD
NOGGING
CLAPBOARDS

POSTHOLE
POSTMOLD

EARTH FLOOR

18 FEET

30 FEET

Figure 8.2. Reconstruction of the "ordinary beginners" house described in the pamphlet *Information and Direction to Such Persons as Are Inclined to America*. The drawing shows an interpretation of a conventional Chesapeake hole-set frame house, with a timber-chimney based on archaeological evidence. From Cary Carson, Norman F. Barka, William M. Kelso, Garry Wheeler Stone, and Dell Upton, "Impermanent Architecture in the Southern American Colonies," *Winterthur Portfolio* 16, no. 2/3 (1981): Fig. 3, 143. Used by permission of University of Chicago Press.

Patuxent Point, a planter's homestead in Calvert County, Maryland. The archaeological site there contains the remnants of a large (20.5 × 40 feet) domestic structure associated with a plantation at Hodgkin's Neck, and a cemetery with 18 human graves. The size of the house, large by contemporary standards, and the adornments such as leaded windows suggest that the house was that of "planters of middling wealth."[10]

The occupation of the Patuxent Point property was short, only about 20 years, between 1660 and 1680, possibly lending support to the financial difficulties of the less wealthy during that time. Much was learned by studying the individuals buried there. The adults appear to have lived about as long as adults of the same time period in England, and they experienced similar health. Historic documents would support the skeletal evidence; most documents seem to indicate that the colonists had plenty to eat. Study of the children's skeletons and teeth, however, contradicts that evidence.

We can learn a great deal about health from skeletal malformations. Skeletal and dental markers of growth arrest often provide information on the quality of life for growing children. The two most commonly used are growth arrests of teeth (enamel hypoplasias) and growth arrests of long bones (Harris lines). They indicate when some physiological disturbance (infection, insufficient food, or several other things) has interfered with growth. Several vitamin and mineral deficiencies cause growth problems. Rickets (vitamin D deficiency) affects the mineralization of bone matrix (osteoid) and results in a bowed deformation of weight-bearing bones such as the legs and pelvis. Scurvy is caused by vitamin C deficiency, which results in bleeding and weak blood vessels that cause bone responses. Anemia causes an expansion of the bone tissue that houses the red-blood-producing cells, usually on the cranial vault and eye orbits.

The children from Patuxent Point, for instance, show signs of retarded growth periods. Markers of stress, low bone density, and bowed long bones all indicate that the diet and health of children (one-third to half of them) were compromised during their early years living in the colony. This makes sense, because adults who grew up in conditions of adequate nutrition experienced normal growth and therefore lack skeletal signs of malnutrition. Thus, the adults who grew up in England under adequate nutritional conditions lack skeletal signs of compromise, whereas those who grew up at Patuxent Point did not have adequate growth conditions. All of the Patuxent children's skeletal responses indicate they spent all or the majority of their growing lives in the Maryland colony in a state of ill health and malnutrition.

We can also tell some things about behavior from the skeleton and teeth. One woman buried at Patuxent Point, with an estimated age of 26–32, died just prior to childbirth—a late-term fetus was found in her pelvic cavity. She had grooves between her front teeth (incisors) that resulted from gripping pins or needles. A man found at the site also had similar grooves, as did a woman from nearby Jordan's Journey Plantation. Repetitive behaviors, such as a seamstress or tailor would perform while holding pins between the teeth, often leave markers of that repetitive use in the teeth or skeleton. Pipe smoking is no exception. Three individuals have facets (worn areas) in their teeth characteristic of pipe smokers: a boy aged 11–12, a young man aged 25–29, and an older female aged 55–60. The older woman had also lost several of her front teeth.

Malaria may have been a problem for those at Patuxent Point. If the early planters were able to keep the mosquitoes away from them, infection rates would be lower. *A. quadrimaculatus*, a vector for malaria, feeds for only a few hours after dusk, a time when people were generally in their homes. Most settlers at that time were generally in bed, as candles were expensive and quite a luxury. Usually only the hearth fires cast what light there was after the sun went down. But the planters lived in houses near the lowland marshes and fields. The house construction did little to keep mosquitoes out, and they were undoubtedly common visitors who shared most dwellings with humans and other mammals.

Life in the Chesapeake colony was particularly hard for indentured servants. William Neale, his wife, two daughters, one son, and two indentured servants settled Leavy Neck in 1662.[11] The 120-acre plantation in Anne Arundel County, Maryland, indicates that Neale was a "middling planter." Neale's house at Leavy Neck was excavated by archaeologists in 2003. It was of earthfast construction, and it had an earthen cellar, which, like many earthen cellars of the time, was filled with garbage—fish and pig parts, chamber pot contents, broken ceramic dishes, and other refuse that accumulated after abandonment, which was around 1677.

Neale's cellar also contained the body of a 15- to 16-year-old boy buried in a shaft too small for him, so his legs were bent to make him fit. He appears to have been hastily dumped into the pit, and from examination of his body, he had had a particularly hard life. Garbage was the clue to the latest time the boy could have died—there was no garbage in the area of the body that dates after the late 1670s, so he must have been buried before that time. The areas where his muscles attached to the bones were well developed, indicating a life of hard labor. Several of the boy's teeth had severe cavities, and the lower jaw (mandible) had a pus-filled infection. The bodies of his vertebrae (spinal column) had shallow depressions called Schmorl's nodes, which are caused by heavy lifting combined with vertebral disc collapse. Some of the lesions on his spine suggest he was experiencing the early stages of tuberculosis at the time of death.

We can also tell some things about the boy by using chemical isotopes. Isotopes have long been used in archaeological and bioarchaeological research. An isotope is formed when an element has the same number of protons but different numbers of neutrons; isotopes are thus different forms of the same element. There are radioactive isotopes that decay through time, such as carbon-14 used for estimating chronological dates, and there are stable isotopes that don't decay through time.

Stable isotopes have been used since the 1970s to estimate two major things: diet and geographic movement (migration). Usually the isotope "signature" is measured using a ratio of two isotopes, for instance, the ratio of carbon-12 to carbon-13, known as "delta ^{13}C" and represented as δ^{13}C. They are measured in parts per thousand (known as per mil, ‰). The isotopes of what a person eats are recorded in the body's tissues, and consequently we can tell a lot about dietary focus by looking at isotopic signatures (Figure 8.3). By examining isotopes obtained from the teeth that formed during early childhood and from later-erupting teeth or bone, we can examine changes in diet between childhood and adulthood. We can use similar isotopes to look at differences between where someone spent their early years and those of their later life.

Carbon is especially useful for determining diet if the diet contains tropical grasses, such as corn. Corn has a signature much different than Eurasian grains such as wheat or barley, because of the type of photosynthesis used to metabolize carbon dioxide from the air. Temperate plants, such as most trees and shrubs, use a photosynthetic pathway (C3) that results in different carbon isotope signatures than tropical plants, like corn, sugar cane, and sorghum (C4 pathway). Someone who primarily ate corn (or any other C4 plant) would have a δ^{13}C signature of –13‰ to –9‰, while someone who ate primarily wheat or barley (C3 plants) would have a δ^{13}C signature

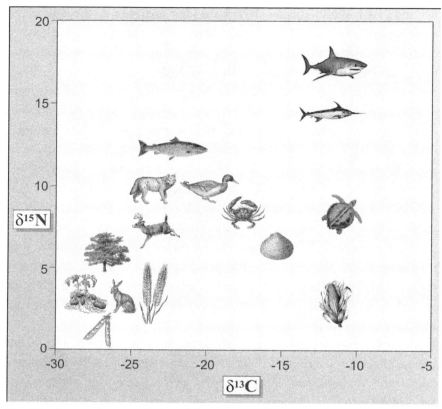

Figure 8.3. Common foods and their stable isotope values. Figure drawn by Susan Brannock-Gaul.

of −20‰ to −17‰. We can therefore make some estimate about how long someone who grew up England had been in the Americas, because once here their diet would have generally included lots of corn, which was the primary New World dietary C4 plant. A $\delta^{13}C$ signature of −21‰ to −18‰ would indicate they lived in England most or all of their lives, and one of −9‰ to −15‰ would indicate they were born America and always lived here. Signatures of −18 to −16 would indicate birth and earlier life in England, but then migration to America. The boy buried in the cellar at Leavy Neck has a $\delta^{13}C$ signature of −19.39‰, indicating that he had not long been eating corn, and therefore had not been in America for long before he died.

Several lesions indicate that even given his short time in America, he had suffered much. His right elbow had been fractured. It was healed, so it happened a while before the time of his death. He also had several unhealed fractures—a lower arm bone, the radius, and several fractured bones of the wrist. The evidence suggests that he was beaten at the time of his death or shortly before. Servants in the early Chesapeake were not always treated well.

Even those who led privileged lives found the early days of the Chesapeake a challenge to their health. In the fall of 1990, two archaeologists working at St. Mary's City, the original capital of Maryland, found something hard in the ground where they were excavating—they thought it was a rock. It turned out to be the stone floor of a chapel. Beneath it were three lead coffins. Lead coffins weren't uncommon in the seventeenth century, but only a few folks could afford them. The occupants must have been important people. After some research, the team of scientists determined that two of the coffins contained adults named Philip and Anne Calvert. Philip was a wealthy man, the younger brother of Cecil Calvert, who founded the Maryland colony. Philip died at age 56 in late 1682 or early 1683. Anne Wolseley Calvert, his wife, was approximately 60 when she died. She had extensive health problems, some of her own making.

At one point in her life, Anne Calvert had fractured her right femur, and it had not aligned correctly when it healed. This left the lower portion where it sits on the tibia twisted. Walking was undoubtedly painful for her. A pus drainage hole (cloaca) shows that it was infected much of her life. She suffered from osteoporosis as well. Anne's dental health was awful. She had lost 20 teeth prior to her death, most probably from a generous consumption of sugar and subsequent cavities. With so few teeth, she probably couldn't eat lots of other things. The final chapter in her story is revealed by elemental analysis of her hair—she had ingested high levels of arsenic, probably in an effort to cure her infection.

The smallest coffin held a child aged five to six years, probably a girl. The child had extensive vitamin D deficiency (rickets), and possible anemia. Clearly, even given the possibility of a diet with sufficient nutrients, lacking knowledge of proper nutrition led to malnutrition for this child. There are some other possible contributing factors, though. Douglas Owsley and Karin Bruwelheide of the National Museum of Natural History, the skeletal researchers who performed the analysis, propose that swaddling might have kept the child from getting enough ultraviolet light, the precursor to vitamin D production. In a similar fashion, rickets became a major problem in England during the industrial revolution, when women and children spent 10–14 hours in dark factories with little sunlight. Whatever the cause, this child of privilege was nonetheless a victim of vitamin and mineral deficiencies.

At the time of the Calverts, the life of privilege in the Chesapeake faced significant challenges. Those of wealth had lands aplenty, but between 1660 and 1750, give or take a few years, major labor shifts occurred in the Chesapeake. Coincident with the financial collapse of tobacco in Virginia, the social and economic situation had improved in England by 1660, and there was less incentive for many people to leave. The rate of emigration dropped between 1660 and 1690 from 18,000 to 13,000. That drop is also reflected in the number of servants, which averaged two per Chesapeake household in 1660; by 1690 it had dropped to two per ten households. Servants began to vanish from most households by 1700, making labor scarce.[12]

Faced with a declining number of indentured servants, Chesapeake planters turned increasingly to African slaves to perform plantation labor, beginning a new era of land development and economic prosperity, at least for some. From 300 in 1650, the number of African slaves increased to 13,000 by 1700, 13 percent of the total Chesapeake population. By 1750 it was 150,000, 40 percent of the population.[13] Simply assuming that all Africans living in the Chesapeake were bound by slavery, however, obscures the complexity of the population dynamics in the colonies. Settlers came from many backgrounds, and in Northampton County on the eastern shore of Maryland, free Africans worked and owned farms alongside settlers from Europe.[14]

By way of comparison with the early settlement of the Chesapeake colony, most settlers in Carolina came initially from Barbados, where sugar was the major crop and slavery had been established as the major form of labor since the 1650s. By 1660 Barbados was the first English colony with more people of African descent than those from Europe: 27,000 as compared to 26,000.[15] By 1680 for every indentured servant there were 17 slaves. A labor force that could work under harsh conditions such as those required by rice thus had a model in the sugar plantations of Barbados.

Carolina, by all accounts, was hot, swampy, and insect-ridden. Between 1670 and 1730, the number of African slaves in South Carolina increased from 1,500 to 20,000—they outnumbered free colonists two to one. Despite the large number of African slaves, a third of the early settlers who came by choice began their colonial experience as indentured servants. The actual demography of Carolina and Barbados is more complicated than those figures would indicate, and they hide a truth that for many years was obscured from view.

As discussed previously, we have come to realize in the past few decades that the slave trade in Indians was substantial. While the origins of the Indian slave trade are debated, the fact that in South Carolina alone in 1708 there were an estimated 1,400 Indian slaves staggers the imagination. There is substantial evidence that a trade in Indians was a vibrant part of the colonial economy. In fact, more Indian slaves were exported from Charleston in the period between 1670 and 1715 than Africans were imported during the same period.[16] Many of those Indian slaves were sent to the West Indies.

In a report on the population in Carolina made in 1708, slaves outnumbered European settlers ("Whites"). Of those slaves, more than 20 percent were Native Americans (Table 8.1). A couple of things in Table 8.1 stand out. First, between 1703 and 1708 the number of Europeans ("Whites" in the table) decreased, except for children, who increased dramatically. Second, while enslaved Africans ("Negro" in the table) and Indians increased by the same number—roughly 1,100—that increase was proportionately far greater for Indians (75%) than for Africans (27%). Indian slavery in early 1700 was a thriving business.

Whether in the Chesapeake or in Carolina, the human costs of the colonial agrarian effort and the labor imposed on those less fortunate can be measured in many ways. The oft-made assumption that servant and slave labor was cheap is incorrect—in fact, the cost of laborers was quite high. It was not the cheapness of labor that placed those poor souls in the fields, but the working conditions. Social and economic stratification dictated that some, those working in the fields, were at greater risk for contracting infectious diseases. Poverty and malnutrition made them more susceptible to infection and less able to recover from it.

Certainly, the loss of life that exceeds the birthrate, as it did for African slaves in South Carolina, is an appreciable statistic. In the Chesapeake, population increase through births did not offset deaths until the end of the seventeenth century.[17] Other costs are harder to measure but are certainly worth considering. Parents in the Chesapeake prior to 1700 were just about as likely to die before their children had reached their teens as children were to die before they reached maturity. Thus, numerous children were enlisted as servants in order to survive. Undoubtedly, the conditions of many children during their growing years included malnutrition and numerous bouts of infectious disease.

Evidence of the impact of malnutrition and disease on children, measured in terms of early mortality, is how we have traditionally assessed children's health. As Paul Ewald, the evolutionary biologist, once noted,

Table 8.1. South Carolina population as reported by the governor and council, Sept. 17, 1708

	Projected for 1703	Reported for 1708	Reported Change
Free men	1,460	1,360	−100
Free women	940	900	−40
Free children	1,200	1,700	+500
White servant men	110	60	−50
White servant women	90	60	−30
Total whites	**3,800**	**4,080**	**+280**
Negro men slaves	1,500	1,800	+300
Negro women slaves	900	1,100	+200
Negro children slaves	600	1,200	+600
Total Negro Slaves	**3,000**	**4,100**	**+1,100**
Indian men slaves	100	500	+400
Indian women slaves	150	600	+450
Indian children slaves	100	300	+200
Total Indian Slaves	**350**	**1,400**	**+1,050**

Source: Wood, *Black Majority*, Table 1, 144. I have used the ancestry terms in Wood's original table. Undoubtedly, he was confronted with the same issue that I was—how to know what criteria were used for classification and through what lens those classifications were made.

mortality is a great measure of success or failure.[18] It is not the best measure, though, nor does it address all of the impacts of children's growth environments. In fact, people interested in nutrition, disease, growth, development, and the relationships between them have come to appreciate the more subtle impacts in the past three decades.

The most prevalent form of childhood malnutrition is protein-energy malnutrition, or PEM. It is called kwashiorkor when the diet includes a sufficient amount of food but is lacking in protein. There are a number of ways of measuring nutritional status. Height and weight measures can be compared to world standards. Low weight for height reflects acute, short-term food shortages, such as during famines, and is called wasting. Children who received inadequate nutrition in their younger years but who later have an adequate diet may be shorter than they would have been if they had consistently had a nutritionally sound diet, a condition called stunting. All of these nutritional impacts have seriously implications for later adult health.

A healthy child grows up and becomes, all things working right, a healthy adult. An unhealthy child, on the other hand, can generally look forward to an unhealthy life and a shorter life span. The health of the mother carrying an unborn child also impacts the later health of the child. And so the cycle of malnutrition goes from a mother who is malnourished to a low-birth-weight baby, who will become a child with stunting. The World Health Organization (WHO) emphasizes that the critical window for adequate nutrition is the 1,000 days between conception and 24 months of age.[19] Stunting leads to a number of later developmental problems that include impaired mental (neurocognitive) development, compromised immune systems, and reduced productivity in later life.

The point of view that early health and nutrition influences later health is part of a larger theoretical framework called life history theory (LHT). LHT emphasizes that resources are limited and that energy is given to three primary life functions: growth, reproduction, and somatic (body) maintenance. Because resources are limited, there are always trade-offs—there is no free lunch. To partition a resource to one function means that it cannot be used for another. Thus, an increased investment in growth means that there may be less energy devoted to maintenance. These trade-offs, known as allocations, can involve the immune system, growth, gestation, and fertility, to name a few.

Let's take the trade-off between investment in growth and immune function—a child who invests more energy in fighting infection will have less energy to devote to growth. Further, a correlative relationship has been observed between growth and the immune system—those with stunted growth tend to suffer more immune system problems. Children who have less access to nutritional resources will have less energy to put into any investment, be it growth or the immune system. Children with adequate access to food will grow better and have healthier immune systems than those who do not.

We have long known that there is a synergistic relationship between malnutrition and infectious disease. Poor nutrition, especially protein deficiency, will lower an individual's resistance to infection and depress the cell-mediated immune response.[20] Infectious disease interferes with nutrition by altering absorption in the digestive system and increasing the physiological need for essential nutrients, again especially protein. Iron availability can be greatly reduced during infection. For children bound in servitude, be it indentured or through slavery, nutrition may have always been a problem, along with frequent bouts of disease. And there were a lot of children bound to servitude.

There are several problems in addressing the issue of nutrition historically. The first is that the narratives regarding the treatment of slaves have followed historical threads. Some of those threads have emphasized the harsh treatment of those in bondage, while others have been apologist, minimizing the harsh treatment and emphasizing misinterpretation of the actual conditions of bondage. Most of the narratives were not written by those bonded or in bondage. Both the variability of the conditions reported in the documents and the interpretive lens of the translator indicate variation regarding how well slaves were provisioned with food, especially with regard to food that contained essential nutrients.

It was certainly common knowledge among plantation owners and other holders of servants that labor was not cheap. Laborers represented an investment, and it was therefore wise to protect that investment. Taking care of laborers through medical intervention and adequate food generally cost less than replacing laborers who died. It also helped to ensure that they were productive. On those points, I think most scholars would agree. It is the policies that followed for which there is disagreement. Some argue that, given the above, at least some slave owners carefully attended to providing a balanced diet, albeit an uninteresting one. Some gave time off to laborers for hunting and fishing. Some provided land to grow food. Providing gardens was well known to enhance the dietary adequacy of slaves, and numerous narratives mention it as sound plantation management.[21]

Historic narratives frequently mention corn, sweet potatoes, rice, and pork in slave diets. There are numerous references to slaves raising pigs, chickens, and vegetables, as well as hunting wild mammals, birds, and fish. The documents also indicate variation in diet due to the policies of particular estate or plantation owners. It is probably safe to say there was tremendous variation in the approach to provisioning slaves, as indicated by the two narratives below:

On Saturday each slave was given ten pounds of cornmeal, a quart of blackstrap [molasses], six pounds of fatback, three pounds of flour and vegetables, all of which were raised on the farm. All of the slaves hunted, or those who wanted to, hunted rabbits, opossums, or fished. . . . Each family was given three acres to raise their chickens or vegetables, and if a man raised his own food he was given ten dollars at Christmas time extra, besides his presents (Narrative of Silas Jackson, Baltimore, Maryland).

There was a great long trough that went across the yard, and that was where we ate. For dinner we had peas or some other sort of vegetables, and corn bread. Aunt Viney crumbled up that bread in the trough and poured vegetables and pot liquor over it. Then she blew the horn and children came running from every which way. . . . We never had anything but corn bread and buttermilk at night. Sometimes that trough would be a sight, because we never stopped to wash our hands, and before we had been eating more than a minute or two what was in the trough would look like real mud what had come off our hands (Narrative of Robert Shepherd, Athens, Georgia).[22]

There are also indications that slave owners hedged their bets and made decisions about the most cost-effective methods of caring for their slaves. They dealt more seriously with acute problems—epidemic diseases, for instance—while letting chronic problems like nutritional deficiencies of vitamin D and iron persist. They may have been more attentive to adults, figuring that with high child mortality rates, it was better to make sure an individual lived past childhood. The historical narratives suggest that the quantity and quality of food often improved for individuals once they reached the age of five. Richard Steckel, an economic historian who has long focused on slave health, suggested that slave children were not typically given meat until they began to work, around the age of ten.[23]

Provisioning on the basis of attaining, or nearly attaining, adulthood was, unfortunately, not the best policy as healthy children grow up to be healthy adults. If we follow the logic of life history theory, resources were being diverted from other biological processes (maintenance and/or reproduction), and any process for children was probably impacted by inadequate nutritional resources. What were some of the probable insults to adequate nutrition that slave children faced? Starting with the earliest post-birth impacts, there is significant indication in the available plantation records that breast-feeding was often hurried and that weaning was rushed, as mothers often returned to the field after three months. Weaning was complicated by the fact that there wasn't an adequate replacement for mother's milk.

The enzyme lactase metabolizes milk sugars (lactose) into absorbable monosaccharides (simple sugars). Without the enzyme, individuals are lactose intolerant and can't process milk properly. If lactose-intolerant individuals drink milk, they can expect gastrointestinal discomfort, cramps, and diarrhea. Some individuals will die from loss of fluids and nutrients, generally a slow wasting death. Therefore, those with the recessive gene that controls lactase production have a reproductive advantage, and the frequency of those individuals in the overall population (or, more correctly, their genes) also goes up.

The rate of lactose intolerance for modern African Americans is roughly 70–77 percent, while for those of European descent it is roughly 5–19 percent. In modern African populations it varies from 0–80 percent, with the highest frequencies in the southern third of the continent. In situations where milk cannot be tolerated or weaning occurs early, gruels made of corn and other starchy grains, easily digested but with many nutritional inadequacies, are substituted for milk. They are not usually a balanced nutritive source. Withholding meat in the early years would likely lead to kwashiorkor (severe protein-energy malnutrition from a diet with insufficient protein).[24]

Historians Kenneth and Virginia Kiple took an interesting approach to examining the whole issue of nutritional adequacy for African slave children, and by extension for adults. They reasoned that if nutrition was adequate for slave populations, then diseases with a nutritional cause should be infrequent.[25] What they found is that historical references to crooked or bandy legs, knock-knee, stooped shoulders, jaundiced complexions, splotchy skin, inflamed and watery eyes, partial blindness, and rotten teeth indicate that nutritionally linked diseases were common for slaves. Among those indicated by the descriptive terms are rickets (vitamin D deficiency), scurvy (vitamin C deficiency), and protein-calorie malnutrition (kwashiorkor and marasmus). The conclusion must be that the apologist historical narratives reporting dietary sufficiency are not entirely accurate, or at least not broadly applicable.

Analysis of the archaeological plant and animal remains found at two plantations on the Cooper River, Yaughan and Curriboo, supports historical descriptions of the slave diet.[26] Yaughan was occupied from 1737 until 1809, Curriboo from at least 1737 until 1849, when the current owner began to subdivide it. From plant and animal analysis, the archaeologists determined several things about slave diet at these sites. It was primarily vegetable and rather monotonous, the mainstays being rice and corn. Meat was scarce and consisted primarily of cows and pigs. Domestic plants and animals were supplemented by hunted and gathered wild foods. At both Curriboo and Yaughan, all cooking and consumption appears to have been done outside, as only one possible hearth was found within the structures. No central kitchen structures were found, so cooking was probably done in various locations across the sites. Analysis of ceramics from the sites suggests that soups, stews, and gruels formed much of the diet, and that eating was done in small groups, given the small size of cooking pots.

To fully estimate the available dietary resources and potential nutritional risks, it would seem prudent to go beyond the written records of diet to other types of data and other forms of inquiry. Again, mortality is often a standard measure of biological stress at the population level. To say that the mortality of infants born into slavery was excessive hardly captures the reality of the situation. Steckel estimates that total loss of life (stillbirths plus infant deaths) before the end of the first year was nearly 50 percent. While reconstructions of mortality based on historical records are always suspect, a contemporary southern planter wrote "Of those born, one half die under one year."[27] Although there were multiple causes, one sure contributing factor is malnutrition. Steckel argues convincingly that given the excess mortality of infants, it made no sense to provide adequate nutrition for them until they became productive adults. Additionally, information on growth provides supporting evidence for a diet lacking in sufficient nutrients.

> The stature of young slave children would trigger alarm in a modern pediatrician's office. At age 4.5 boys on average reached only centile 0.2 and girls attained only 0.5. Progress was slow for many years thereafter. Upward movement through the centiles, or catch-up growth, occurred after age 4.5, but the first centile of modern standards was not reached until age 6.5 in females and 7.5 in males. . . . Sustained

catch-up growth took place after age 13.5 in girls and about age 16.5 in boys, and by adulthood males reached centile 27.1, and females reached 28.4.[28]

As Steckel says, "Comparative heights suggest that children from the slums of Lagos, Nigeria, and from urban areas of Bangladesh had an environment for growth superior to that of American slave children."[29] Clearly, children were not that healthy at an early age if their growth was so stunted. Their growth deficit began before birth. Slave newborns weighed on average about 2,500 grams (approximately 5.5 pounds). Modern newborns average 3,450 grams (approximately 7.6 pounds). That would suggest that mothers were also unable to provide adequate nutritional support for the growing fetus, or that they suffered from infections during pregnancy. Just as an example of the impact of infection, contemporary African women infected with *Plasmodium falciparum* malaria had newborn children weighing 263 grams below those of women who were not infected.[30]

In sum, although some nutritional historians and economists contend that the overall adult slave diet, while monotonous, probably came close to the recommended dietary allowance (RDA) for adults, it seems unlikely, given the descriptions of diet presented by the slaves themselves. Archaeological data regarding what slaves ate, and the analysis of historical records of growth and mortality, bring to doubt the picture of adequate diets presented by some historical narratives. There seem to be data from several sources that suggest that growth was retarded and that diseases of nutritional inadequacy were common.

Any nutritional problems experienced by servants, slaves, or colonists would likely have been exacerbated by intestinal parasites. Dirt floors and farm fields placed people at risk for contracting hookworm (*Necator americanus*) and roundworm (*Ascaris lumbricoides*). In seven states (Alabama, Georgia, Louisiana, Mississippi, North and South Carolina, and Virginia) during the year 1849–50, worms were cited as the cause of death for a collective 1,708 people. Ninety-six of those deaths were of children aged nine and younger.[31] Clearly, given the attention to worms in the narratives of slave owners, they were a major health issue. Colonel Landon Carter reported a worm as long as six inches coming out of a newborn on his Shirley plantation in Virginia.[32]

The two most common species of worms have quite different methods of transmission. Roundworm eggs are ingested, and sanitation of dwellings is a major factor in transmission. Hookworms hatch in warm, moist soil and burrow into the feet. Again, sanitation is an issue, but it extends beyond the house to yards and fields. Neither of the worms generally causes death, but they certainly could exacerbate other infectious and nutritional problems. If the worm burden is high enough, severe complications such as congestive heart failure can occur. Both hookworm and roundworm are major health issues in contemporary global populations.

Hookworm in particular is a good reminder that the living conditions that often accompany poverty are usually associated with increased risk for several diseases. Despite its late clinical diagnosis in 1893, characteristic descriptions make it clear that it was present in human populations long before. Hookworm came to public attention in 1903 when it became apparent that it was one of the most prevalent infections of rural southern populations. The popular depiction of "hillbillies" was, in fact, largely based on the high prevalence of hookworm infections in rural southern populations. Victims of hookworm disease show a characteristic set of symptoms that include pronounced anemia, often accompanied by diarrhea, and sometimes a slight fever. Hookworm is particularly prevalent among children, and it affects their development—they develop anatomical deformities and lack mental acuity. It is not usually a fatal disease, but it afflicts the sufferer with lethargy. A single infection can last up to a decade or more.[33]

Alongside poor nutrition, crowded living conditions and poor sanitation can be blamed for many of the annual infections.[34] In slave housing on plantations, respiratory infections—such as the common cold, pleurisy, pneumonia, whooping cough, tuberculosis, and diphtheria—were common in the winter months. Transmission of respiratory infections was enhanced by close quarters. Sanitation was often poor. The best toilet facilities one could hope for were privies, and they were often of such poor design that they were infrequently used. The summer months often saw a rise in the rates of intestinal infections such as dysentery, typhoid fever, and cholera.

Unfortunately, we can assume that many of these infections were underreported. Studying human skeletons has given us further information on the quality of life for African slaves. Jennifer Olsen Kelley and Larry Angel of the Smithsonian Institution considered the life stresses of slavery in several Chesapeake plantation slaves.[35] Like other researchers, they treated mortality (longevity) as a measure of quality of life. Eighteenth-century females lived until 36 on average, males until 30. The nineteenth century saw a reduction in female life span to 35, and an increase for males to 36. In either century, average length of life was short. Growth defects of enamel, enamel hypoplasias, were half as frequent in the nineteenth century as the eighteenth, indicating an improvement in health.

As with indentured servants, hypertrophic (enlarged size due to enlarged cell size) muscle attachments were common among Chesapeake slaves. Arm muscles were typically larger, leaving characteristic developments on the skeleton. Arthritis early in life was common—shoulder and neck vertebrae exhibited breakdown and arthritis, as did hips and elbows. These developments were most extreme in the turn-of-the-century individuals from Catoctin Furnace, an iron forge from Frederick County, Maryland.

In a South Carolina rural population from near Charleston, Ted Rathbun studied the remains of 36 people buried between 1840 and 1870.[36] The average age at death was about the same as in Virginia and Maryland, with females living until 35 and males until 40. Anemia was a significant health problem and affected 35 percent of adults and 80 percent of children. Harris lines ranged in frequency from 45 percent for men to 18 percent for women. General markers of infectious disease were very common—69 percent of males, 60 percent of females, 80 percent of children. Thus, infection and malnutrition went hand in hand.

For the rural slaves Rathbun observed, growth-arrest markers in teeth and bones were common—92 percent of males and 70 percent of females exhibited growth arrests. Skeletal markers of heavy labor—enlarged muscle and tendon attachment sites and osteoarthritis—were ubiquitous. Women seemed to be more affected in the neck, knee, and shoulder joints; men more commonly were affected in the hip and elbow. Interestingly, lead was relatively high in the bone elements, a difference from many slaves.

Lead poisoning serves to remind us that wealth and access to scarce resources don't always shield one from negative consequences. Lead has proven to be an interesting element to study in this regard, because it often indicates social-status and resource-access differences. It was typically obtained through ingestion of lead-contaminated beverages, such as rum and wine, lead storage vessels, or lead dinner ware. It is generally highest for Europeans, as documented at Newton Plantation in Barbados.[37] Thus, while wealth has its privileges, constant exposure to lead caused lead poisoning in some wealthy individuals.

Poverty creates a web of inescapable suffering for many people. Appreciating the scope of its impacts is difficult. Mortality rates for early childhood are only one measure of the health and living conditions of a population. About the last quarter of the nineteenth century, mortality rates dramatically decreased for many industrial nations. Improved hygiene had a lot to do with it, as did better nutritional standards and health care. Even today, in many nonindustrial nations one of every five children will die before the age of five.[38] For people living in villages in Bolivia or Indonesia or many other parts of the world, the fact that I have only one child, and have ever had only one child, is inconceivable. Adults in those villages have usually buried at least a couple of children.

What we have come to appreciate in the past few decades is just how important the health of the mother is for the developing child. The first few years of the child's life are also extremely influential on later health. With substandard living conditions, nutritional deprivation, and hard work in poor working conditions, living a long life was generally not possible. Many of those who built the fields and factories of America generally did so under the weight of limited resources and impoverished health.

PART IV

Measuring the Lands

9

Measured Lands and Multitudes

Cities, like dreams, are made of desires and fears, even if the thread of their discourse is secret, their rules are absurd, their perspectives deceitful, and everything conceals everything else.

Italo Calvino, *Invisible Cities*

At all seasons of the year, there is an amount of sickness and death in this, as in all large cities, far beyond those of less densely peopled, more airy and open places, such as country residences. . . . These circumstances have never been investigated in this city [New York], as they should be.

John H. Griscom, *The Sanitary Condition of the Laboring Population of New York, with Suggestions for Its Improvement*

Cities did not come immediately to the colonial landscape; there was first the measuring and ordering of things. One of the first tasks of the early settlers in America was to chronicle the major coastal landmarks, rivers, bays, and harbors, and then record those on maps. Some of the earliest observations of the lands, wildlife, and people of burgeoning Atlantic America were made by surveyors such as William Bartram and John Lawson. They provided the grid for early landscape modification. The second task was to subdivide the lands into portions, recording those portions as to owners and proprietors (Figure 9.1). It is as if, in so doing, one can bring order to chaos.

It is not that the earlier Indians had neglected to make landscape modifications. They burned tracts to manage deer and plantings, built residences, channeled water. In some areas of the Americas, the modifications were fairly extensive. Take, for example, the cliff dwellings of Mesa Verde, or the semi-subterranean pit houses of Chaco Canyon, or the large

Figure 9.1. *Mahantango Valley Farm*, late nineteenth century, artist unknown. Courtesy National Gallery of Art, Washington.

urban centers of Cahokia and Teotihuacan. Nowhere, though, did the level of built environment reach the extent or proportions of Atlantic colonial cities.

Measured lands in the colonies began with farmsteads and plantations, and they often took the ordered form of the European landscape. Fences, enclosures, outbuildings, and such all transformed natural landscape to the built environment. Early on, human settlements were connected primarily by waterways, but roads soon channeled people and products between farms and came to connect them with one another, and then to larger places, the cities where multitudes settled. Cities were the ultimate reformation of the landscape, and they became in many ways the petri dishes of the colonial process. There, people and pathogens congregated, often in large numbers, often in shadows and in enclaves stratified by access to proper housing, food, and other necessities of life.

Many early cities took on the appearance of Europe. The first artist's view of New Amsterdam depicts houses along the shore that look like those of Amsterdam. As the fingers of piers reached out into the urban harbors, and the limbs of cities reached outward onto the landscape, the transformation was immense. Not only was there deforestation, but grids often set the patterns of streets, residences, shops. James Oglethorpe designed Savannah around squares, in the same design as architect Christopher Wren used for the rebuilding of London after the Great Fire of 1666. Early maps of Boston, Charleston, New York, and Savannah all affirm that the organization of the urban lands was well under way by the early eighteenth century (Figures 9.2–9.4).

The Chesapeake really had no major cities prior to 1800. There were generally fewer cities in the southern portion of Atlantic America than in the north, reflecting perhaps the more agrarian economy of the South as compared to the industrial leanings of the North. In the South were Charleston and Savannah. In the North were Boston, New York, and Philadelphia, but neither Charleston nor Boston exerted the influence of New York or Philadelphia.[1]

There were major differences between Charleston and the cities of the North. Charleston acted primarily as a point of product exportation—rice, indigo, and naval stores—and as a port of commerce in the slave trade. Fewer people came to settle, at least by choice, through the port of Charleston. New York and Philadelphia, on the other hand, were settled

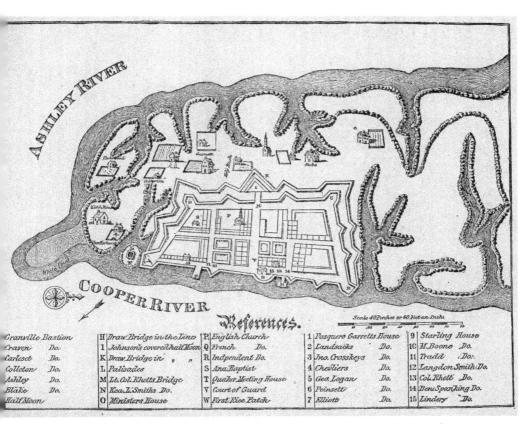

References.

Granville Bastion		H	Draw Bridge in the line	P	English Church	1	Pasquero Garretts House	9	Starling House
Craven	Do.	I	Johnson's covered half Moon	Q	French Do.	2	Landsacks Do.	10	M. Boone Do.
Carlosb	Do.	K	Draw Bridge in " "	R	Independent Do.	3	Jno. Crosskeys Do.	11	Tradd Do.
Colleton	Do.	L	Palisades	S	Ana Baptist	4	Chevliers Do.	12	Langdon Smith Do.
Ashley	Do.	M	Lt. Col. Rhetts Bridge	T	Quaker Meeting House	5	Geo. Logan Do.	13	Col. Rhett Do.
Blake	Do.	N	Kea. L. Smiths Do.	V	Court of Guard	6	Poinsett Do.	14	Benj. Spanking Do.
Half Moon		O	Ministers House	W	First Rice Patch	7	Elliott Do.	15	Lindery Do.

Figure 9.2. Charleston about 1704, when the town was roughly 40 years old. Library of Congress, reproduced from *Great American Homes: Historic Charleston*, Shirley Abbott, Oxmoor House, Birmingham, Alabama, 1988.

by Dutch and Quaker merchants who channeled the productive yields of the Hudson Valley, Long Island, Delaware, and Pennsylvania into a larger Atlantic trading system. It was a highly effective system that by the close of the colonial era dominated a large portion of the Atlantic coastal region from the St. Lawrence River to Baltimore. New York was the port of entry for millions of European immigrants.

From the founding of New Amsterdam in 1625, the financially sound Dutch East India Company made sure the colonists had the provisions they needed to successfully clear land and establish an agricultural base. New Amsterdam did not have the "starving time" that Jamestown settlers

Figure 9.3. Savannah in 1734, as depicted by Peter Gordon and printed in William de Brahm, *History of the Province of Georgia*, 1849.

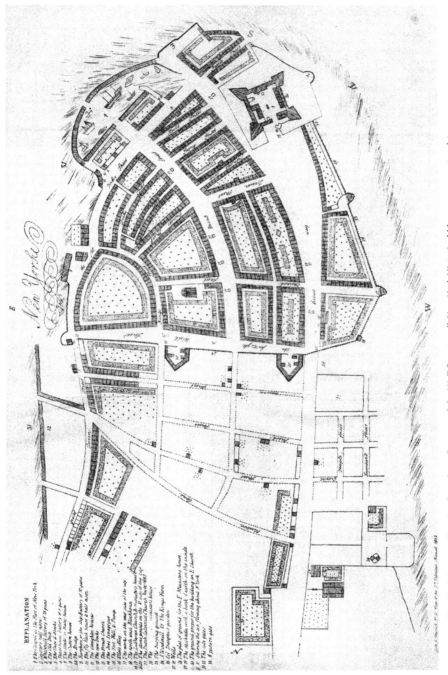

Figure 9.4. New York in 1695, showing Broadway Street and the Wall Street wall. New York Historical Maps, www.nyctourist.com.

had suffered. That initial period of prosperity, however, was soon over-shadowed by other problems.

By 1650, with a population of 1,000, New Amsterdam had outgrown its early charm. As with any city, a sedentary population aggregated into a confined space created issues of sanitation. So it has been since societies traded the nomadic life for one of permanent dwellings. Even with only a few thousand people, hygiene is always an issue—dirt, dust, excrement, dead animals, food wastes—they all pile up. One solution in early New York was to allow hogs to roam freely through the city and eat many of the accumulated organic materials. The problem was they left other re-mains in their place.

Within the walls that became Wall Street, New Amsterdam stank. Sew-age spilled into the canal that provided passage from Manhattan. Pri-vate wells suffered both from brackish water and from bacterial pollu-tion. Underground sewers drained some of the water, but the smell was reported as noxious. By 1644 ordinances were issued against throwing trash into the street. An ordinance was issued in 1648 to keep hogs and goats from running in the streets. In 1656 soldiers were ordered to shoot free-running hogs. The year 1657 saw another ordinance against throwing trash into the street. And so it went for New York. As one of the most rap-idly growing cities along the Atlantic, and certainly later as the gateway to America, growing population numbers, shrinking available land, and poverty continued to make sanitation in New York a major problem well into the nineteenth century.

Imagine New York in the 1650s, smaller than now but with many of the same architectural features. Streets are laid out with houses along them. A single canal, the Heere Graft, has just been built along Broad Street to provide drainage and docking facilities. Horses are the predomi-nant mode of transport for humans, garbage, nightsoil, milk, and water. Dogs, goats, pigs, and even cows wander through the streets. Animals are nearly as common as humans, and dead animals regularly adorn the street. That remained commonplace for two centuries: "In May of 1853, for example, the City Inspector reported that 439 large dead animals had been removed from the streets along with the bodies of 71 dogs, 93 cats, 17 sheep, 4 goats, and 19 hogs."[2] Butchers and tanners operate shops near many of the residences. There is no sewage system, and freshwater is not all that easy to come by—the first public wells, all nine of them, are mostly brackish. Street manure is picked up two or three times a week by contractors, but that schedule is at best theoretical.

Privies were the subject of many conversations in early New York. The sewage problems became so extreme that in May 1658 city officials were pressed to order removal of all privies having their outlet level with the ground. The design, which facilitated the access of the privy materials to hogs, both created a great stench and was a nuisance to those walking by who had to evade the frequent eruptions of the privy deposits. Requiring privies without such street access, however, just created other sanitation problems—they eventually had to be emptied of their contents.

> WHEREAS many, even the greatest part of the burghers and inhabitants of this City build their privies even with the ground with an opening towards the street, so that hogs may consume the filth and wallow in it, which not only creates a great stench and therefore great inconvenience to the passers-by, but also makes the streets foul and unfit for use,—therefore. . . . the Burgonmasters and Schepens, herewith order and command, that all and everybody. . . . shall break down and remove such privies coming out upon the street.[3]

Sources of freshwater continued to be an issue. In a region surrounded by salt water, freshwater had to be obtained from either springs or rivers. Ponds, rivers, and shores tended to be popular places to dump anything that people were trying to remove. Dumping finally led to the filling in of the Heere Graft—by 1675 it had become impossible to keep it clean, although it is also said that it was abandoned because it impeded traffic.

Whether north or south, cities served as the portal through which passengers, products, and pathogens entered and departed. Cities were initially located on navigable waterways and served as the major ports. They provided a source of infected and susceptible hosts in constant, measured time. Immigration, be it forced or by choice, is an emotionally and physically stressful event. The oceanic passage to America generally lasted two months at sea in cramped conditions with limited nutritional resources. Immune systems were undoubtedly compromised. Scurvy (vitamin C deficiency) was extremely common due to the absence of fresh fruit. Mosquitoes probably bred in the numerous water containers hauled on ships. Because many people were already malnourished and immune-compromised prior to the journey, illness commonly broke out during the voyage. Direct transmission of any infectious disease was easy because the next available person probably wasn't any farther away than a few inches. For all those reasons, ships often represented delivery of the next epidemic.

The period between 1700 and 1800 for most cities was a time of epidemics, for many reasons. For one, there was constant movement into port cities from elsewhere. Population growth was exponential. From 1700 to 1760 the population of New York rose from 19,000 to 117,100, while that of Philadelphia rose from 18,000 to 183,700. Many of those were immigrants from Europe with rural backgrounds. In the early 1790s about 3,000 immigrants came to New York each year.

Major population growth in Charleston occurred through the importation of slaves. The actual numbers of enslaved Africans who arrived in Charleston but soon departed for the low country and other destinations, is immense. In a five-year period, between 1735 and 1740, an estimated 66 shipments of African slaves arrived in Charleston—11,562 people total, 1,559 of them below the age of 10. When you consider that estimates of deaths during the Middle Passage were about 20 percent, the number of those torn from their homelands is even more staggering.[4] The immense immigration combined with the speed and magnitude of population increase simply exceeded the capacity of cities to plan effectively for growth, especially when it came to housing and sanitation.

Most diseases that plagued New York and other cities were facilitated by poverty and inadequate sanitation. Poverty was commonplace in New York, just as it was in most cities in Europe, partly because the impoverished of Europe came to America seeking a better life, partly because of the nature of available jobs, partly just because the city was going through growing pains. The majority of the labor force—indentured and free servants, and slaves—were poor. Wealth separated the common laborer from those more fortunate, and the arrival to the city of thousands per year kept wages low. There was always someone willing to work for starvation wages.

In parts of the city, poverty was ubiquitous, and once the cycle of poverty began, it usually did not improve. Poverty did not go unnoticed, but relief was differentially provided. Support for the impoverished began through charity and churches in the early eighteenth century. In 1736 the city built an almshouse. New York was hardly unique in having an almshouse, and the frequency with which they appeared was a testament to the sheer numbers of the destitute (Figure 9.5). However, it was common for keepers of the almshouses to deny charity to strangers and "sturdy beggars" who could work but had no job. No aid was provided for those who were seen primarily as medical concerns—the insane or the chronically ill. There was generally no aid for those who were not European Caucasians; Indians or Africans were not provided aid unless they were very young or very old. Women received aid only when they proved that they were morally fit. Later, in the early nineteenth century, relief societies such as the Society for the Relief of Poor Widows with Young Children began to offer further aid.

The squalid living conditions that characterized the impoverished persons, combined with malnutrition, could hardly have provided a better environment for the transmission of infectious disease. Many of the diseases that plagued the population of New York and other urban centers were crowd diseases—they need a sufficient number of susceptible hosts to sustain an infection (Table 9.1). When they circulated more or less continuously among populations, they became diseases of childhood, the only group of susceptible hosts, and they became less dangerous to adults—that did not happen until after 1850.

One of the most serious crowd diseases was smallpox, once among the most deadly diseases in the world. Smallpox appeared in New York as early as 1675 and visited the city on at least seven other occasions in epidemics. The 1731 bills of mortality that list the cause of death as smallpox for those buried in New York's cemeteries list 477 Europeans (7 percent of their population) and 71 Africans (5 percent of their population). The lower death rate for Africans may be due to the West African practice of inoculation for smallpox—smallpox variolation (vaccination) was known very early to be effective.[5] Beginning in 1752 smallpox was a regular visitor to New York. Alexander Colden wrote on August 21, 1757, that smallpox was epidemic: "The Bells are ringing every day & five or Six Children buried of an Evenning."[6]

Measles spread through the Atlantic colonies in 1713, and there were some cases in New York. New England was the first region to suffer, with Boston taking heavy casualties. Scattered outbreaks of measles occurred

Figure 9.5. *Berks County Almshouse, 1878*, by Charles C. Hofmann. Courtesy National Gallery of Art, Washington.

Table 9.1. Epidemic diseases in New York City, 1600–1900

Disease	Years Affected	Total Deaths
Cholera	1832–34, 1849, 1854, 1866	13,193
Diphtheria	1745, 1755, 1768	9,403
Influenza	1789–90	*
Malaria	1668	*
Measles	1713, 1729, 1788	*
Smallpox	1679, 1702, 1731, 1738, 1739, 1745, 1752, 1756–66, 1804, 1824, 1834–35, 1848, 1851, 1852–54, 1865, 1872, 1875	8,608
Typhus/Typhoid	1847, 1848, 1851, 1864, 1865	5,951
Yellow Fever	1702, 1743, 1795, 1803	1,150

Notes: *Figures given for deaths are limited to the period 1798–1900. Some diseases have no figures. Data from Duffy, *Epidemics in Colonial America* and *A History of Public Health in New York City 1625–1866*; Condran, "Changing Patterns of Epidemic Disease in New York City," 27–41.

in New England, New York, and New Jersey from 1739 to 1741. In 1747–48 measles appeared in widely separated localities in South Carolina, Pennsylvania, New York, Massachusetts, and Connecticut. The prevalence of measles among adults in America indicates that, like smallpox, it did not become endemic until late in the colonial period. The intervals between epidemics permitted the development of a new group of susceptibles due to the scattered population density on the landscape. It continued, alongside smallpox, to be one of the great causes of mortality among infants until relatively recently. For instance, mortality from measles in New York City was 21.9 of 100,000 in 1840; by 1930 it was 2.1 of 100,000.[7]

A new disease appeared in New Hampshire in 1735 that was clearly diphtheria, and it swept through the Atlantic colonies in succeeding years.[8] Diphtheria is spread by human contact and is usually attributed to a respiratory infection, although subcutaneous spread through cuts does occur. The principal victims are those under the age of puberty. It is similar in some respects to scarlet fever. Names for it included throat distemper, throat ail, canker ail, throat disease, pestilential sore throat, and a few others.

Diphtheria shows fairly distinct clinical symptoms: swelling, redness, and tenderness of the throat, and later the appearance of grayish-white specks or patches and the gradual formation of a yellowish-colored false membrane over all the mucous surfaces of the throat. As this membrane thickens and spreads down the larynx and trachea, breathing becomes increasingly difficult, and in severe cases death results from suffocation. Sometimes bleeding comes from the nostrils, and there is a fetid discharge. The ecology of diphtheria is internal rather than external, that is to say a body system ecology. Diphtheria is caused by a gram-positive bacillus called *Corynebacterium diphtheriae*. It is a normal inhabitant of the upper respiratory tract of human beings and is not found in any other animals, nor does it produce disease in other species of animals. Only a small number of humans who harbor the bacillus will ever develop diphtheria.

In 1735 diphtheria was accompanied by a severe form of scarlet fever. Scarlet fever, another childhood disease, was also a constant source of mortality in the nineteenth century. Between 1860 and 1865, however, scarlet fever accounted for 1,082 of the deaths of known cause in New York, as compared to 1,414 deaths from cholera and 3,313 deaths from consumption during the same years.

Measles, smallpox, pleurisy, scarlet fever, whooping cough, diphtheria, yellow fever, and other diseases flourished in Charleston as they did in many eighteenth-century cities. Of course they didn't all arrive via Atlantic crossings, but the volume of oceanic traffic that came and went through Charleston's ports undoubtedly contributed to infectious disease outbreaks. In 1711 Commissary Johnston wrote " . . . for the small Pox, Pestilential fevers, Pleurisies, and fluxe's have destroyed great numbers here of all Sorts, both Whites, Blacks, and Indians,—and these distempers still rage to an uncommon degree."[9]

One disease that was less of a problem in Charleston was malaria. Lord Adam Gordon noted in 1764–65 that although malaria was prevalent in the Carolinas, Charleston was free of it. According to those who lived in Charleston, the absence was because "the air being mended by the Number of Fires in Town, as much as to its cool Situation, on a point, at the junction of the two navigable Streams, called Ashley and Cowper Rivers."[10] Malaria was a disease largely of the coastal lowlands along the Atlantic and into the interior—it reached as far north as Illinois and a bit farther westward. It did reach into some cities, but it tended, because of the reproductive and resting habits of the *Anopheles* mosquito, to be primarily a disease of rural agrarian landscapes.[11] Yellow fever, on the other hand, was a disease primarily of cities, especially port cities, which it haunted along the Atlantic and Gulf coasts for two centuries.

Yellow fever, for several reasons, is more serious than malaria. The latter, while it sometimes killed the very young and the very old, tended to subject those it infected to months of debilitation but not death. While most cases of yellow fever are mild, 10–20 percent proceed to the classic yellow fever cases with high fever, jaundice, and severe hemorrhages leading to the "black vomit" with a high mortality. Yellow fever is extremely variable in its appearance, ranging from a mild influenza to the characteristic jaundice of the skin (cf. Rush, "The Yellow Fever: Some Family Letters [1793]"). It often resembles a cold and is "one of the most innocuous diseases of childhood."[12]

The central nervous system can be involved in yellow fever—symptoms are slurred speech, brisk tendon reflexes, and lacking coordination of the limbs. During the first three days of the infection, the fever can reach 104 degrees Fahrenheit, with an abrupt onset that is accompanied by chills, severe headache, nausea, vomiting, abdominal pain, and distressing pain in the back. Later, after a period of calm, the fever returns and the patient vomits either fresh blood or altered blood with a black color. Bleeding may take place from the eyes, nose, mouth, bladder, rectum and other organs.

As with malaria, one of the most accepted theories about the transmission of yellow fever was that vapors rising from wetlands, "miasmas," caused the disease. Although the connection between insect vectors and disease transmission was not made until the early twentieth century, the correlation between water and the disease was made as early as 1692. Dr. Elihu Smith notes that in New York the yellow fever epidemic was localized in one area that was "the lowest, flattest and most sunken part of the whole city." He characterized that scene as "swampy, and abound[ing] with little pools and puddles of stagnant water." Heavy rains had occurred, and, he said, "clouds of musketoes, incredibly large and distressing" were common that summer.[13] Ironically, this earliest account contains all the information needed to link the disease to its vector. Yet, mosquitoes, as the vector of malaria, or any other disease for that matter, would not be firmly demonstrated until the early 1900s when the connection between yellow fever and mosquitoes was made.[14]

The mosquitoes responsible for urban yellow fever are known as "container mosquitoes"—they prefer to breed in objects that hold freshwater in smaller quantities. The list of acceptable breeding sites is large—bottles, jars, cans, basins, gourds, tires, birdbaths, pots, pans, pools, runoff basins, washtubs, drainage ditches, to name a few—many are in your backyard. The primary mosquito vector is *Aedes aegypti*. *Aedes* likes interior domestic spaces as resting environments, is day-active, and rarely travels far from home on its own power. All of its breeding and feeding preferences make it a perfect urban disease vector.

I use the term "urban disease vector" because yellow fever is one of many diseases for which the disease ecology varies. Many years ago, and for a long time, there was a distinction made between urban and rural yellow fever because the disease cycles seemed so different. Sylvan (or jungle) yellow fever affects several nonhuman primates and is transmitted by canopy mosquitoes. When humans are affected, they are usually people who had forest contact, such as tree cutters. Urban yellow fever is transmitted by mosquitoes inhabiting lower elevations, frequently container-breeding mosquitoes such as *Aedes*. Urban and sylvan yellow fever were distinguished as separate diseases in 1934, but it has since become clear that it is not the pathogens but the disease ecology—different vectors, different zones of infection—that is different.

There are early reports of yellow fever for New York in 1626, Boston in 1691, and Charleston in 1693. Between 1702 and 1800 yellow fever visited the United States 35 times—between 1800 and 1879, only two years went by without yellow fever epidemics. After 1822 yellow fever was primarily a disease of southern port cities. It was often called "stranger's fever," because those principally affected were immigrants from Europe where the disease was not present, and colonists who arrived in the South from the North.

Yellow fever may have started earlier in the North, but once it began cycling in epidemics, it was a regular visitor to Charleston and other southern ports. Between 1693 and 1876 (the last Charleston epidemic), Charleston experienced epidemics of yellow fever during 34 years (see Table 9.2). For 24 of those epidemics, total estimated mortality was recorded at 4,265. The only city that rivaled Charleston for constancy of yellow fever impacts was New Orleans. During the same period, New Orleans experienced 38 epidemics of yellow fever, including the last recorded U.S. epidemic in 1905.

In 1702, when a major yellow fever epidemic occurred in New York, one Anglican missionary reported that New York was "a very mournfull Towne there dyeing near 20 Persons dayly for some Months."[15] Between 1702 and 1822, yellow fever epidemics swept through New York 19 times, with an estimated mortality of 5,091.[16] Smallpox and yellow fever led the city council to a policy of quarantine in 1738. In June of that year, a quarantine anchorage was established off Bedloe's Island for vessels coming from infected ports. By 1760 a "pesthouse" was placed on Bedloe's Island as well.

Table 9.2. Major yellow fever epidemics, 1693–1905

	Charleston	Philadelphia	New York
No. of epidemics	34	18	19
Total deaths	4,265+	12,914	5,091

Source: Patterson, "Yellow Fever Epidemics and Mortality in the United States, 1693–1905."

Yellow fever visited Philadelphia 18 times between 1693 and 1822, about as many times as it visited New York. The mortality, however, was an estimated as 2.5 times greater—by one count 12,914 died in those epidemics. Dr. Benjamin Rush, a signer of the Declaration of Independence, was particularly observant of the yearly conditions of the weather, climate, and health of his fellow Philadelphians. Rush practiced medicine there, and his notes on yellow fever are among the best historical documents referring to the disease.[17] His observations include conditions that seem parsimonious, such as the mosquito vector, increased rain, and waterfront origins. However, they also indicate his belief that yellow fever was a disease caused by putrid miasmas attributed to rotting coffee, oysters, fish, and other noxious substances at the Arch Street Wharf.

A description of yellow fever in New York in 1798 and the public health measures taken to prevent the epidemic bear witness to the misunderstanding of the important issues underlying yellow fever transmission:

On August 13 Oothout addressed a circular to 15 merchants, accusing them of storing "putrid or spoiled beef" on their premises and urging them to get rid of it immediately. A few days later he positively forbade a contractor to dig into one of the docks in order to prepare a foundation for a new building because of the danger of disturbing unwholesome dirt. On August 20 he submitted a long report to the Mayor in which he mentioned that there had been nine deaths from the fever. He noted that clean gravel had been spread over certain notoriously filthy lots, and he pressed for more speed in draining the water from Lispenard's meadow. In response to several requests that garbage and offal be removed more frequently, Oothout stated that, if it was agreeable, he would hire five scavengers at a cost of 12 shillings per day per man to remove the garbage on Monday, Thursday, and Saturday.

Despite vigilance of the health officials, around August 24 the number of cases and deaths increased sharply, and a mass exodus got under way. Thousands began fleeing from the city, and businessmen started removing their offices and places of business from lower Manhattan to Greenwich Village, at that time a small rural community. By the end of August the number of yellow fever victims had climbed to over a hundred. What was more significant, the fever was now appearing in districts that had hitherto been exempt.

The health commissioners redoubled their efforts, inspecting cellars, storage places, and carefully examining barrels of salted meat and other perishables. With respect to the latter, John Oothout issued orders that the inspectors must insist upon boring into all barrels to be sure that the meat was not spoiled, adding the following injunction: "Do not be sparing in the use of quick lime where you find the cellars offensive!"[18]

The year 1793 proved to be one of an extremely widespread and lethal yellow fever outbreak. Several diseases are reported preceding the 1793 epidemic, and it is likely that many continued to be present during it. These include influenza, scarlatina, and mild bilious remittent fever, particularly in children. Rush also kept journals for these diseases. Everyone who could leave Philadelphia fled the city and the contagion during the 1793 epidemic. In fact, Rush sent his wife and children away. On September 18, Rush wrote to his wife, "Parents desert their children as soon as they are infected, and in every room you enter you see no person but a solitary black man or woman near the sick. Many people thrust their parents into the streets as soon as they complain of a headache."[19] The only people left in Philadelphia were either those who couldn't flee or those whose civic duty was to stay and help with the ill.

While Philadelphia shared many of the urban characteristics of New York, it also differed from New York in a couple of ways. For one, Philadelphia was located up the Schuylkill River, and so it was surrounded by freshwater. That provided Philadelphia with a good water supply, although it still suffered problems of sanitation. The freshwater also fostered the reproduction of mosquitoes carrying malaria and yellow fever. Another major difference was that after the latter 1700s, most of Philadelphia's 2,500 Africans were free. Poverty still characterized their condition, but in the late 1780s Absalom Jones and Richard Allen formed the Free African Society, an aid group organized by Africans.

There was a notion by the 1793 epidemic that people of African descent suffered yellow fever far less frequently and severely. Rush was particularly attuned to it, and he made a personal plea to the Free African Society for help in the hospitals. The genetic theory of African immunity did not hold, however, and more than 300 citizens of African descent died in the epidemic, a proportion about even with the other deaths. Worse than that, Matthew Carey, a major historian of the epidemic, accused the black hospital workers of profiteering and theft. A narrative defense by the founders of the Free African Society is perhaps one of the first African political documents in America.

> We feel ourselves hurt most by a partial, censorious paragraph, in Mr. Carey's 2d edition of his account of the sickness, &c. in Philadel-phia, pages 76 and 77, where he asperses the blacks alone, for having taken the advantage of the distressed situation of the people.
>
> When the people of colour had the sickness and died, we were imposed upon, and told it was not with the prevailing sickness, until it became too notorious to be denied; then we were told some few died, but not many. Thus were our services extorted at the peril of our lives. Yet you accuse us of extorting a little money from you.
>
> The bill of mortality for the year 1793, published by Matthew White-head and John Ormrod, clerks, and Joseph Dolby, sexton, will con-vince any reasonable man that will examine it, that as many co-loured people died in proportion as others. In 1792 there were 67 of our colour buried, and in 1793, it amounted to 305: thus the burials among us have increased more than fourfold. Was not this in a great degree the effects of the services of the unjustly vilified coloured people?[20]

From the founding of New Amsterdam, there were individuals of Afri-can descent in New York. In the early 1700s, African slaves constituted 20 percent of the population, but the Dutch allowed their slaves to own property and trade.[21] Some became landowners through the "freedom dues" granted by the Dutch East Indies Company. When the English took charge of the city, slave numbers increased dramatically, although their historic visibility did not.

Historic documents are scant regarding the circumstances of African health in the eighteenth century, but the plight of Africans brought to New York during that century is revealed through their burials in the New York African Burial Ground (NYABG). In 1989, while preparing the construction of a 34-story federal office building at 290 Broadway street, the burial ground was rediscovered. It was excavated between 1991 and 1992, and analysis of the buried individuals occurred over the next decade or so before the Africans were placed again to rest.[22]

The burial ground was established in 1712 and was last used in 1794. The individuals buried there bear witness to the difficult lives of impoverished and enslaved Africans who lived in New York at that time. The analysis of several markers of nutrition, health, and disease shows that children buried in the NYABG frequently experienced delayed growth and development due to a combination of stresses that included malnutrition, disease, and work-related stress. Infant mortality was much higher than for others in New York City. Both Africans and European Americans died frequently before the age of two, but the mortality for African children under two was nearly twice that of European Americans, 55 percent as compared to 28 percent, respectively. If an African child lived until 15, however, he or she was likely to live until at least 30 or 40. Even then, the life of adults was difficult—muscle hypertrophy and osteoarthritis for both adult men and women indicate elevated work stress.[23]

The growing years were undoubtedly affected by malnutrition, although there is little documentation about it. We get some sense of diet from the narrative of John Jea, who was born in Old Calabar (West Africa) in 1773; his presents the only known narrative by someone who lived in New York at this time. Jea had been brought with his parents and siblings to New York when he was two and a half years old. His Dutch owners fed the family a mixture of "Indian corn pounded, or bruised and boiled with water . . . and about a quart of sour buttermilk poured on it; for one person two quarts of this mixture, and about three ounces of dark bread, per day, the bread was darker than that usually allowed to convicts, and greased over with very indifferent hog's lard."[24] The bones of buried Africans verify that there were dietary deficiencies. Cranial indicators of anemia were present for about half of the individuals. Bowed legs indicating vitamin D deficiency (rickets) were present in about a tenth of those buried in the cemetery.

Adults buried in the NYABG were twice as likely as children to have skeletal indicators of infectious disease if they also had indicators of nutritional inadequacy. Children who were seriously malnourished and infected by various ailments may have not lived long enough to develop the telltale lesions of infection. Adults who exhibited lesions both of malnutrition and infection may well support the contention that childhood health affects later adult health.

All skeletal and dental indicators show that those Africans who had lived to adulthood experienced heavy physical labor and often suffered from malnutrition and infectious disease. The worst of the labors, it seems, frequently fell upon the "Negroes." In the earliest days of New York, as human wastes began to pile up, they were given the task of carrying tubs of waste outside the city. In the spring of 1800, a law was passed requiring that all privy pits and sinks must be cleaned out. The job again fell to the black population. Many became sick and some died, with symptoms reported as "catarrhs and redness of the eyes, nausea, vomiting, pains in the belly, bloody stools, and fever."[25]

Africans undoubtedly suffered differential mortality in New York throughout its history. While Africans made up 10 percent of the New York population between 1800 and 1825, they accounted for a higher proportion of total deaths. In 1821, for instance, there were 550 African deaths of 3,542 total deaths in New York. Their 15.5 percent death rate that year is even more astounding given that they only made up 8 percent of the population. In the same year, of 715 deaths attributed to consumption, 105 of those were of individuals of African descent. With worsening health conditions in the city slums, mortality rates increased in later years. In 1824 African deaths were 718 out of 4,341 (16.5 percent), and in 1825 they were 875 of 5,018 (17.4 percent).[26]

You may recall that in the early 1790s, about 3,000 immigrants came to New York each year. Between 1825 and 1829, the yearly figure rose to 12,000. In the thirty-year period from 1830 to 1860, New York's population jumped from about 200,000 to 800,000.

The demand for housing created by this influx challenged every conceivable structure. Warehouses, cellars, shanties, and almost any building with a roof became a residence, while avaricious builders, unrestricted by sanitary and building codes, threw up flimsy tenements lacking even the most elementary sanitary conveniences. In the tenement areas one or two privies often served 50 or more individuals. The New York City drainage system was designed primarily to carry off surface water rather than sewage, although, it should be added, the thousands of overflowing privies and cesspools made the distinction purely academic.[27]

It was the sanitary officers, city inspectors, and doctors who frequently gave the impoverished a voice. Dr. Benjamin McCready wrote a treatise on occupational health in 1837, noting that the health of the laborers and their living situation were linked by "the confined and miserable apartments in which they are lodged . . . the cupidity of landlords has tempted them to build up narrow alleys with small wooden tenements."[28] Dr. John Griscom, another sanitary officer, notes in 1842 that the poor were "like cattle, in pens, . . . compel[led] . . . to swallow poison with every breath."[29] In an 1850 discourse titled, "The Sanitary Condition of the Laboring Population of New York, with Suggestions for Its Improvement," Griscom detailed the many issues of poverty and health, focusing primarily on sanitary conditions.

> It is often said that "one half of the world does not know how the other half lives." . . . Sanitary regulations affect the pauper class more directly than any other, because they live in situations and circumstances which expose them more to attacks of disease. They are more crowded, they live more in cellars, their apartments are less ventilated, and more exposed to vapors and other emanations, &c., hence, ventilation, sewerage, and all other sanitary regulations, are more necessary for them, and would produce a greater comparative change in their condition.[30]

Tenement housing reached a new level of development after 1850, ironically in an effort to provide the poor with housing. People were stuffed into small apartments, most alongside alleys that were no more than six feet wide, with the usual minimal sanitary facilities (Figures 9.6–9.7).

> Our people, especially the more destitute, have been allowed to live out their brief lives in tainted and unwholesome atmospheres, and be subject to the silent and invisible encroachments of destructive agencies from every direction, without one warning voice being raised to point to them in their danger, and without an effort to rescue them from their impending fate. . . .
>
> The tenements, in order to admit a greater number of families, are divided into small apartments, as numerous as decency will admit. Regard to comfort, convenience, and health, is the last motive. . . .
>
> At No. 50 Pike-street is a cellar about ten feet square, and seven feet high, having only one very small window, and the old fashioned, inclined cellar door. In this small place, were lately residing *two families consisting of ten persons*, of all ages.[31]

Figure 9.6. Ceru family, 143 Thompson St., near tenement, N.Y. Library of Congress Prints and Photographs Division Washington, D.C. 20540 USA http://hdl.loc.gov/loc.pnp/pp.print.

City inspector F.I.A. Boole reported in 1864 that two tenements housed 900 people, 440 adults and 460 children. Each measured 18 by 180 feet and was five stories high, which would allow 38.9 square feet per person, if one counted the basement as a sixth floor. A family of five could count on 194.4 square feet under the same assumptions. By the early 1860s there were demands for housing reform that culminated in 1865 in the *Report of the Council of Hygiene and Public Health*.

Those who lived in tenement housing were among the most frequent victims of poverty and chronic illness. Infectious diseases had haunted the impoverished in New York for a couple of centuries, but tenement housing represented the urban petri dish that allowed them to flourish. Mortality from the combined epidemics that raged through New York

Figure 9.7. Row of tenements, 260 to 268 Elizabeth St., N.Y. Library of Congress Prints and Photographs Division Washington, D.C. 20540 USA http://hdl.loc.gov/loc.pnp/pp.print.

between 1650 and 1900 would be difficult to calculate without considering deaths from chronic illness, chronic malnutrition, and chronic poverty. Exact figures are difficult to come by for the earlier years, but by 1809 John Pintard of the city inspector's office had compiled mortality statistics for the years from 1802 through 1808. Annually during those years mortality ranged from 1,930 deaths to 2,352. During the same period Pintard reported that 440 deaths per year were due to consumption, the most common cause of death. Pintard listed croup as the leading cause of infant deaths, although diarrheal diseases were undoubtedly a major cause—one-fourth of infants died before age one, and one-third by age two.[32]

Cholera was one of those diseases that frequented the poorer segments of New York in the nineteenth century. It is a disease of populations and of sanitation. It first ravaged New York in 1832 and by September of that year had caused an estimated 3,000 deaths. It has characteristically been more prevalent in urban areas, but during epidemics it has reached into rural areas. Unclean water, whether from rivers, drainage ditches, leaky sanitation systems, or street drains, is the primary route of disease transmission. Cholera is caused by a comma-shaped, gram-negative bacterium with a flagellum (which makes it motile), *Vibrio cholerae*, first isolated in 1883 by Robert Koch in Egypt and Calcutta. The infection is spread by infected humans through their excretions to water or by flies landing on food or drink once they have acquired the bacteria from excreta. It can also be acquired from eating contaminated raw shellfish.

Cholera causes profuse watery diarrhea, vomiting, circulatory collapse, and shock.[33] The diarrhea results from the failure to reabsorb water, delivered in large amounts from the bloodstream to the intestine, and all other symptoms of the disease are attributable to water and salt depletion. They include weakened pulse, thickening of the circulating blood, suppression of urination, loss of tissue fluids, muscular spasms, and shock. Mortality is quite high—reaching 50 percent and upward in epidemics, but not everyone who contracts the bacterium becomes infected. There may be some natural immunity, thought perhaps to be tied to stomach acidity. The bacteria adhere to the intestinal wall and produce and secrete a toxin that is the actual cause of the disease. The toxin prevents the absorption of water and electrolytes (salts) from the intestine into the circulation.

One of the highlights of epidemiology involves urban cholera and the work of Dr. John Snow. He was a distinguished doctor known for his work in the administration of anesthetics—he was the one to introduce the use of chloroform to Britain, administering it to Queen Victoria during the births of two of her nine children. When cholera raged in London in the late summers of 1849 and 1854, Snow noted that the disease tended to break out in highly localized areas of London, usually poorer ones.

In an investigation sure to challenge any modern-day detective, Snow made the connection between cholera and water transmission, centering his final attentions on a public water pump located in a sector of town known as Soho. In that particular region, in September of 1854, more than 600 people died, and Snow suspected that the public water pump on Broad Street was a major culprit in the transmission. His observations were further supported by the fact that the only folks in the area who seemed not to be ill during the epidemic were the workers at the local brewery—they drank beer instead of water!

His map of cholera cases near the Broad Street pump is a standard in

Map 9.1. Snow's map of cholera in the city of London, Published by C. F. Cheffins, Lith, Southhampton Buildings, London, England, 1854, in John Snow, *On the Mode of Communication of Cholera*, 2nd ed., John Churchill, New Burlington Street, London. Redrawn by Susan Brannock-Gaul.

courses on epidemiology to this day (Map 9.1). When he was convinced he understood the route of infection, he drew water from the pump, let it stand a couple of days, and found that it turned stinky and formed a scum. Lacking further proof at the time, he nonetheless persuaded the officials to remove the pump handle. After that, cholera cleared up. The pump is still there, and the visitor to London can visit it on what is now known as Broadwick Street. Across the way, on the site of the original brewery building, lies John Snow's Pub. It remains a site of pilgrimage for visitors of all sorts, especially academics and health officers.

Two major cholera epidemics occurred in New York in 1849 and 1866, and it was cholera more than any other disease that finally created the urgent need to clean up the city. Sanitation commissions were established, public health consciousness was raised, and in 1842 New York got its first water system, the Croton aqueduct. In 1850 an underground sewage system was added. Attention to water quality, it seems, reached a critical level in the 1850s on multiple continents. Other issues of infectious disease received less attention.

Typhus, the disease of crowding and insufficient hygiene discussed in chapter 6, was directly associated with the overcrowded immigrant vessels, where it ran its course during long voyages. In 1818 city inspector George Cuming listed typhus as the second leading cause of death.[34] Prior to the 1840s typhus was largely an institutional disease in New York caused by crowding and poverty, but a dramatic increase of immigrants in the 1840s and 1850s brought with it numerous cases of typhus. In three late summer months in 1847 some 467 typhus cases were admitted to New York Hospital, and the Academy of Medicine decided a special committee was needed to study the situation. By 1851 mortality from typhus reached nearly 1,000. Tenement slums created an ideal climate for the vectors, and with an ideal immune-suppressed set of hosts, it became an endemic disease. It is a disease that rarely affects the well off and which ravages those who are impoverished. Public concern was limited because it was not a common disease of the wealthier New York inhabitants.

> In the summer of '42, a number of cases of Typhus fever, of a very severe type, occurred in a building in the rear of No. 49 Elizabeth street, under circumstances which left no doubt as to its local origin. . . . This was a double frame house, three stories in height. It stood in the centre of the yard. Ranged next the fence, where [sic] a number of pig styes and stables, which surrounded the yard on three sides. From the quantity of filth, liquid and otherwise, thus caused, the ground, I suppose, had been rendered almost impassable, and to remedy this, the yard had been completely boarded over, so that the earth could nowhere be seen. These boards were partially decayed, and by a little pressure, even in dry weather, a thick greenish fluid could be forced up through their crevices. The central building was inhabited entirely by negroes. In this building there occurred, in the course of six weeks, nine cases of Typhus fever.[35]

Consumption (tuberculosis) was another disease that attracted less attention than many diseases, partly because it was not a disease that suddenly struck people down. It also tended to affect the poorer segments of society. Nonetheless, consumption caused more deaths in New York than any other disease, twice as many as the next-closest competitor in 1848. For most years between 1800 and 1850, consumption killed more people than cholera, smallpox, yellow fever, and typhus combined.[36] TB was notoriously a disease of malnutrition, poverty, and close living conditions with limited ventilation, and high rates of tuberculosis were unsurprising within the squalid living conditions of back-alley tenements.

Historic documents probably tell only part of the story of health and disease among the impoverished living in urban environments. Examination of the actual individuals who lived during the 1800s provides additional information about the success or failure of those living in the city to mitigate the multiple challenges to their health. Monroe County Poorhouse in Rochester, New York, gives us a sense of the complex relationships between poverty, nutrition, and health. It was used between 1826 and the end of the Civil War, roughly 1865. Approximately 300 skeletons were excavated from the poorhouse cemetery by the Rochester Museum and Science Center in 1984.[37] By comparing historic records from the town of Brighton and the Mt. Hope Cemetery, the causes of death for children and adult females were compared to skeletal indicators. The most frequent cause of death listed in the records for children and adult females was consumption (29–39 percent of children; 27–38 percent for adult females). Children commonly died of gastrointestinal complaints (18–31 percent), and other respiratory diseases (6–18 percent). Following consumption, the most frequent causes of death for adult females were typhus fever (19 percent) and cholera (12 percent).

Many bouts of infectious disease undoubtedly occurred alongside nutritional deficits and chronic health problems. We know from the skeletal remains recovered from the Monroe County Poorhouse that most women in this situation died young—between 20 and 30. Diets consisting primarily of carbohydrates, such as corn, were common for the impoverished. Unfortunately, many of the carbohydrate dietary staples turned rapidly in the mouth into sugars that led to tooth decay. Dental care during the mid-nineteenth century was generally not available, and the teeth from the Monroe County Poorhouse inhabitants illustrate this unavailability.

Dental health for those folks was abysmal, with high rates of cavities, periodontal disease, early tooth loss, and abscesses in the jaws.

According to historic sources, the most common causes of death for urban free African Americans were tuberculosis, cholera, and respiratory fevers.[38] Burials of free African Americans at the First African Baptist Church (FABC) in Philadelphia give us further information on health in the early 1800s. The cemetery was used between 1823 and 1841. It was rediscovered during a subway expansion and excavated in 1983–84.[39] Muscle hypertrophy was common, undoubtedly due to severe physical labor. Surprisingly, osteoarthritis was slight in expression, although 76 percent had skeletal changes of osteoarthritis. Malnutrition seems to have been a problem, as indicated by tibial bowing due to rickets—27 percent of adults seem to have experienced rickets as children. Anemia was common, with 70 percent of those buried there affected. Some of those affected may have suffered from genetic anemia, sickle cell, but modern African Americans who have the trait number around 12 percent. Thus, the investigators speculate that the high frequency of anemia in this population must be due to a combination of hereditary anemia and dietary iron deficiency. Three or four people had active tuberculosis. In Philadelphia life seems to have been harder on African American women than men, with an average age at death of 39 for women; men died at 45, six years later.

Angel and his coworkers suggest that one occupational hazard that may have placed women from the FABC more at risk was proximity to the Schuylkill River, where cholera could be contracted. Records of the congregation buried at the FABC show that 50 percent of the females were laundresses. The well-developed triceps and pectoral muscles of the arms in several females are likely due to repeated movements of laundering. All in all, the observations suggest that nutrition was not great during the growth years, occupational stress was frequent, and tuberculosis affected the poor in Philadelphia as it did in New York.

We can compare the health of Africans interred at the FABC with that of German immigrants buried in the Voegtly Cemetery in Pittsburgh, Pennsylvania. The cemetery at the Voegtly Church and parsonage was used between 1833 and 1861. It was located in Old Allegheny Town, a popular place for Swiss-German immigrants to settle during the time.[40] The professions of only 10 men were listed—all were in the trades, except for one veterinarian. Church records indicate 823 people were buried on the site; 799 of those had ages recorded. Mortality was high for those under age one (39 percent), and continued to be high between one and five years (24 percent). In fact, only 29 percent of those in the cemetery lived past 20 years of age. The average age at death given in the historical records was 15 for all individuals—15 years for females and 16 years for males. Study of the skeletons yielded a slightly lower age of death, 14 years for all individuals. The causes of death were listed in the parish records for 151 people; some of these, in order of frequency, were stillbirth (29 percent), cholera (8 percent), consumption (7 percent), typhoid (5 percent), and scarlet fever (3 percent).

As at the Monroe County Poorhouse, dental disease affected many of the folks interred at Voegtly Cemetery. Cavities, abscesses, and early tooth loss were common. Only two individuals showed any signs of dental care or restoration. Skeletal fractures were common, and some had become infected. Several people suffered bone infections, many probably associated with systemic disease processes. Arthritis of the shoulder, elbow, and spine was common, and extreme in some cases. Study of skeletons also gives us some insight into repeated behaviors that leave characteristic signatures on bones and teeth. In the case of Voegtly Cemetery, nine men showed the characteristic wear from clenching pipestems in their teeth— one of these also had a notch from a smaller object, likely a pin associated with his profession as a tailor. All in all, those buried at Voegtly Cemetery support the view of health woven throughout this conversation for those inhabiting cities during the mid-nineteenth century.

Thankfully, during the last half of the nineteenth century, voices like those of Griscom and other sanitary officers inaugurated sanitation reforms that improved the lives of many city dwellers. The installation of a sewage and water system in New York in 1850 began the process of distributing clean water to residences and taking organic and nonorganic wastes away from residences and public areas. Other social programs made inroads on health reforms. Child mortality decreased dramatically by 1930. In 1840 approximately 190 of every 1,000 infants born in New York never reached age one; in 1870 that figure had reached 200. By 1930, after health reforms had taken hold, fewer than 70 infants per 1,000 died in the first year of life.[41]

Yet urban centers continue to obscure the poverty that haunts the lives of many residents. Hidden in the shadows of society, on the perimeter of towns, countless numbers can predict their well-being no further in the future than their next meal, and perhaps not that far. Despite the progress we've made on sanitation and infection, there remains much to be done.

Epilogue

A documentary film made in the 1990s shows actual film clips of a deadly epidemic. People are dying by the thousands, and amidst scenes of panic-stricken crowds and huge makeshift wards full of people in hospital beds, survivors talk about their experiences as children during one of the greatest mortality events in recorded history. Those interviewed live in the United States, but they are speaking about a pandemic that reached around the world.

The film is called *Influenza 1918*, and it originally aired as an *American Experience* episode on PBS. It brings home many messages to the students I teach, well over 50 percent of whom had no idea that an epidemic of flu occurred in 1918. They are usually stunned that the flu could kill so many, that such a large-scale epidemic occurred here in America, and that there could actually still be (as of the 1990s) as many survivors of the epidemic as are interviewed in the film. Most disturbing for the students, I think, is that they are confronted with the fact that epidemic disease and mass death are not only about "someone else."

Between September 1918 and June 1919, ten short months at the end of World War I, 675,000–800,000 Americans died of influenza and pneumonia. When compared to the number of Americans killed in combat in World War I, World War II, the Korean War, and the Vietnam War combined—somewhere around 423,000—the influenza epidemic of 1918–1919 was far more deadly in ten months than the combined years of those wars.[1] The global impact was even greater—one-fifth of the world's population was infected with this deadly virus. Fifty million people died of influenza in 1918 across the world, compared to the 16 million who perished in World War I. Within months, influenza had killed more people than any other illness in recorded history.

The first wave of the 1918 influenza epidemic occurred in the spring of 1918. While it took far fewer victims than the second wave would, doctors noticed that the virus seemed to spread more quickly than it ever had before. The rate at which the disease killed young adults is another distinction of the spring flu; the mortality rates for this flu were highest for the 20- to 29-year age group. Unfortunately, America's public health system did not realize how quickly it would reach epidemic proportions and for the most part ignored it.

The rapidly advancing American war effort contributed to the lack of attention paid to the victims of the spring flu. In March 1918, some 84,000 Americans left for Europe, and in April 118,000 followed. The global war machine ensured that the flu would be spread far and wide. Between April and May of 1918, flu appeared among British, German, and French forces in Europe. An estimated eight million Spaniards caught it by the end of June, giving the disease its nickname "Spanish influenza."

By the end of August 1918, the second wave of influenza broke out in Boston, and it spread with remarkable speed. Even so, Boston did not take any measures to protect its citizens against the epidemic for several more weeks. What was especially troubling is that Boston, one of America's most important port cities for shipping troops and equipment to the front lines in Europe, seemed to have much more important things to worry about— the Boston Street Railway strike, the Boston Red Sox victory in the World Series, the upcoming Senate vote on women's suffrage.

Across America, doctors warned health departments that dire consequences might result if the right precautions were not taken. They urged cities to quarantine the sick and restrict attendance at large public gatherings, yet patriotic war fervor led many communities to resist the advice and continue to hold large rallies. Large public gatherings in support of the war, such as parades, bond rallies, and loan drives, brought masses of people together to breathe on one another and spread the flu. People who did not appreciate the amount of danger they were in ignored closing orders for schools, churches, theaters, and other places of public meetings. By not restricting such mass meetings, the government merely offered more chances for its citizens to become infected with the flu virus.

Many cities refused to halt their massive public transportation networks until the flu felled hundreds of transit authority employees and forced them to do so. In Washington, just a day after officials acknowledged the epidemic in the capital, 13 million men crammed into federal buildings to register for the draft and cough and sneeze on one another at the same time. As most Americans remained unaware of the full magnitude of the epidemic, flu spread across the country.

The flu did not discriminate. Although it first struck urban cities, it soon moved into rural areas, from the densely populated East Coast to the remotest parts of the Southwest. Urban dwellers fell victim to the flu most rapidly. Crowded, dirty, and poorly ventilated living conditions contributed to the spread of the disease. The large immigrant populations who had little or no experience with public health principles of sanitation and quarantine factored into the problem as well. They could not speak enough English to communicate with doctors, nurses, or public health officials. These people had little confidence in either medical or political officials in America, and they often had no money to pay for treatment. The flu afflicted over 25 percent of the U.S. population, and in one year the average life expectancy in the United States dropped by 12 years.

Hospitals overflowed with patients during the epidemic and had to set up emergency expansion quarters; this only intensified the shortage of medical personnel. Nurses were in short supply. Overwork and overexposure to the disease soon took their toll on those fighting it, decimating their forces even more. Although masks were mandated midway through the epidemic, they did little to prevent the spread of the flu from patients to the medical personnel or fellow citizens.

Yet, while the flu ravaged American cities and country, the war went on. The military continued to ship boatloads of soldiers into Europe. The tight quarters offered for traveling soldiers guaranteed the rapid spread of any respiratory illness among troops. During the day, three men crammed themselves into every double seat on the trains. In the sleeping cars, one man slept in the upper bunk and two in the lower. The intense physical training the men underwent in camps only helped to weaken their resistance and make them more susceptible to the disease. On the battlefield, the sick were crammed into trenches next to those still susceptible, but who themselves would often soon be ill. Those who had succumbed to flu were taken on trains and in ambulances, often into pockets of those who were not sick, and the speed of transport enabled what Paul Ewald has called "attendant-borne transmission," possibly creating more virulent forms of the virus.[2]

Most discussions of the 1918–19 influenza epidemic emphasize the virulence of the flu virus. A single mutation or multiple mutations are often invoked to explain that virulence. It appears from investigations of the genetic structure of the 1918 flu virus that it did have a unique structure, but that is normal.[3] The influenza virus mutates perhaps faster and more successfully than any other pathogen that commonly afflicts humans. The literature on the number of species it travels through and mutates in before returning to humans is immense.[4] But again, that is normal and has probably been going on for millennia.

Christopher Wills perhaps said it best in his book on plagues—they do not occur in a vacuum.[5] In 1918 the condition of the world mattered as much as what strain of influenza was predominant, and the condition of the world was anything but normal. Europe had drawn significant portions of the world into war, and as it drew the United States in, it fueled the fire of influenza in multiple ways. It was not just a virulent form of the influenza virus that ravaged the world in 1918–19. It was frequent movement within the United States as well as across the Atlantic, aggregated troops in transport vehicles and in trenches, aggregated populations at home in public gatherings, increased mobility of infected people among those not yet affected, famine and poverty, poor living conditions, and a host of other environmental factors. The conditions—environmental, social, economic, and political—were perfect for an epidemic.

Prologue

1. Ward, *Navigator*.

Chapter 1. The Transformation of Native America

1. The scenes depicted by White were actually made famous through de Bry's engravings; the original drawings by White were not known until much later. There are generally differences between the White drawings and the engravings of the same scenes made by de Bry. Some have speculated that de Bry used a different set of drawings to construct his engravings (Hulton, *America 1585*).

2. On the problems with accuracy and deception, see Kuhlemann, "Between Reproduction, Invention and Propaganda: Theodor De Bry's Engravings after John White's Watercolours." Milanich points out that de Bry never left Europe and that all of his engravings are based on art created by other people. Inaccuracies include Brazilian shells, clubs, and headdresses in the engravings of Florida Indians, incorrect depictions of houses, and entire scenes lifted from other artists (Milanich, "Devil in the Details").

3. The demography of native populations has been heavily debated for decades. Alchon, in the appendix, gives a thorough review of the methods used to estimate populations prior to and following contact, and the debates surrounding those estimates (Alchon, *Pest in the Land*). Regardless of the number of people estimated to inhabit the Americas at the time of European arrival, Native American populations (as a combined sample) continued to decline in numbers and reached their lowest numbers in the late 1800s (Thornton, *American Indian Holocaust and Survival*; Ubelaker, "North American Indian Population Size, A.D. 1500–1985").

4. López de Gómara, *Cortés*, 204–5.

5. Cortés, *Letters from Mexico*, 263.

6. Many people see epidemics in central Mexico in 1519, Guatemala in 1520, and Peru in 1525 as part of a single pandemic that spread from Mexico, but that is

disputed. Regardless of whether it was one pandemic or several epidemics, Henry Dobyns estimates that "ninety percent of the population of civilized Mesoamerica and Andean America perished by 1568" (Dobyns, "Disease Transfer at Contact," 276). He attributes their decimation to new diseases such as smallpox and influenza, which in many cases ravaged populations before direct contact with European explorers and settlers. Other sources that discuss the impacts of newly introduced diseases from Europe include Cook, *Born to Die*; Cook and Lovell, *Secret Judgments of God*; Crosby, "Conquistador y Pestilencia," *Columbian Exchange*, "Virgin Soil Epidemics as a Factor in the Aboriginal Depopulation of America," *Ecological Imperialism*; Diamond, *Guns, Germs, and Steel*; Dobyns, *Their Number Become Thinned*; Henige, *Numbers from Nowhere*; Ramenofsky, *Vectors of Death*, "Diseases of the Americas, 1492–1700"; Smith, *Archaeology of Aboriginal Culture Change in the Interior Southeast*; Stannard, *American Holocaust*; Verano and Ubelaker, *Disease and Demography in the Americas*.

7. Dobyns, for instance, arrived at a hemispheric estimate of population by taking the nadir figures and multiplying them 20 to 25 times based on the assumption of high population losses due to epidemics (Dobyns, "Estimating Aboriginal American Population"). Cook did a similar thing for Peru by determining what diseases had been responsible for two or three epidemics, concluding that smallpox was responsible for the first two, and measles for the third. He then calculated possible rates of mortality at 33–50 percent for the first epidemic, and 25–30 percent for the second two. He finally corrected the population numbers using the estimated prior loss (Cook, *Demographic Collapse, Indian Peru, 1520–1620*).

8. Anthropology is the study of humans and their closest nonhuman biological relatives, the nonhuman primates. With specialties ranging from those who study human biology, to those who study the material culture of the human past (archaeologists), to those who study the economic, political, and social fabrics of contemporary and recent historic groups, anthropologists tend to take fairly broad and encompassing views of "what it is to be human."

9. Diamond, *Guns, Germs, and Steel*, 29.

Chapter 2. Of Plagues and Peoples

1. Michelson, "Adam's Rib Awry? Women and Schistosomiasis." The article is a review article that reports on the survey of several previously published studies of schistosomiasis in different parts of the world.

2. The earliest domesticated plants and animals occurred in the Middle East beginning about 10,500 B.P. in the area known as the Fertile Crescent, and in the Nile Valley of Egypt. Domesticates in the Near East and Egypt included wheat, barley, sheep, and goats. A couple of centuries later, by 10,000–7,000 B.C., farmers raised domesticated plants such as lentils in the Indus Valley of India and Pakistan. About the same time along the Yangtze and Huang Ho (Yellow) river valleys in China, rice

and millet became more prevalent. Mediterranean populations were engaged in agriculture by 8,500 B.C. and cultivated such crops as asparagus, broccoli, grapes, and olives (McNeill, *Plagues and Peoples*, 69–132; Smith, *Emergence of Agriculture*).

3. McNeill, *Plagues and Peoples*, 54–93.

4. In Egypt the best evidence for smallpox occurs in two sources, ancient mummies and texts. In Egypt at least 31 cases of skeletal and mummy tuberculosis have been dated to 3,700–1000 B.C. (Sandison and Tapp, "Disease in Ancient Egypt"; Roberts and Buikstra, *Bioarchaeology of Tuberculosis.)* Three mummies show signs of smallpox rashes on the skin. One is Ramses V (died in 1157), another died in 1570, and a third in 1085, demonstrating that the disease affected Egyptians as early as 1570 B.C. (Sandison and Tapp, "Disease in Ancient Egypt").

Clashes, recorded in cuneiform Hittite tablets, that occurred in northern Syria between the Hittite empire during the reign of Suppiluliumas I (1380–1346 B.C.) and the Egyptians resulted in a disease epidemic that could have been smallpox. The disease originated among their captives and spread to the Hittite army and civilian populations. The epidemic continued for some 20 years, killing Suppiluliumas I and his son within a year (Hopkins, *Princes and Peasants*, 16).

In addition to smallpox and tuberculosis, the twelfth-century B.C. mummy Nahkt, known by its curation number as ROM 1 (Royal Ontario Museum), had been exposed to quartan malaria. The ova of both bilharzia and either beef or pork tapeworm found in the intestines indicate chronic health problems (Millet et al., "ROM I: Mummification for the Common People"). Approximately 30 percent of Egyptian mummies (including ROM 1) show signs of Harris lines, a growth arrest due to nutritional and disease problems (Sandison and Tapp, "Disease in Ancient Egypt").

In northern China after 5,000 B.P. increased rates of porotic hyperostosis (anemia), carious lesions, and stature reduction are likely linked with a dietary shift to increased reliance on millet (Pechenkina et al., "Diet and Health Changes at the end of the Chinese Neolithic").

At Alepotrypa Cave in Greece, Papathanasiou ("Health Status of the Neolithic Population of Alepotrypa Cave, Greece") reports declining health in the late Neolithic. Increased rates of anemia and infectious disease are also reported for the southern Levant (Eshed et al., "Paleopathology and the Origin of Agriculture").

5. McNeill, *Plagues and Peoples*, 161–207.

6. Procopius, *Wars of Justinian*, Book 2, ch. 22: 29, 22: 37, 122–23.

7. Procopius, *Wars of Justinian*, Book 2, ch. 23: 9, 23: 12, 123.

8. Glacial and pollen evidence suggests that glacial retreat in the Alps caused milder winters and drier summers that facilitated agriculture (Gottfried, *Black Death*, 24). This milder weather enabled the tremendous political and social change that occurred between A.D. 800 and 1200. However, by the late twelfth century, the Alpine glaciers began to advance, causing colder and wetter weather. The "Little Ice Age" was disastrous for agriculture, because more-northern pasture

lands had to be abandoned as the glaciers advanced (Gottfried, *Black Death*, 23). Fodder crops and pasture were turned over to the raising of wheat in an intensive land use pattern. The monocropping of wheat led to other problems, such as low protein levels for many peasants. Living standards stagnated and then began to decline after 1250 (Gottfried, *Black Death*, 23–30; Hays, *Burdens of Disease*; Karlen, *Man and Microbes*).

9. Further reading on the history of the Black Death: Karlen, *Man and Microbes*; Wheelis, "Biological Warfare at the 1346 Siege of Caffa"; Pollitzer, *Plague*; Gottfried, *Black Death*; Nikiforuk, *Fourth Horseman*; Gregg, *Plague!*; Scott and Duncan, *Biology of Plagues*; Zinsser, *Rats, Lice, and History*. Detailed local responses are described in the literature of the time, the most famous pieces being that of the Italian Boccaccio in his *Decameron*, and of the Englishman Chaucer in his *Canterbury Tales*. Wheelis, "Biological Warfare at the 1346 Siege of Caffa," points out that even though de' Mussi's narrative is consistent with the known facts of the plague and biological warfare, the importance of Caffa in the overall plague epidemic is "anecdotal at best" (974). Plague was undoubtedly being disseminated through multiple localities.

10. McNeill, *Plagues and Peoples*, 150.

11. Cantor, *In the Wake of the Plague*; Tuchman, *Distant Mirror*.

12. Pavlovsky, *Natural Foci of Human Infections* and *Natural Nidality of Transmissible Diseases*. "A natural nidus is a micro-scale region constituted of a living community, among the members of which a disease agent continually circulates, and the habitat conditions necessary to maintain that circulation in the disease system" (Meade and Emch, *Medical Geography*, 100); see also Wills, *Yellow Fever, Black Goddess*.

13. Black rats are often cited as a recent immigrant species to medieval Europe, having come out of the tropics with the Crusaders across the Indian Ocean to the Mediterranean (Meade and Emch, *Medical Geography*, 115; Wills, *Yellow Fever, Black Goddess*, 65). However, archaeological evidence (Armitage et al., "New Evidence of the Black Rat in Roman London"; Rackham, "*Rattus rattus*") demonstrates that black rats lived in Roman-era contexts in Britain during the first centuries A.D.

14. Scholars have been puzzled by records of high infection rates during the winter months, because plague is a warm-weather disease (Cohn, *Black Death Transformed*; Scott and Duncan, *Biology of Plagues*). The plague's arrival in Russia was delayed until 1351, good evidence that it was not carried along international trade routes by river transport, or it might have reached Russia from the Crimean Sea much earlier. Other cities located on trade routes, for instance—Milan—seem to have escaped the plague (Nutton, "Introduction," 8). These and other contradictory factors have been suggested as evidence for an alternate disease presence of anthrax, which is caused by a much hardier organism, is characterized by pustules with a jet-black center, precipitating the voiding of black blood, and has a pul-

monary form (Pollitzer, *Plague*). Undoubtedly, other illnesses accompanied the plague. Illnesses such as pneumonia would not have been recognized or described as separate from the plague. Other ancillary diseases might have been typhus, smallpox, and anthrax.

15. Discussions of the historic descriptions of the Black Death epidemic and whether it was *Yersinia pestis* can be found in Byrne, *Black Death*; Carmichael, "Universal and Particular"; Cohn, "Black Death Transformed," "Epidemiology of the Black Death"; Jankrift "Language of Plague"; Nutton, "Introduction"; Scott and Duncan, *Biology of Plagues*. Examples of new approaches to historical documents include DeWitte and Hughes-Morey, "Stature and Frailty during the Black Death"; DeWitte and Slavin, "Between Famine and Death"; Wood et al., "Temporal Dynamics of the Fourteenth-Century Black Death." The archaeology of plague cemeteries is discussed in Antoine, "Archaeology of 'Plague'"; Grainger et al., *Black Death Cemetery*.

16. The current molecular information and interpretation are undoubtedly changing. Molecular studies that have produced positive data for *Yersinia pestis* DNA from purported plague cemeteries (e.g., Drancourt et al., "*Yersinia pestis Orientalis* in Remains of Ancient Plague Patients"; Raoult et al., "Molecular Identification by 'Suicide PCR' of *Yersinia pestis* as the Agent of Medieval Black Death"; Wiechmann and Grupe, "Detection of *Yersinia pestis* DNA in Two Early Medieval Skeletal Finds from Aschheim [Upper Bavaria, 6th Century A.D.]") have been countered by negative evidence (e.g., Gilbert et al., "Absence of *Yersinia pestis*-Specific DNA in Human Teeth from Five European Excavations of Putative Plague Victims"). The current interpretations as I write this, again already out of date, are based on finer-grained DNA analyses (e.g., Haensch et al., "Distinct Clones of *Yersinia pestis*") and protein capsule antigen information (e.g., Pusch et al., "Yersinial F1 antigen and the Cause of Black Death"; Bianucci et al., "Technical Note," "Plague Immunodetection in Remains of Religious"). A draft genome of the plague pathogen was published in 2011 (Bos et al., "Draft Genome of *Yersinia pestis*").

17. Further reading on multiple introductions of plague and their associated support data are Cohn, "Epidemiology of the Black Death"; Haensch et al., "Distinct Clones of *Yersinia pestis*"; Schmid et al., "Climate-Driven Introduction of Black Death"; Walløe, "Medieval and Modern Bubonic Plague." Climate fluctuation reading includes Schmid et al., "Climate-Driven Introduction of Black Death"; Stenseth et al., "Plague Dynamics Are Driven by Climate Fluctuations."

18. Karlsson, "Plague without Rats"; Hufthammer and Walløe, "Rats Cannot Have Been Intermediate Hosts."

19. Gregg, *Plague!*; Meade and Emch, *Medical Geography*, 116; Fritz et al., "Surveillance for Pneumonic Plague in the United States during an International Emergency"; Ruiz, "Plague in the Americas."

20. Further reading on precolumbian New World agriculture: Chapman and Watson, "Archaic Period and the Flotation Revolution"; Cowan and Watson, *Ori-

gins of Agriculture; Erickson, "Lake Titicaca Basin," "Agricultural Landscapes as World Heritage."

21. Further reading on precolumbian New World diseases: Buikstra, "Diseases of the Pre-Columbian Americas"; Cohen and Armelagos, *Paleopathology at the Origins of Agriculture*; Cohen and Crane-Kramer, *Ancient Health*; Hutchinson, "Treponematosis in Regional and Chronological Perspective from Central Gulf Coast Florida"; Hutchinson et al., "Temporal and Spatial Variation in the Pattern of Treponematosis in La Florida"; Larsen, "Biological Changes in Human Populations with Agriculture"; Powell, "Endemic Treponematosis and Tuberculosis in the Prehistoric Southeastern United States"; Roberts and Buikstra, *Bioarchaeology of Tuberculosis*. One effect of the numerous nutrition deficits and health problems detailed in the above sources would be immune suppression.

22. Chagas' disease (South American trypanosomiasis) is spread by certain types of the "cone-nosed bug," also known as "assassin bugs," "kissing bugs," and the "triatomid bug." Assassin bugs live in the walls of adobe mud houses, preferably those with thatch roofs, providing the insects ample opportunity to breed in cracks and crevices of the walls and for them to come forth at night and bite their victims. Those particular types of domiciles are the primary epidemiological factor in Chagas' disease (Coimbra, "Human Settlements, Demographic Pattern"; Forattini, "Chagas' Disease").

Only a small proportion of those infected actually show symptoms of the disease. Early clues to a possible infection include local swelling around a bite, followed by swelling of a lymph gland or by a fever—at this stage a blood test can confirm the disease. The long-term complications are serious: damage to the heart, and paralysis of the intestine and esophagus. There is no effective and safe treatment; at present, there is no drug that can penetrate the macrophage cells and kill the parasite without harming the host. The disease is currently present in South and Central America and most prevalent in Brazil. An estimated 16–18 million people in this region suffer chronically from the disease; 50,000 die each year from it. An estimated 20,000 new cases appear each year in Brazil alone.

Forattini ("Chagas' Disease") argues that a major factor in the spread of Chagas' disease was the establishment of animal pens adjacent to residences in South America. Apparently, many of the triatomine species were originally sylvatic, with only a few species oriented to other vegetation zones (Coimbra, "Human Settlements, Demographic Pattern"; Forattini, "Chagas' Disease"). Natural environmental changes and human clearing of forests enlarged the triatomid territory beyond the tropical lowlands into the highlands.

Rothhammer and coworkers ("Chagas' Disease in Pre-Columbian South America") reported on the autopsy of 22 mummies from Quebrada de Tarapacá in Chile dated between 470 B.C. and A.D. 600. Nine of those exhibited clinical manifestations (megacolon, cardiomegaly, and megaesophagus) often resulting from Chagas' disease. Rothhammer and coworkers suggest that Chagas' became endemic with the "adaptation of *T. infestans* to permanent human dwellings in the central and southern highlands before 500 B.C." (Rothhammer et al., "Chagas' Disease in Pre-Columbian South America," 497; see also Shimkin, "Models for the Downfall").

Generally confined to the discovery of at most a couple of individuals, mummies from the Chinchorro society along the Atacama coast of Chile offer a very early (5,000–2,000 B.C.) and extensive glimpse of precontact New World health. Arriaza estimates that at least 282 individuals have been recovered (Arriaza, *Beyond Death*). Study of their feces (Reinhard and Auderheide, "Diphyllobothriasis in Pre-Columbian Chile and Peru: Adaptive Radiation of a Helminth Species to Native American Populations") showed that 19 percent of the Chinchorros were infected with fish tapeworm parasites. A secure diagnosis of tuberculosis in a Chilean individual who lived about A.D. 700 was first made by Allison and coworkers (Allison et al., "Documentation of a Case of Tuberculosis in Pre-Columbian America"). Since then, Salo and coworkers ("Identification of *Mycobacterium tuberculosis* DNA in a Pre-Columbian Mummy") have used DNA evidence to show that a Peruvian suffered from tuberculosis. Mummified individuals from Alaska and the Aleutian Islands provide evidence that coronary artery disease was common, as were intestinal parasites (Zimmerman, "Alaskan and Aleutian Mummies").

Chapter 3. Virginity and Virulence

1. Crosby, "Virgin Soil Epidemics as a Factor in the Aboriginal Depopulation of America," 289.

2. Burnet and White, *Natural History of Infectious Disease*.

3. For a discussion of the skeletal lesions associated with congenital syphilis, see Hutchinson and Richman, "Regional, Social, and Evolutionary Perspectives on Treponemal Infection."

4. For further reading on the earlier molecular research on syphilis, see Centurion-Lara et al., "Flanking Region Sequences"; Fraser et al., "Complete Genome Sequence of *Treponema pallidum*, the Syphilis Spirochete"; Kolman et al., "Identification of *Treponema pallidum* Subspecies"; Wills, *Yellow Fever, Black Goddess*.

5. Fairly recent molecular research on the relationships between the treponemal pathogens is summarized in Šmajs et al., "Genetic Diversity in *Treponema pallidum*," and Giacanni and Lukehart, "Endemic Treponematoses."

6. Crosby, "Virgin Soil Epidemics as a Factor in the Aboriginal Depopulation of America," *Ecological Imperialism*.

7. Much of the current skeletal research on the evidence for treponemal infection in prehistoric North America can be found in Powell and Cook (eds.), *The Myth of Syphilis*. European information, including much on the debate of New World or Old World origin, is contained in Dutour et al., *L'Origine de la syphilis en Europe*, and Harper et al., "Origin and Antiquity of Syphilis Revisited." Two suggested cases

of syphilis from Europe before A.D. 1493 are from Greece (Henneberg and Henneberg, "Treponematosis in an Ancient Greek Colony of Metaponto, Southern Italy, 580–250 BCE"), and France (Pálfi et al., "Paléopathologie de la série de Costebelle, Hyères [France], Var [3e–5e siècles après J.-C.]").

8. Harper et al., "On the Origin of the Treponematoses"; Mulligan et al., "Molecular Studies in *Treponema pallidum* Evolution."

9. Tuberculosis could manifest itself as abscesses of the lymph nodes that burst through the skin of necks, armpits, or groins—the liquids from the abscesses run, leaving sores and then scars ("scrofulous TB"). Or it could appear as wasting of the lungs and adjacent tissues ("consumption" or "phthisis"). For further reading on both TB and the history of TB, see Buikstra, *Prehistoric Tuberculosis in the Americas*; Dubos and Dubos, *White Plague*; Morse, "Prehistoric Tuberculosis in America," "Tuberculosis," "Ancient Disease in the Midwest"; Roberts and Buikstra, *Bioarchaeology of Tuberculosis*.

10. From Morse, "Prehistoric Tuberculosis in America," 489:

(1.) Tuberculosis of the spine usually involves one to four vertebrae. Involvement of more vertebrae does occur, but this is rare.

(2.) Bone destruction occurs with little or no bone regeneration.

(3.) As the disease advances, the bone in the vertebral bodies becomes eroded and decalcified. Under the pressure of body weight the spine collapses forward to give the characteristic deformity, the *angular kyphosis*.

(4.) Involvement of the neural arches and transverse and spinous processes of the vertebrae is rare.

(5.) Extra vertebral "cold" abscesses are frequent. In the cervical and upper dorsal region these can occur posteriorly, and the sinus tracks can open externally. In the lower thoracic and lumbar areas, abscesses will develop anteriorly and occasionally rupture into the peritoneum or proceed to the psoas area, but they will almost never open through the skin posteriorly.

(6.) Massive regeneration of the bone is a great rarity, and even spontaneous fusion is uncommon. That is why, before tuberculosis of the bone was treated with specific antituberculous drugs, so many cases necessitated surgical intervention.

11. The following is Buikstra's summary, in "Introduction," of Cockburn's argument in *Evolution and Eradication of Infectious Diseases*, pages 220–21:

(1.) Sufficiently large, settled populations, which are necessary for the support of this disease, did not exist, pg. 89.

(2.) Native American populations show classic characteristics of groups experiencing a new infection: Death rates are high and all age groups develop the pathology, pg. 85.

(3.) Native American groups tended to show the classic symptoms of populations experiencing tuberculosis for the first time: glandular, rather than pulmonary involvement, pg. 93.

(4.) There is no satisfactory domestic animal to serve as an intermediate host or reservoir for the disease, a necessary factor as the pathogen spread to a human host.

12. From Hrdlička, *Tuberculosis among Certain Indian Tribes of the United States*, 1:

(1.) No reference to the prevalence of this disease among the Indians is made by the writers who reported on the period of the earliest contact of the whites with the various tribes.

(2.) There are to this day among the Indians a scarcity of remedies and lack of specialized forms of treatment for this disease.

(3.) In many tribes the testimony of the old Indians is to the effect that diseases of the kind were unknown or but seldom seen among them in their early days, or in the still earlier times of which information had come down to them.

(4.) The old men and women in many of the tribes are remarkably free from signs of tuberculosis of the lymph nodes and bones.

(5.) The whites who have been long in contact with the Indians, particularly in the Southwest, all speak of the spread of the disease within their memory, while the observations of explorers and men of science indicate a progressive decrease in most localities as we recede into the past.

(6.) As yet no bones of undoubtedly pre-Columbian origin have been found that show tuberculosis lesions, and such lesions are very rare in Indian bones dating from the period of the earliest contact with the whites.

(7.) The Indian presents everywhere a greater susceptibility to the disease than the white man; this means a lesser immunization of his system, indicating the more recent introduction of the infection into his race.

(8.) It is to be assumed on purely logical grounds that the disease must have been much less frequent among the Indians in former times when they lived a more natural and active life, were better inured to hardships, and, with exception of particular localities and periods, were better provided with suitable food.

13. The Bartlett-Black model for measles states there need to be at least 250,000 people to maintain continuous transmission (Cliff et al., *Measles*). There are, of course, many diseases that can be maintained in small populations, such as several of the helminthic worms (e.g., pinworm). They are not, however, crowd diseases.

14. A general discussion of pathogen evolution is presented in Freeman and Herron, *Evolutionary Analysis*. A few further readings on pathogen evolution would include Frank and Schmid-Hempel, "Mechanisms of Pathogenesis and the Evolu-

tion of Parasite Virulence"; Schmid-Hempel and Frank, "Pathogenesis, Virulence, and Infective Dose"; and Weiss, "Virulence and Pathogenesis."

15. These data came from Dubos and Dubos, *White Plague*, 191; Cummins, *Primitive Tuberculosis*, 110; Bushnell, *Study in the Epidemiology of Tuberculosis*, 157–61.

16. The anthropologist Mascie-Taylor gives a more detailed historical example ("Biological Anthropology of Disease," 2). In Denmark, during World War II, 300 students were exposed in a poorly ventilated room to a teacher who had developed tuberculosis. Of the student group, 94 had not yet been vaccinated and had no natural infection as determined by a skin reaction test. Yet 24 escaped infection and remained tuberculin-negative; 29 experienced subclinical infection; of the remaining 41 students who showed evidence of primary tuberculosis, only 14 developed progressive pulmonary disease.

17. Since the early application of ancient DNA (aDNA) to detect tuberculosis (Salo et al., "Identification of *Mycobacterium tuberculosis* DNA in a Pre-Columbian Mummy"), numerous other studies have produced molecular evidence of New World tuberculosis (e.g., Braun et al., "DNA from *Mycobacterium tuberculosis*"; Raff et al., "Tuberculosis in the New World") and Old World tuberculosis (e.g., Nicklish et al., "Rib Lesions in Skeletons from Early Neolithic Sites"; Zink et al., "Molecular History of Tuberculosis"). The evolution of the pathogen, however, remains unclear (see Brosch et al., "New Evolutionary Scenario"; Donoghue, "Insights into Ancient Leprosy and Tuberculosis").

Chapter 4. Merchants and Maladies

1. I take this characterization from the title of a wonderful treatise on the early era of French and Iroquois relations by Trigger, *Natives and Newcomers*. I should say some things about the terms used to refer to groups of people.

The classifications used for groups of humans based on appearance and/or geographic distribution are part of an oscillating landscape of debate. Racial classifications are among the most highly debated. Bound satisfactorily by neither biology nor culture, they continue to be used to describe human individuals and populations. I have endeavored in this book to use terms that largely can be accepted by descendants of the characters in the book. Nonetheless, I also acknowledge the terms used historically at times, not because they are at all acceptable, but because to hide them from the fact that they were used sanitizes the social context in which they were used to justify discrimination.

I have not erased terms used historically like "negro," despite a general agreement they are not acceptable. I have used the term "slave" as it is used in the literature I consulted, despite the fact that it is clear that the term refers to people of varying ancestry. Unfortunately, many historical documents do not discuss ancestry, but only bondage. Another term, "indentured servant," also combines people from multiple backgrounds and varies in meaning. My goal was not to become enmeshed in debates about the labels themselves, which are sometimes very specific (e.g., tribal names) and sometimes very generic (e.g., "Indian"). The important point is that the labels embodied a social and economic context in which people were treated differently and for whom discrimination increased risk for exposure to poverty, malnutrition, and impacts on their health.

Finally, because nearly all of the accounts presented by people bound or bonded in the text are translations through the lens of those more educated and fortunate, I have taken the liberty to slightly alter them linguistically. As is true today, linguistic variation such as dialect can be a lens of class distinction, and it will always be unclear to what degree that class distinction was imposed on those who were not penning their own accounts.

2. A very well-written and informative book on the trade in cod throughout history, and its current use, is Kurlansky, *Cod*.

3. Cartier, "Memoir of Jacques Cartier," 26.

4. For further reading on the development of the fur trade in the Northeast, see Cronon, *Changes in the Land*, 22; Eccles, "Fur Trade in the Colonial Northeast"; Sauer, *Sixteenth-Century North America*, 269–70; Taylor, *American Colonies*, 99; Trigger, *Children of Aataentsic*, 209.

5. Taylor, *American Colonies*, 164–66.

6. Thwaites, Reuben Gold (ed.), *Jesuit Relations*.

7. Le Jeune, "Relation of 1634," *Jesuit Relations* 7: 106–15.

8. Van den Bogaert, *Journey into Mohawk and Oneida Country*. For a comprehensive summary of seventeenth-century disease epidemics in the Northeast, see also Snow, "Disease and Population Decline in the Northeast."

9. Van den Bogaert, *Journey*, 4–5. A castle is a large village. A palisade is in this time period generally constructed of logs placed side by side in the ground vertically so as to form a defensible wall.

10. Lalemont, "Relation of 1640," *Jesuit Relations* 19: 8–93.

11. Smallpox has considerable antiquity, and an excellent set of discussions about that history can be found in Hopkins, *Princes and Peasants*, and Crosby, "Smallpox." The evidence that India was the original home of smallpox relies heavily on historical tradition. India was one of the earliest places with records of smallpox epidemics, and Hindu mythology and Brahmin traditions support a lengthy antiquity of the disease there. Despite this long record, there is only scant evidence that it was present prior to A.D. 1500. Most evidence prior to that date is in mythology, particularly through worship of the Hindu goddess of smallpox, Shitala mata.

Recent DNA evidence may help to clarify the origin of smallpox (Li et al., "On the Origin of Smallpox"). It indicates that the two primary clades of variola virus (VARV) likely diverged from an ancestral rodent-borne variola-like virus either 16,000 years ago or 68,000 years ago, depending on which historical records (East

Asian or African) are used to calibrate the molecular clock. A molecular clock uses rates of molecular change or fossils to deduce the time when two species diverged.

As discussed in chapter 2, there is both historic and paleopathological evidence for smallpox early in Egypt and the adjacent Near East. In Greece and the Mediterranean, Hopkins (*Princes and Peasants*) reports that the epidemic known as the Plague of Athens, which occurred during the Peloponnesian War (431–404 B.C.), originated in Ethiopia, spread to Egypt and Libya, and then descended on Athens via the port of Piraeus in the spring of 430 B.C. It raged for two or three years, destroyed a quarter of the Athenian army and many citizens, and then spread east to Persia. The illness was characterized in the writings of Thucydides by headache, malodorous breath, cough, retching, convulsions, loss of memory, sleeplessness, diarrhea, and a rash of small sores over the whole body. It was lethal and contagious, but those who survived were immune. Most deaths occurred on the seventh or ninth day of the illness. In 2001 a mass grave was discovered that belonged to the years of the Plague of Athens. DNA indicating typhoid (*Salmonella enterica serovar Typhi*) was extracted from three skeletons, but since typhoid was likely endemic in the classical Greek world, it is probably not the cause of the Plague of Athens (Littman, "Plague of Athens.")

Another epidemic (also maybe smallpox) occurred among North African (Carthaginian) soldiers besieging Syracuse in 395 B.C. This epidemic arrived from Libya as well. The Chinese first suffered a disease that matches the descriptions of smallpox in 243 B.C., when the invading Huns brought it with them (the Chinese referred to it as Hunpox). After this time the Chinese also had a goddess of smallpox.

Smallpox was eradicated in 1975 as a result of a global immunization effort spearheaded by the World Health Organization (WHO) and is no longer an active infection, but stored viral material makes its return always a threat when biological warfare comes up. Consequently, I treat the discussion here in the present tense. The viruses that cause smallpox are *Variola minor*, which causes a mild disease with death rates of 1 percent or less, and *Variola major* with a mortality rate of 25–30 percent. The incubation period for smallpox is about 12 days, with sudden onset marked by high fever, headache, back pain and muscle pain, vomiting in children, convulsions, and a rash that appears more densely on the face, palms, and soles of the feet. The rash generally begins two to five days after the onset of symptoms. A few days after the onset of the rash, it turns to pustules, which in extreme cases are confluent and almost always indicate a lethal infection. Drying and crusting of the pustules generally occurs on the eighth or ninth day after the first eruptions, and the scabs fall off three to four weeks after onset of the infection.

12. Thwaites, *Jesuit Relations*, 7: 221, 8: 43, 87–89, 12: 265. For many of the diseases discussed in this section, there is room for disagreement on the exact disease—many were characterized by fevers and spots.

13. Measles is a viral disease of the genus Morbillivirus of the family *paramyxo-*

viridae (Cliff et al., *Measles*). It is transmitted by contact of susceptible persons with the nose and throat secretions of infected persons, primarily by droplet spread. It enters the human body through the mucous membranes of the respiratory tract. It can occur by direct contact but also by indirect contact with soiled articles or by airborne transmission. Although the virus does not survive drying on a surface, it can survive drying in microdroplets in the air. There is no reservoir for measles other than human beings, which means that a continuous chain of susceptible contacts is necessary to sustain transmission.

Few susceptibles escape the disease following first exposure, and as a result measles is uncommon after the age of 10 years and rare after 15 in populations where the chain of transmission is continuous. In temperate climates epidemics of measles always begin in the winter and reach a peak in the late spring. There is nearly always a cyclical variation in incidence: epidemics are recorded irregularly every two or three years in larger communities and at similar or longer intervals in rural or semirural populations. In the United States measles epidemics were transmitted in the classroom of elementary schools; when measles was introduced, most, if not all, of the susceptible children would have measles in two weeks. Estimates are that at least 80 percent of all preschool children were infected by school-aged siblings.

Before the introduction of measles vaccines, about 400 measles deaths per year were recorded in the United States, a death-to-case ratio of 1:10,000. In Africa, where protein-deficient diets are common, as many as 5 percent of all children die from measles. Measles mortality is highest for the very young and the very old. There is significant evidence that malnutrition exacerbates the effects of measles. In some areas the disease takes on a different form: the rash becomes dark red-purple, and skin exfoliates extensively, exposing large areas to bacterial infection. Mortality rates are also different—in the late 1970s in Indonesia, for instance, it was 26 percent.

The origin of measles is unknown. Francis Black has noted that populations of a sufficient size (250,000 according to the Bartlett-Black model) to allow for a continuous chain of transmission would not have developed until at least 2500 B.C. It may have arisen as an adaptation of other viruses of the same genus, which include bovine rinderpest and canine distemper (Cliff et al., *Measles*). The first credible account of measles was written in A.D. 910 by the Persian physician Rhazes in his *Treatise on the Small-pox and Measles*. Measles was probably confused in the early literature with smallpox. With its fever and spots, a descriptive account of measles could easily have been confused with smallpox.

The most famous epidemiological study of measles was conducted by Peter Panum and was reported in his *Observations Made during the Epidemic of Measles on the Faroe Islands in the Year 1846* (1940). During this epidemic, which lasted from April to October of 1846, more than 6,000 of the 7,782 inhabitants were stricken with the disease. Because this was an isolated island population, the previous epidemic had been in 1781, a 65-year span.

At other world localities, however, the colonial experience proceeded at a slower rate, and recorded epidemics did take a heavy toll on previously unexposed populations. High mortality rates were reported for several virgin-soil populations in the Pacific during the nineteenth century. These include 40,000 deaths out of a population of 150,000 in Hawaii in 1848; 20,000 deaths, constituting 20 to 25 percent of the population in Fiji in 1874/1875 (another estimate for Fiji is "not less than 40,000," constituting 27 percent—Corney, "Behaviour of Certain Epidemic Diseases in Natives of Polynesia"); and 645 deaths out of 8,845 cases in Samoa in 1911, constituting 7 percent. In Fiji, in 1874, 40,000 out of an estimated 150,000 natives lost their lives in a period of three months. Equally high mortality rates have been reported for other "virgin soil" populations such as the Yanomamo of Brazil. It is now prevalent in all parts of the world, with small pockets of nonimmune populations. In fact, measles is one of the most contagious diseases known.

Much of the high mortality in those populations has been attributed to the same factors that still affect unvaccinated populations in the developing world today— lack of supporting care, lack of treatment for complications, and malnutrition. More recent studies of well-nourished populations where medical care was available are also recorded. In 1951 in southern Greenland, for instance, in one district 4,257 persons out of a population of 4,400 contracted measles—77 died of the experience. Iceland had similar experiences, both Greenland and Iceland being relatively isolated localities until recently, when only the age of faster boat and air travel has resulted in spreading the relatively short-lived measles virus. Another factor cited is the faster spread within the island between outer settlements and the major urban center of Reykjavik.

The evidence of the disease in the American colonies during the 1600s is limited. The Jesuits report in 1645 a disease resembling measles among the French and Indians, but we must remember that smallpox was also present during this time in the area.

14. Snow, "Disease and Population Decline in the Northeast." Scarlet fever was identified as early as 1675 but could be mistaken for smallpox, measles, and diphtheria. Scarlet fever often accompanied other diseases, such as during the smallpox epidemic of Boston in 1702. John Marshall claimed that "smallpox was attended with a sort of feaver called the scarlett feaver" (Duffy, *Epidemics in Colonial America*, 130). It occurred again in Boston in 1735–36 in conjunction with diphtheria. Between 1860 and 1865, scarlet fever accounted for 1,082 of the deaths of known cause in New York, as compared to 1,414 deaths from cholera and 3,313 deaths from consumption during the same years, although consumption likely conflated any number of diseases characterized by "wasting." See also Hardy, "Scarlet Fever."

15. François Le Mercier, "Relation of 1637," *Jesuit Relations* 13: 98–105; Crosby, "Influenza" and *Epidemic and Peace, 1918*.

16. See note 3, chapter 1, for literature on the subject of native depopulation following European contact. There is a massive literature.

17. I have previously written about the difficulties of recognizing the archaeological signature of disease epidemics: Hutchinson, *Tatham Mound and the Bioarchaeology of European Contact*; Hutchinson and Mitchem, "Correlates of Contact." One good example of a plague cemetery is discussed in Grainger et al., *Black Death Cemetery, East Smithfield, London*.

18. What follows is a description of the Feast of the Dead at Ossossané in 1636 (excerpted from Kidd, "Excavation and Identification of a Huron Ossuary," 372–75; account originally published in Thwaites 1896–1901: X: 279–305).

Twelve years or thereabout having elapsed, the Old Men and Notables of the Country assemble, to deliberate in a definite way on the time at which the feast shall be held to the satisfaction of the whole Country and of the foreign Nations that may be invited to it. The decision having been made, as all the bodies are to be transported to the Village where is the common grave, each family sees to its dead, but with a care and affection that cannot be described: if they have dead relatives in any part of the Country, they spare no trouble to go for them; they take them from the Cemeteries, bear them on their shoulders, and cover them with the finest robes they have. In each village, they choose a fair day, and proceed to the Cemetery, where those called *Aiheonde*, who take care of the graves, draw the bodies from the tombs in the presence of the relatives, who renew their tears and feel afresh the grief they had the day of the funeral. I was present at the spectacle, and willingly invited to it all our servants; for I do not think one could see in the world a more vivid picture or more perfect representation of what man is.

. . . For, after having opened the graves, they display before you all these Corpses, on the spot, and they leave them thus exposed long enough for the spectators to learn at their leisure, and once for all, what they will be some day. The flesh of some is quite gone, and there is only parchment on their bones; in other cases, the bodies look as if they had been dried and smoked, and show scarcely any signs of putrefaction; and in still other cases they are still swarming with worms. When the friends have gazed upon the bodies to their satisfaction, they cover them with handsome Beaver robes quite new: finally, after some time they strip them of their flesh, taking off skin and flesh which they throw into the fire along with the robes and mats in which the bodies were wrapped. As regards the bodies of those recently dead, they leave these in the state in which they are, and content themselves by simply covering them with new robes. Of the latter they handled only one Old Man, of whom I have spoken before, who died this Autumn on his return from fishing: this swollen corpse had only begun to decay during the last month, on the occasion of the first heat of Spring; the worms were still swarming all over it, and the corruption that oozed out of it gave forth an almost intolerable stench; and yet they had the courage to take away the robe in which it was enveloped, cleaned it as well as they could, taking the matter off by handfuls, and put the body into a fresh mat and robe, and all this without showing any horror at the corruption . . .

The bones having been well cleaned, they put them partly into bags, partly into fur robes, loaded them on their shoulders, and covered these packages with another beautiful hanging robe. As for the whole bodies, they put them on a species of litter, and carried them with all the others, each into his Cabin, where each family made a feast to its dead.

. . .

The whole Company arrived with their corpses about an hour after Midday, and divided themselves into different cantons, according to their families and Villages, and laid on the ground their parcels of souls, almost as they do earthen pots at the Village Fairs. They unfolded also their parcels of robes, and all the presents they had brought, and hung them upon poles, which were from 5 to 600 toises in extent; so there were as many as twelve hundred presents which remained thus on exhibition two full hours, to give Strangers time to see the wealth and magnificence of the Country. I did not find the Company so numerous as I had expected; if there were two thousand, persons, that was about all. About three o'clock, each one put away his various articles, and folded up his robes.

Meanwhile, each Captain by command gave the signal; and all, at once, loaded with their packages of souls, running as if to the assault of a town, ascended the Stage by means of ladders hung all round it, and hung them to the cross poles, each Village having its own department. That done, all the ladders were taken away; but a few Chiefs remained there and spent the rest of the afternoon, until seven o'clock, in announcing the presents which were made in the name of the dead to certain specified persons.

"This," said they, "is what such and such a dead man gives to such and such a relative." About five or six o'clock, they lined the bottom and sides of the pit with fine large new robes, each of ten Beaver skins, in such a way that they extended more than a foot out of it. As they were preparing the robes which were to be employed for this purpose, some went down to the bottom and brought up handfuls of sand. I asked what this ceremony meant, and learned that they have a belief that this sand renders them successful at play. Of those twelve hundred presents that had been displayed, forty-eight robes served to line the bottom and sides of the pit; and each entire body, besides the robe in which it had been enveloped, had another one, and sometimes even two more, to cover it. That was all; so that I do not think each body had its own robe, one with another, which is surely the least it can have in its burial; for what winding sheets and shrouds are in France, Beaver robes are here. But what becomes then of the remainder? I will explain in a moment.

About seven o'clock, they let down the whole bodies into the pit. We had the greatest difficulty in getting near; nothing has ever better pictured for me the confusion there is among the damned. On all sides you could have seen them letting down half-decayed bodies; and on all sides was heard a horrible din of confused voices of persons, who spoke and did not listen; ten or twelve were in the pit and were arranging the bodies all around it, one after another. They put in the very middle of the pit three large kettles, which could only be of use for souls; one had a hole through it, another had no handle, and the third was of scarcely more value. I saw very few Porcelain collars; it is true, they put many on the bodies. This is all that was done on this day.

All the people passed the night on the spot; they lighted many fires, and slung their kettles. We withdrew for the night to the old Village, with the resolve to return next morning, at daybreak, when they were to throw the bones into the pit; but we could hardly arrive in time, although we made great haste, on account of an accident that happened. One of the souls, which was not securely tied, or was perhaps too heavy for the cord that fastened it, fell of itself into the pit; the noise awakened the Company, who immediately ran and mounted in a crowd upon the scaffold, and emptied indiscriminately each package into the pit, keeping, however, the robes in which they were enveloped. We had only set out from the Village at that time, but the noise was so great that it seemed almost as if we were there. As we drew near, we saw nothing less than a picture of Hell. The large space was quite full of fires and flames, and the air resounded in all directions with the confused voices of these Barbarians; the noise ceased, however, for some time, and they began to sing,—but in voices so sorrowful and lugubrious that it represented to us the horrible sadness and the abyss of despair into which these unhappy souls are forever plunged.

Nearly all the souls were thrown in when we arrived, for it was done almost in the turning of a hand; each one had made haste, thinking there would not be room enough for all the souls; we saw, however, enough of it to judge the rest. There were five or six in the pit, arranging the bones with poles. The pit was full, within about two feet; they turned back over the bones the robes which bordered the edge of the pit, and covered the remaining space with mats and bark. Then they heaped the pit with sand, poles, and wooden stakes, which they threw in without order. Some women brought to it some dishes of corn; and that day, and the following days, several Cabins of the Village provided nets quite full of it, which were thrown upon the pit.

. . .

As to the rest of the twelve hundred presents, forty-eight robes were used in adorning the pit. Each whole body had its robe, and some had two or three. Twenty were given to the master of the feast, to thank the Nations which had taken part therein. The dead distributed a number of them, by the hands of the Captains, to their living friends; some served only for show, and were taken away by those who had exhibited them. The Old Men and the notables of the Country, who had the administration and management of the feast, took possession secretly of a considerable quantity; and the rest was cut into pieces, as I have said, and ostentatiously thrown into the midst of the crowd. However, it is only the rich who lose nothing, or very little, in this feast. The middle classes and the poor bring and leave there whatever they have most valuable, and suffer much, in order not to appear less liberal than the others in this celebration. Every one makes it a point of honor.

19. For a lengthy discussion of ossuaries and mortuary rituals, see Hutchinson and Aragon, "Collective Burials and Community Memories."

20. Jackes, "Osteological Evidence for Smallpox," "Mortality of Ontario Archaeological Populations."

21. Taylor, *American Colonies*, 365–66.

Chapter 5. Commerce and Consequence

1. Lalemont, cited in Trigger, *Children of Aataentsic*, 358; originally in Thwaites 1896–1901, 4: 207.

2. Trigger, *Children of Aataentsic*, 208.

3. A great resource is a film by Brian Weiss, *The Turtle People*, College Station: Penn State Media, 1972.

Another example of the seductive nature of economic change is found farther north. It occurs among the Skolt Lapps, who live near the Arctic Circle in Finland. Their traditional subsistence regime was formed of fishing and the herding of reindeer. Reindeer were especially important and were used for food, transportation, shoes and clothing, and antler for various tools and other objects. Consequently, much of the winter activity for the traditional Lapps focused on reindeer herds. In the 1960s the Lapps began a rapid adoption of snowmobiles on the premise that it would make herding easier and more economically advantageous. The first machine arrived in 1962, and by 1971 there were 70 in the area. The machines were considered prestigious, and a certain amount of status was conferred to those owning one.

The consequences of this adoption of snowmobiles, however, was far-reaching. With the machines came the need for parts, gasoline, oil, and other mechanical goods that created a huge dependency on the outside world. Traditional skills, now replaced by snowmobile technology, also resulted in a need for outside support in the form of mechanics. All of this meant a huge increase in the need for cash, and accordingly men were forced to spend great amounts of time involved in wage labor. Furthermore, the adoption of the machines resulted in a decline in herd size, because the animals are afraid of the machines. They run away, and there is some evidence that they reproduce less efficiently. The end result is that many Lapp men are no longer herders at all, with few economic alternatives. Their dependency on a cash economy, with fewer job opportunities, has made them poorer than ever, both financially and culturally, since in Lapp society the essence of manhood is being a herder of reindeer. See Pelto, *Snowmobile Revolution*.

4. Cronon, *Changes in the Land*, 22.

5. Sources cited here for the decline in fur-bearing animals are: Sagard, *Histoire du Canada*, 585; Thwaites, *Jesuit Relations*, 8: 57; Thwaites, *Jesuit Relations*, 4: 207; Biggar, *Works of Samuel de Champlain*, 5: 232; Cronon, *Changes in the Land*, 99.

6. General sources for this discussion include Ethridge, "Introduction"; Trigger, "Early Iroquoian Contacts with Europeans," *Children of Aataentsic*, and *Natives and Newcomers*.

7. Paul Ragueneau, "Relation of 1648–49," *Jesuit Relations* 34: 122–37.

8. Wray et al., *Adams and Culbertson Sites*, 255. The evidence for population differences is based on nonmetric traits, skeletal and dental markers that are genetically conservative and thus are used to gauge distance between populations, a study known in human osteology as biological distance. Wray et al., *Tram and Cameron*.

9. Usner, "Economic Relations in the Southeast until 1783."

10. Silver, *New Face on the Countryside*, 92. Usner, "Economic Relations in the Southeast until 1783," 391, gives the total for 1750 as 100,000. Silver, *New Face on the Countryside*, 93, gives the total for 1750 as 150,000. It is worth noting that the same number of deerskins was being shipped from New Orleans at that time, but through French trade networks that began in 1699.

11. With regard to closed hunting seasons and other regulatory laws: Cowdrey, *This Land, This South*, 56; Marten, "Southeastern Indians and the English Trade in Skins and Slaves," 319; Bartram, *Travels*, 165, 170–72, 181–82. Specifically, they had to have planted and tended 5,000 corn hills; Silver, *New Face on the Countryside*, 96. Cowdrey, *This Land, This South*, 57.

12. The term "militaristic slaving societies" comes from Ethridge, "Introduction." A few good sources on Indian slavery are: Gallay, *Indian Slave Trade* and *Indian Slavery in Colonial America*; Snyder, *Slavery in Indian Country*.

13. Gallay, *Indian Slave Trade*, 298–99.

14. Silver, *New Face on the Countryside*, 74–76.

15. Kelton, *Epidemics and Enslavement*, 144–47.

16. Ethridge, "Introduction," 39.

17. All three diseases are described on the CDC website (www.cdc.gov/) as well as in numerous other places.

18. A genomic analysis of human and microbial DNA from the 5,200-year-old Tyrolean Ice Man found *Borrelia burgdorferi* and indicates that he likely suffered from Lyme disease (Keller et al., "New Insights into the Tyrolean Iceman's Origin and Phenotype as Inferred by Whole-Genome Sequencing").

19. Ostfeld, "Ecology of Lyme-Disease Risk"; Ostfeld, *Lyme Disease*.

20. Wills, *Yellow Fever, Black Goddess*, 15. The reference to the Navajo legend also comes from Wills, 16.

Chapter 6. Contested Colonies

1. Barnwell, "Tuscarora Expedition," 53.

2. The numbers come from Gallay, *Indian Slave Trade*, 283. Kelton, *Epidemics and Enslavement*, 168, gives somewhat different numbers of hundreds killed by fire, 170 killed outside of the palisade, and 400 sold into slavery. It seems Moore, the commander of the Second Expedition of the Tuscarora War, was very specific in his numbers. He reports having taken 392 prisoners and 192 scalps, and thought at least 200 people were burned inside the fort, with 166 who had fled (Moore's estimates presented in Gallay, *Indian Slave Trade*, 298).

3. Askew, "Neoheroka Fort."

4. Kelton, *Epidemics and Enslavement*, 203–6.

5. Kelton, *Epidemics and Enslavement*, 201.

6. Gallay, *Indian Slave Trade*, 330.

7. Silver, *New Face on the Countryside*, 92–93. The French lost their trade flexibility after they ceded the Southeast as a consequence of the French and Indian War. Following the Treaty of Paris in 1763, Georgia traders seized the opportunity to trade with Creeks and Cherokees. Between 1764 and 1773, more than 500,000 deerskins were exported from Savannah.

8. Borneman, *French and Indian War*.

9. Other impacts of conflict include migration, ecological imbalance, lack of sleep, overcrowding, poor sanitation, suppressed immunity, death in overwhelming proportions, rape, and psychological trauma. Dirks, "Famine and Disease"; Scott and Duncan, *Biology of Plague*; Walter and Schofield, "Famine, Disease and Crisis Mortality in Early Modern Society"; Wills, *Yellow Fever, Black Goddess*.

10. Book of Revelation 6: 1–8.

11. Scrimshaw, "Interactions of Malnutrition and Infection."

12. Anderson, *Crucible of War*, 236–38.

13. Anderson, *Crucible of War*, 462–63.

14. Knox, *Historical Journal of the Campaigns in North America*, vol. 2, 374–75.

15. Knox, *Historical Journal of the Campaigns in North America*, vol. 2, 16.

16. Crosby, "Smallpox."

17. Dixon, *Smallpox*, 219–20.

18. Thompson, "To Save the Children."

19. Thompson, "To Save the Children," 438.

20. This is the cartoon "The Cow Pock" by British satirist James Gillray. It caricatures a scene at the Smallpox and Inoculation Hospital at St. Pancras, showing Edward Jenner administering cowpox vaccine to frightened young women, and

cows emerging from different parts of people's bodies. The cartoon was inspired by the controversy over inoculating against the dreaded disease smallpox. The inoculation agent, cowpox vaccine, was rumored to have the ability to sprout cowlike appendages. A serene Edward Jenner stands amid the crowd. A boy next to Jenner holds a container labeled "VACCINE POCK hot from ye COW"; papers in the boy's pocket are labeled "Benefits of the Vaccine." The tub on the desk next to Jenner is labeled "OPENING MIXTURE." A bottle next to the tub is labeled "VOMIT." The painting on the wall depicts worshipers of the golden calf.

21. Thompson, "To Save the Children," 443–46.

22. For reading on British military sites in the Northeast, see Starbuck, *Great Warpath*; Jabez Fitch's account is on page 65. Rogers' Rangers was an independent colonial unit of fighters during the French and Indian War led by Colonel Robert Rogers. They were a light brigade, credited with bold and ingenious stealth. They became the chief scouting agency of the British army and were often used for gathering intelligence about the enemy and other special operations. Several of the rangers were leaders for the colonists in the American Revolutionary War.

23. Technically, the French and Indian War ended on February 10, 1763, when France, Britain, and Spain signed the Treaty of Paris. Pontiac's War, or Pontiac's Rebellion, named after the Ottawa leader, was a war that was launched in May of 1763 by a loose confederation of Native American tribes, primarily from the Great Lakes region, the Illinois Country, and the Ohio Country. They were dissatisfied with British postwar policies in the Great Lakes region, particularly those led by Major General Jeffrey Amherst. An excellent source, from which much of the discussion on this and the French and Indian War was taken, is Anderson, *Crucible of War*.

24. Anderson, *Crucible of War*, 541.

25. For further reading on typhus, see Harden, "Epidemic Typhus." Rickettsia are smaller than most bacteria but are still visible under the light microscope. Unlike common bacteria, they are obligate intracellular parasites—they must metabolize and multiply only inside living cells, a characteristic they share with viruses. Until recently they were characterized as something between bacteria and viruses, but later research revealed that they were indeed bacteria. Pathological rickettsia were discovered by Howard Taylor Ricketts, who died of typhus while investigating the same disease in Mexico.

26. For further reading on the role of famine in plagues, see Dirks, "Famine and Disease"; Scott and Duncan, *Biology of Plagues*; Walter and Schofield, "Famine, Disease and Crisis Mortality in Early Modern Society"; Wills, *Yellow Fever, Black Goddess*. The specific reference to Ireland comes from Dirks, "Famine and Disease," 161.

27. Kimball, *Correspondence of William Pitt*, 292.

28. Hopkins, *Princes and Peasants*, 258–60. *Inoculated* is another term for *variolated* and, again, is not synonymous with *vaccination*.

29. Shallow as it may seem, more than once I've watched the 1992 movie ver-

sion of *The Last of the Mohicans* directed by Michael Mann. The quote comes from Colonel Edmund Munro's description of the inevitable approach of the French general Montcalm and his army. Many scenes were filmed in my home state of North Carolina—part of the allure.

30. For information on the Fort William Henry massacre, see Starbuck, *Massacre at Fort William Henry*, especially page 65; Liston and Baker, "Reconstructing the Massacre at Fort William Henry."

Chapter 7. Landscapes and Liabilities

1. For further reading regarding the emigration of the poor from England to Virginia, see Taylor, *American Colonies*, 117–37.

2. For further reading regarding the establishment of the Chesapeake colony, see Taylor, *American Colonies*, 138–57.

3. Beverly, *History and Present State of Virginia*, 119.

4. Hoffer, *Brave New World*, 123–56.

5. There are numerous primary and secondary sources for the Roanoke colony. A few recommended ones are Quinn, *Roanoke Voyages*, for a quintessential piece, and Kupperman, *Roanoke, the Abandoned Colony*.

6. Percy, *Observations Gathered out of "A Discourse of the Plantation of the Southern Colony in Virginia by the English, 1606,"* 28.

7. Smith, *Complete Works of Captain John Smith, 1580–1631*, 2: 28.

8. Percy, *Observations Gathered out of "A Discourse of the Plantation of the Southern Colony"*, 34. The quoted material spans August 24 through sometime between September 5 and 11.

9. Percy, "A True Relation of the Proceedings and Occurrences of Moment which have happened in Virginia from the Time Sir Thomas Gates was shipwrecked upon the Bermudas," 158–59.

10. Taylor, *American Colonies*, 130; Kelso, *Jamestown*, 161–66.

11. Horn et al., *Jane*. There is also an hour-long video on Jane (Schmidt and Givens, *Jane*).

12. Purchas, *Pilgrimes*, vol. 4, p. 1753, cited in Blanton, *Medicine in Virginia in the Seventeenth Century*, 65.

13. While species or subgroups of *Shigella* most often cause human disease, bacteria from several other genera can invade the intestinal mucosa and cause dysentery, including *Campylobacter*, *Salmonella*, *Yersinia*, and *Escherichia coli* (Patterson, "Bacillary Dysentery," 43).

14. Wyatt, *Letter of Sir Francis*, 117.

15. Kiple, *Cambridge Historical Dictionary of Disease*, 345.

16. See, for instance, Wills, *Yellow Fever, Black Goddess*, 135–41, for a fuller version of Mary Mallon's life.

17. For a summary of the settlement of Carolina, see Taylor, *American Colonies*, 222–44.

18. For further reading on rice agriculture in Carolina, see Carney, *Black Rice*; Doar, *Rice and Rice Planting in the South Carolina Low Country*; Edelson, *Plantation Enterprise in Colonial South Carolina*; Porcher and Judd, *Market Preparation of Carolina Rice*.

19. Taylor, *American Colonies*, 237–38.

20. Wood, *Black Majority*.

21. Doar, *Rice and Rice Planting in the South Carolina Low Country*, 9–10.

22. Carney, *Black Rice*, 88.

23. Doar, *Rice and Rice Planting in the South Carolina Low Country*, 8.

24. Carney, *Black Rice*, 92.

25. Humphreys, *Malaria*, 20.

26. Humphreys, *Malaria*, 9, 23.

27. Baird, *History of the Huguenot Emigration to America II*, 393.

28. William Fitzhugh to Henry Fitzhugh, July 18, 1687, in Davis, *William Fitzhugh and His Chesapeake World*, 229. For other sources regarding malaria in Virginia, see Blanton, *Medicine in Virginia in the Seventeenth Century*, 50–55; Duffy, *Epidemics in Colonial America*, 207; Rutman and Rutman, "Of Agues and Fevers."

29. Peters and Gilles, *Tropical Medicine and Parasitology*, 26.

30. Rutman and Rutman also propose *A. crucians* as a significant vector of malaria in Virginia, but that claim is not supported by other research (see Humphreys, *Malaria*).

31. Dubisch, "Low Country Fevers," 644; Rutman and Rutman, "Of Agues and Fevers," 36. To complicate things even more on the issue of preferred hosts, recent experimental research suggests that human blood-feeding rates by *A. quadrimaculatus* may vary with proximity to the larval hatching and resting sites of the mosquito. Truls and coworkers found that the feeding preference for *A. quadrimaculatus* was for ruminants, equines, lagomorphs, and canines. When the resting mosquitoes are collected indoors, the human blood-feeding rate can be as high as 93 percent, but when collected outdoors the maximum rate is 18 percent (Truls et al., "Human Blood-Feeding Rates among Sympatric Sibling Species of *Anopheles quadrimaculatus* in Northern Florida."

Female *A. quadrimaculatus* deposit eggs on the surface of still freshwater, preferring sunlit streams, ponds, and lakes with aquatic vegetation (Carpenter and LaCasse, *Mosquitoes of North America [North of Mexico]*). Feeding occurs at night; during the day they rest inside dark buildings and shelter in dark corners. Flight activity is highest for a short period after dark and is limited the remainder of the night (Carpenter et al., "Mosquitoes of the Southern United States East of Oklahoma and Texas"). Flight range is usually less than one mile. Adult females live generally no more than two weeks during the summer. However, their development slows in colder months, and fertilized adult females can overwinter in protected shelters such as barns, tree holes, and other dark protected areas—the malaria parasite does not survive that period generally.

32. Desowitz, *New Guinea Tapeworms and Jewish Grandmothers*, 21–22.

33. Humphreys, *Malaria*, 9, 24.

34. Another, the genetic blood condition glucose-6-phosphate dehydrogenase deficiency (G6PD, for short) provides some protection against falciparum malaria. Here's the real whammy: *P. vivax* is fairly rare in sub-Saharan Africa, because about 95 percent of the population lacks an antigen called the Duffy antigen. Antigens are molecules or parts of molecules that are attached to viruses, bacteria, or even pollen grains and which allow the immune system to recognize "self" or "non-self" (Mielke et al., *Human Biological Variation*, 93). The absence of this antigen apparently prevents *P. vivax* from infecting the blood cells (Young et al., "Experimental Testing of the Immunity of Negroes to *Plasmodium vivax*"). See Desowitz, *New Guinea Tapeworms and Jewish Grandmothers*, 59–74, for further discussion of malaria and sickle-cell disease.

35. As early as the 1950s, Frank Livingstone observed that clearing for agricultural fields was instrumental in the rising rates of malaria in Africa (Livingstone, "Anthropological Implications of Sickle-Cell Gene Distribution in West Africa").

Chapter 8. Poverty and Pestilence beyond the Big House

1. One of those is Kovacik, "Health Conditions and Town Growth in Colonial and Antebellum South Carolina."

2. Mary Anderson, *Narrative of Mary Anderson*.

3. Robert Glenn, *Narrative of Robert Glenn*.

4. Artifacts are the material remains left by past societies, such as cooking pots and spears; features are the collective remains of a process, things like burials and trash pits. Features often contain artifacts, but it is the entire collective feature that allows for interpretation. For instance, a single cooking pot (an artifact) holds far different meaning if it is associated with a burial than it does if it is associated with a trash pit.

5. For further reading on the garbage project: Rathje, *Rubbish!* For further reading on the archaeology of privies: Balicki, "Wharves, Privies, and the Pewterer"; Carnes-McNaughton and Harper, "Parity of Privies"; Crist, "Babies in the Privy"; Fisher et al., "Privies and Parasites"; Heck and Balicki, "Katherine Naylor's 'House of Office'"; Mann et al., "Reconstruction of 19th-Century Surgical Techniques"; Stevens and Ordoñez, "Fashionable and Work Shoes from a Nineteenth-Century Boston Privy."

6. The terms of indentured servants were particularly hard before the 1640s, and many lost their lives during their servitude. While the overall Chesapeake population grew from 350 in 1616 to 13,000 in 1650, the growth was largely due to

immigration, as mortality remained at 25 percent until 1650 (Taylor, *American Colonies*, 134). It was higher for indentured servants. Between 1625 and 1640 Virginia's population increased by only 7,000, despite the immigration during that period of 15,000 indentured servants (Taylor, *American Colonies*, 143). Consequently, houses and the garbage associated with them (plates, cups, tools) did not differ much, as they would if immense economic differences existed.

7. Hoffer, *Brave New World*, 124.

8. Carson et al., "Impermanent Architecture in the Southern American Colonies."

9. Kelso, *Kingsmill Plantations 1619–1800*, 19.

10. King, "Living and Dying in the 17th Century Chesapeake."

11. For further reading about the Chesapeake colony during the seventeenth century, see Owsley and Bruwelheide, *Written in Bone*, and Walker, *Written in Bone*. Both books are associated with an exhibit at the National Museum of Natural History, Smithsonian Institution, created by Douglas Owsley and Karin Bruwelheide.

12. Taylor, *American Colonies*, 153.

13. Hoffer, *Brave New World*, 387.

14. See Breen and Innes, *Myne Owne Ground*.

15. All demographic figures, unless otherwise noted, are from Taylor, *American Colonies*, 212–44.

16. See Braund, *Deerskins and Duffels*, for more on trade. A few good works on the Indian slave trade and Indian slaves in the colonies are Gallay, *Native Slave Trade*; Grinde, "Native American Slavery in the Southern Colonies"; Stanwood, "Captives and Slaves"; Lauber, *Indian Slavery*. The quantitative figure for South Carolina is from Grinde, "Native American Slavery in the Southern Colonies," 41.

17. Hoffer, *Brave New World*, 141.

18. Ewald, *Evolution of Infectious Disease*.

19. WHO, "Childhood Stunting: Challenges and Opportunities." For further reading on growth, development, and life history, see Barker, *Mothers, Babies, and Disease in Later Life*, "Fetal Origins of Coronary Heart Disease"; Ellison, "Evolutionary Perspectives on the Fetal Origins Hypothesis"; Kuzawa, "Developmental Origins of Life History"; McDade, "Life History Theory and the Immune System"; Stearns, "Issues in Evolutionary Medicine."

20. Wiley and Allen, *Medical Anthropology*, 340–41.

21. For discussions on slave gardens and the dietary provisioning of slaves, see De Bow, "Plantation Management-police"; Deetz, *Flowerdew Hundred*; Covey and Eisnach, *What the Slaves Ate*.

22. Jackson, "Narrative of Silas Jackson, Baltimore, Maryland"; Shepherd, "Narrative of Robert Shepherd, Athens, Georgia."

23. Steckel, "Dreadful Childhood," "Peculiar Population," "Birth Weights and Infant Mortality among American Slaves."

24. Cicely D. Williams was a doctor at a time when female doctors were limited

in number. She was trained during WWI at Oxford and devoted her life thereafter to global health, especially nutritional health. While working in Ghana in the early 1930s, she made the connection between a wasting condition confused at the time with pellagra (niacin; vitamin B3 deficiency) and protein-calorie malnutrition. She published her observations first in 1933, but they are more extensively known from her 1935 article in the British medical journal the *Lancet*. I quote from that article: "The name 'kwashiorkor' indicates the disease the deposed baby gets when the next one is born, and is the local name in the Gold Coast for a nutritional disease of children associated with maize diet" (Williams, "Kwashiorkor," 1151).

25. Kiple and Kiple, "Slave Child Mortality"; see also Kiple and Himmelsteib King, *Another Dimension to the Black Diaspora*.

26. Wheaton et al., "Vaughan and Curriboo Plantations," 296–97.

27. Affleck, "On the Hygiene of Cotton Plantations and the Management of Negro Slaves."

28. Steckel, "Peculiar Population," 726. Growth is often measured in centiles (percentiles). Fifty percent of the population, in terms of height, is expected to be below the fiftieth centile, 90 percent below the ninetieth centile, and so forth.

The two-year age difference between boys and girls is normal; girls experience adolescence and its associated biological changes about two years earlier, on average, than boys. See also Steckel, "Women, Work, and Health under Plantation Slavery in the United States," 43–60.

When normal growth is interrupted by systemic disease or environmental conditions (often nutritional), it often resumes at a faster rate than the normal growth rate for age during remission. This accelerated growth phase is called the "catch-up growth" phenomenon (it is also called "compensatory growth"), which may or may not lead to normal size for age by the end of puberty.

29. Steckel, "Dreadful Childhood," 430. Steckel's data come largely from plantation records. For instance, his "Birth Weights and Infant Mortality among American Slaves" used data from "11 units that grew cotton, rice, or sugar in South Carolina, Georgia, Alabama, and Louisiana between 1786 and 1865." Throughout this paper he refers to several other sources of data, depending on the measures he is discussing.

30. Jellife, "Low Birth-Weight and Malarial Infection of the Placenta."

31. The data come from a compendium of causes of mortality done by DeBow, "Mortality Statistics, the Seventh Census," cited in Kiple and Kiple, "Slave Child Mortality," 298.

32. Carter, *Diary of Colonel Landon Carter of Sabine Hall, 1752–1778*, vol. 1, 205–6.

33. Marcus, "South's Native Foreigners."

34. Savitt, *Medicine and Slavery*.

35. Kelley and Angel, "Life Stresses of Slavery." They examined individuals from seven eighteenth-century Virginia sites and two from Maryland; one Maryland turn-of-the-nineteenth-century site; and four nineteenth-century Virginia sites

and nine from Maryland. The total sample was 92 adults from 25 sites. All but those from Catoctin Furnace, the turn-of-the-century site, were farm or plantation slaves.

36. Rathbun, "Health and Disease at a South Carolina Plantation." There were 13 males, 15 females, and 8 children.

37. Corruccini et al., "Osteology of a Slave Burial Population from Barbados, West Indies."

38. World Health Organization (WHO), "Under Five Mortality Rates."

Chapter 9. Measured Lands and Multitudes

1. For overviews of the early history of New York and the middle colonies, see Hoffer, *Brave New World*, 189–218; Taylor, *American Colonies*, 246–72.

The changing place of Charleston is evident when examining population trends. By 1800 Charleston had fallen to fifth place, and twenty-second place by 1860. In 1900, with a population of 55,807, it was the sixty-eighth-largest American city. While it remained a major economic port until the mid-nineteenth century, by 1900 the more industrial cities of the North had surpassed it economically (Coclanis, *Shadow of a Dream*, 115).

2. Unless otherwise noted, the discussions, statistics, and observations regarding New York health come from Duffy, *History of Public Health in New York City 1625–1866*. This book is essential for anyone interested in New York history, public health, or colonial health. The quote is from the *Daily Times*, June 8, 1853, cited in Duffy, *History of Public Health in New York City*, 377.

3. Records of New Amsterdam, I, 31, cited in Duffy, *History of Public Health in New York City*, 18.

4. Wood, *Black Majority*, appendix C, 341. The Middle Passage was the trip made from West Africa to the Caribbean by vessels transporting African slaves.

5. Duffy, *History of Public Health in New York City*, 54.

6. Alexander Colden to Cadwallader Colden, August 21, 1757, in *The Letters and Papers of Cadwallader Colden III, 1743–1747*, New York Historical Society Collections 1919, LII, New York, 1929, vol. 5176, cited in Duffy, *History of Public Health in New York City*, 57.

7. Measles mortality figures for New York City between 1840 and 1930 indicate a trend toward a more endemic situation, probably combined with malnutrition and lacking health care.

*1840–45 = 21.9/100,000
*1870 = 42.3/100,000
*1900 = 16.2/100,000
*1930 = 2.1/100,000

(Cliff et al., *Measles*)

8. There is some feeling that the modern form of diphtheria did not arise until quite late, one conjecture being 1857 (Duffy, *Epidemics in Colonial America*, 115). There remains quite a bit of disagreement over the earliest dates. Some say that the first epidemics recorded for the Americas occurred in 1659 in the eastern colonies, where diphtheria continued to appear in pockets throughout the 1700s, often causing several deaths within a town, often multiple deaths within a family, with most being children. Towns that remained unaffected neighbored others that were severely affected. Lionel Chalmers in his *Account of the Weather and Diseases of South Carolina* (1776) reported that "an angina resembling that which is called putrid, appears now and then amongst us, but never epidemically that I have observed." He noticed as well that it usually affected children under 10 or 12 years of age. Despite his feelings about epidemics, however, he described an epidemic that occurred during the fall of 1770 having all characteristics of diphtheria—inflammation of the throat, tonsils, and eustachian tubes; these parts gradually became ulcerated, which sometimes caused discharge from the nose, a hoarse voice, and an extremely fetid odor. When the infection spread down into the glottis, the patient died.

The key thing to understand about diphtheria is that in severe infections, the bacterium produces an extracellular substance called an exotoxin. Diphtheria exotoxin is a protein and stimulates the production of an antibody (antitoxin) that neutralizes the activity of the toxin. This is the critical factor in whether an individual will suffer more morbid consequences of the infection. People who have been exposed to the disease previously or who have been vaccinated usually produce the antitoxin on first exposure and therefore don't suffer the later problems of diphtheria. The importance of the toxin is that it is absorbed through the mucous membranes into the general circulation, and its two major actions are on the heart and the peripheral nerves, although other organs can be affected. Heart failure due to myocarditis is the most common cause of death following diphtheria. Neurologic complications can set in as late as a month or six weeks after the onset of the infection. Antitoxin is carried across the placental boundary from mother to child, and this protects the child for a period of a few weeks.

Not all diphtheria bacilli produce the toxin, and so outbreaks of epidemics require basically three things: a carrier who has a virulent strain, a supply of susceptible persons, and close association of persons. In epidemics of diphtheria, clinical disease occurs in both vaccinated and unvaccinated persons. Thus, vaccination does not necessarily prevent the development of infection and the disease. This should be expected, since the bacillus has the capacity to invade and multiply and bring about pseudomembrane formation independent of its capacity to produce exotoxin. Of particular importance, however, is the fact that mortality from the disease in epidemics is found almost exclusively among the unvaccinated.

9. Johnston, page 99, cited in Wood, *Black Majority*, 77.

10. Duffy, *Epidemics in Colonial America*, 212–13.

11. An excellent historical source for malaria in the interior is by Drake, *Malaria in the Interior Valley of America.*

12. The quote is from Commission of Medical Officers, *Report of the Commission of Medical Officers Detailed by Authority of the President to Investigate the Cause of Yellow Fever.*

For further reading on yellow fever, see La Roche, *Yellow Fever, Considered in Its Historical, Pathological, Etiological, and Therapeutical Relations*; Humphreys, *Yellow Fever and the South*; Warren, "Landmarks in the Conquest of Yellow Fever"; Ashburn, *Ranks of Death*, 30; Patterson, "Yellow Fever Epidemics and Mortality in the United States, 1693–1905"; Keating, *Yellow Fever Epidemic of 1878, in Memphis, Tennessee*; Carrigan, "Yellow Fever."

Diseases often confused with yellow fever are infectious hepatitis, leptospirosis (Weil's disease), dengue, malaria, smallpox (before the rash), influenza, measles, dysentery, plague, typhus, scurvy, and many of the tickborne diseases (Carter, *Yellow Fever*). The two diseases that most closely mimic yellow fever for the modern doctor, however, are dengue (carried by the same mosquito) and rift valley fever (Tholler, "Virus"). Once the disease has been survived, lasting immunity is conferred on the individual.

13. Winslow, *Conquest of Epidemic Disease*, 211.

14. The suggestion that a mosquito might be the vector of yellow fever was first made by Dr. Josiah Noh of Mobile in 1848, followed by Dr. Louis Beauperthuy in Venezuela in 1854. It was a paper by Dr. Carlos J. Finlay of Havana, Cuba, in 1888, however, which contributed finally to the investigation of mosquitoes. Ultimately, the loss of military forces to yellow fever in Havana prompted the assignment of J. Walter Reed and a team of investigators from the United States Army Hospital staff to Havana in 1900. After quickly eliminating bacterial causes from the possible etiology of the illness, they began investigating mosquitoes following the previous suggestion of Finlay. Members of the team allowed themselves to be bitten by mosquitoes that had bitten yellow-fever patients and in all cases succumbed to yellow fever.

For two more years the team worked at Camp Leazar, named for the first casualty from the team, to fully investigate other possible vectors. In 1902 they were able to announce that the vector of yellow fever is the mosquito *Aedes aegypti*; we now know there are other species as well. Probably the most successful test occurred in 1901, when the swamps and low-lying areas were drained in Havana. Campaigns were made to eliminate all breeding places for mosquitoes. The number of yellow fever cases declined dramatically, and within a short period of time only a few remained. Panama was the next target for drainage of swampy areas, and these two cases of reproductive prophylaxis were overwhelmingly successful in controlling yellow fever.

15. Duffy, *History of Public Health in New York City*, 35.

16. Patterson, "Yellow Fever Epidemics and Mortality in the United States, 1693–1905," table in footnote 40.

17. Rush, "Yellow Fever."

18. Duffy, *History of Public Health in New York City*, 107.

19. Foster et al., "Philadelphia Yellow Fever Epidemic of 1793," 91.

20. Jones, *Narrative of the Proceedings of the Black People during the Late Awful Calamity in Philadelphia in the Year 1793*.

21. Hoffer, *Brave New World*, 203.

22. Rankin-Hill et al., "Demographic Overview of the African Burial Ground and Colonial Africans of New York."

In total, 419 skeletons were excavated from less than a city block, a fraction of those who were buried in the 5.5–6 acres of land the cemetery once occupied. Of those excavated, 301 had sufficient preservation for analysis. Subadults constituted 43 percent of the sample, adults 57 percent.

An excellent television documentary on the African Burial Ground is *Slavery's Buried Past*, from the series *The New Explorers* by Bill Curtis, 1996.

23. A summary of the information learned from the African Burial Ground can be found in Barrett and Blakey, *Life Histories of Enslaved Africans in Colonial New York*.

Original data reports and discussions pertinent to the information presented in this discussion come from Blakey et al., "Discussion." See also Null et al., "Osteological Indicators of Infectious Disease and Nutritional Inadequacy"; Blakey et al., "Childhood Health and Dental Development."

24. Gates and Andrews, "Life, History and Unparalleled Sufferings of John Jea, the African Preacher." Another informative volume is Berlin and Harris, *Slavery in New York*.

25. Duffy, *History of Public Health in New York City*, 183.

26. Duffy, *History of Public Health in New York City*, 260. John Duffy gives mortality figures for the nineteenth century, and I have seen no earlier ones.

27. Duffy, *History of Public Health in New York City*, 274.

28. Benjamin W. McCready, *On the Influence of Trades, Professions and Occupations, New York*, cited in Duffy, *History of Public Health in New York City*, 525.

29. Duffy, *History of Public Health in New York City*, 525.

30. Griscom, *Sanitary Condition of the Laboring Population of New York, with Suggestions for Its Improvement*, 4–5.

31. Griscom, *Sanitary Condition of the Laboring Population of New York, with Suggestions for Its Improvement*, 4, 6, 7, 10.

32. Duffy, *History of Public Health in New York City*, 257–61.

33. The history of cholera prior to 1817 is sketchy, and while there is little doubt that it has occurred for a lengthy period of time, exact references are unclear. There are a few accounts of diseases characterized by diarrhea and rapid death in Portu-

guese explorers' accounts of the 1500s (Correia and Garcia da Orta). Cholera seems to have long been endemic in the Ganges River Delta of India and Bangladesh. Since 1817 it has spread outside of India, and most agree that there have been seven pandemics of cholera recorded since that time. The first six of the outbreaks were due to the classic strain of cholera, 01, but the seventh was a new strain called El Tor. The 1991 epidemic was marked by yet another new strain, 0139.

Treatment of cholera is relatively simple. Provide a mixture of glucose and salts in the right balance, and the nutrients can both be tolerated. This simple solution, however, was not discovered until 1964, and since then, it has saved countless lives.

It turns out that *Vibrio cholerae* live in mildly salty, nutrient-rich water as normal flora. They do not make cholera toxin, however, and at some distant time in the past acquired the right DNA combination to turn a normal and benign estuarine bacterium into the more deadly one that it is now.

34. Duffy, *History of Public Health in New York City*, 259. Humphreys debates, however, the antiquity of typhus in the colonies (Humphreys, "Stranger in Our Camps").

35. B. W. McCready, letter reported in Griscom, *Sanitary Condition of the Laboring Population*, 18.

36. Duffy, *History of Public Health in New York City*, 447.

37. Higgins and Sirianni, "An Assessment of Health and Mortality of Nineteenth Century Rochester"; Sutter, "Dental Pathologies among Inmates of the Monroe County Poorhouse." The ranges given for cause of death reflect differences between figures given in the Brighton town clerk's records and those from the Mt. Hope Cemetery records.

38. Census records from 1838 kept by the Pennsylvania Abolition Society, City of Philadelphia cemetery returns, and Savitt, *Medicine and Slavery*.

39. There were 75 adults, about evenly divided between the two sexes, 33 infants under one year of age, and 27 children. Angel et al., "Life Stresses of the Free Black Community as Represented by the First African Baptist Church, Philadelphia, 1823–1841"; Rankin-Hill, *Biohistory of 19th Century Afro-Americans*; see also Roberts and McCarthy, "Descendant Community Partnering in the Archaeological and Bioanthropological Investigation of African-American Skeletal Populations."

Angel et al., "Life Stresses," cite an anemia figure of 70 percent. Rankin-Hill, *Biohistory*, cites a figure for anemia of 53 percent. It is not uncommon for researchers to cite different figures based on sample differences or different criteria for inclusion or exclusion of certain individuals. In either case, over half of the people in the cemetery experienced anemia.

40. Ubelaker et al., *Human Remains from Voegtly Cemetery, Pittsburgh, Pennsylvania*. The average age at death as determined from study of skeletons was 37 for females and 38 for males. The reason the ages are higher for the skeletons than for the historical records is that it is difficult to estimate sex from the skeletal remains of children. Consequently, the majority of the sample, those who died prior to

about age 15, are lost from those used to estimate age of death in sex-differentiated categories.

Cause of death was listed for only 151 of the individuals. Causes of death are listed selectively here. For the entire list, see Ubelaker et al., *Human Remains from Voegtly Cemetery*, 21.

41. Condran, "Changing Patterns of Epidemic Disease in New York City," 33.

Epilogue

1. Most information cited in this discussion comes from two sources: Crosby, *Epidemic and Peace, 1918*; Hoehling, *Great Epidemic*. The specific quantitative figures cited here are from Crosby, "Virgin Soil Epidemics," 206–7.

2. Ewald theorizes that the type of pathogen transmission has a lot to do with pathogen virulence. Transmission routes such as arthropod vectors or artificial vectors such as ambulances enable more virulent forms of pathogens to evolve, because the mobility of the host is not required for their transmission (Ewald, *Evolution of Infectious Disease*).

3. Taubenberger et al., "Initial Genetic Characterization of the 1918 'Spanish' Influenza Virus"; Tumpey et al., "Characterization of the Reconstructed 1918 Spanish Influenza Pandemic Virus"; Taubenberger and Reid, "Archaeovirology."

4. Webster, "Influenza"; Webster and Walker, "Influenza": "The world is teetering on the edge of a pandemic that could kill a large fraction of the human population."

5. Wills, *Yellow Fever, Black Goddess*.

Primary Sources

Affleck, Thomas. "On the Hygiene of Cotton Plantations and the Management of Negro Slaves." *Southern Medical Reports* 2 (1851): 429–36.

Anderson, Mary. "Narrative of Mary Anderson, near Raleigh, North Carolina." In *When I Was a Slave: Memoirs from the Slave Narrative Collection*, edited by Norman R. Yetman, 1–5. Mineola, NY: Dover, 2002.

Baird, Charles W. *History of the Huguenot Emigration to America, II.* New York: Dodd, Mead, 1885.

Barnwell, John. 1908. "The Tuscarora Expedition: Letters of Colonel John Barnwell." *South Carolina Historical and Genealogical Magazine* 9: 28–54.

Bartram, William. *Travels through North and South Carolina, Georgia, East and West Florida, the Cherokee Country, the Extensive Territories of the Muscogulges, or Creek Confederacy, and the Country of the Choctaws.* New York: Dover, 1988 [Reprint of 1791].

Beverly, Robert. *The History and Present State of Virginia.* Chapel Hill: University of North Carolina Press, 1947.

Biggar, Herbert. P. *The Works of Samuel de Champlain.* 6 vols. Toronto: Champlain Society, 1922–36.

Blanton, Wyndham B. *Medicine in Virginia in the Seventeenth Century.* Richmond, VA: William Byrd Press, 1930.

Boccaccio, Giovanni. *The Decameron.* New York: Dell, 1973.

Carter, Landon. *The Diary of Colonel Landon Carter of Sabine Hall, 1752–1778,* vol. 1. Edited by Jack P. Greene, 205–6. Richmond: Virginia Historical Society, William Byrd Press, 1965.

Cartier, Jacques. "A Memoir of Jacques Cartier, Sieur de Limoilou, His Voyages to the St. Lawrence, a Bibliography and a Facsimile of the Manuscript of 1534." Excerpted in *Interpreting a Continent: Voices from Colonial America*, edited by Kathleen DuVal and John DuVal, 24–29. Lanham, MD: Rowman and Littlefield, 2009.

Chalmers, Lionel. *Account of the Weather and Diseases of South Carolina*. London: Edward and Charles Dilly, 1776.

Chaucer, Geoffrey. *The Canterbury Tales: A Selection*. Edited by Donald R. Howard. New York: Signet Books, 1969.

Chilam Balam of Chumayel. *The Book of Chilam Balam of Chumayel*. Translated by Ralph L. Roys. Norman: University of Oklahoma Press, 1967.

Commission of Medical Officers. *Report of the Commission of Medical Officers Detailed by Authority of the President to Investigate the Cause of Yellow Fever*. Washington, DC: Government Printing Office, 1899.

Cooper, James Fenimore. *The Last of the Mohicans: A Narrative of 1757*. New York: Harper and Row, 1965 [Reprint of 1826].

Corney, B. G. "The Behaviour of Certain Epidemic Diseases in Natives of Polynesia with Special Reference to Fiji." *Epidemiological Society of London Transactions (New Series)* 3 (1883): 76–94.

Cortés, Hernan. *Letters from Mexico*. Translated and edited by Anthony R. Pagden. New York: Grossman, 1971.

Davis, Richard Beale, ed. *William Fitzhugh and His Chesapeake World, 1676–1701: The Fitzhugh Letters and Other Documents*. Chapel Hill: University of North Carolina Press, 1963.

De Bow, James D. B. "Plantation Management-police." *De Bow's Review, Agricultural, Commercial, Industrial Progress, and Resources* 14 (1853): 175–81.

Doar, David. *Rice and Rice Planting in the South Carolina Low Country*. Contributions from the Charleston Museum VIII, Charleston, South Carolina, 1936.

Drake, Daniel. *Malaria in the Interior Valley of America*. Originally published as *A Systematic Treatise, Historical, Etiological, and Practical on the Principal Diseases of the Interior Valley of North America as they appear in the Caucasian, African, Indian, and Esquimaux Varieties of Its Population*. Urbana: University of Illinois Press, 1964 [Reprint of 1850].

Finnley, John. "Narrative of John Finnley, Fort Worth, Texas." In *When I Was a Slave: Memoirs from the Slave Narrative Collection*, edited by Norman R. Yetman, 39–42. Mineola, NY: Dover, 2002.

Frethorne, Richard. Letter to his father and mother, March 20, April 2 and 3, 1623. In *The Records of the Virginia Company of London*, edited by Susan Kingsbury, vol. 4, 58–62. Washington, DC: U.S. Government Printing Office, 1906–35.

Glenn, Robert. "Narrative of Robert Glenn, Raleigh, North Carolina." In *When I Was a Slave: Memoirs from the Slave Narrative Collection*, edited by Norman R. Yetman, 46–51. Mineola, NY: Dover, 2002.

Granberry, Mary Ella. "Narrative of Mary Ella Grandberry, Sheffield, Alabama. In *When I Was a Slave: Memoirs from the Slave Narrative Collection*, edited by Norman R. Yetman, 61–62. Mineola, NY: Dover, 2002.

Griscom, John H. *The Sanitary Condition of the Laboring Population of New York, with Suggestions for Its Improvement*. A discourse delivered on the 30th December 1844, at the Repository of the American Institute, Harper Brothers, New York. Republished by Arno Press, New York, 1970 [Reprint of 1845].

Hariot, Thomas. *A Brief and True Report of the New Found Land of Virginia*. New York: Dover, 1972 [Reprint of 1590].

Hrdlička, A. *Tuberculosis among Certain Indian Tribes*. Bureau of American Ethnology Report No. 34, Washington, DC: Government Printing Office, 1908.

Hulton, Paul. *America 1585: The Complete Drawings of John White*. Chapel Hill: University of North Carolina Press, 1984.

Jackson, Silas. "Narrative of Silas Jackson, Baltimore, Maryland." In *When I Was a Slave: Memoirs from the Slave Narrative Collection*, edited by Norman R. Yetman, 73–76. Mineola, NY: Dover, 2002.

Jenner, Edward. *An inquiry into the Causes and Effects of* Variolae Vaccinae, *a Disease, Discovered in Some of the Western Counties of England, Particularly Gloucestershire, and Known by the Name of Cow Pox*. London: Sampson Low, 1798.

Jones, Absalom. *A Narrative of the Proceedings of the Black People during the Late Awful Calamity in Philadelphia in the Year 1793, and a Refutation of Some Censures Thrown upon Them in Some Late Publications*. Philadelphia: Independence National Historic Park, 1969.

Keating, John M. *The Yellow Fever Epidemic of 1878, in Memphis, Tennessee*. Memphis: Howard Association, 1879.

Kimball, Gertrude Selwyn, ed. *Correspondence of William Pitt When Secretary of State with Colonial Governors and Military and Naval Commissioners in America*. New York: Macmillan, 1906.

Knox, John. *An Historical Journal of the Campaigns in North America for the Years 1757, 1758, 1759, and 1760*. Edited with introduction, appendix, and index by Arthur G. Doughty. Toronto: Champlain Society, 1914–16.

Lahontan, Baron Louis-Armand de Lom d'Ares. *New Voyages to North-America*, vol. 2. Chicago: A. C. McClurg, 1905 [Reprint of 1703].

Lalemont, Jérôme. "Relation of 1640." *Jesuit Relations* 19: 8–93.

La Roche, Réné. *Yellow Fever, Considered in Its Historical, Pathological, Etiological, and Therapeutical Relations*. 2 vols. Philadelphia: Blanchard and Lea, 1855.

Lauber, Almond Wheeler. *Indian Slavery in Colonial Times within the Present Limits of the United States*. Williamston, MA: Corner House, 1979 [Reprint of 1913].

Le Jeune, Paul. "Relation of 1634." *Jesuit Relations* 7: 106–15.

Le Mercier, François. "Relation of 1637." *Jesuit Relations* 13: 98–105.

López de Gómara, Francisco. *Cortés: The Life of the Conquerer by His Secretary*. Translated and edited by Lesley Byrd Simpson. Berkeley: University of California Press, 1965.

Mussi, Gabriele de'. *Historia de Morbo*. Translated and published in A. W. Henschel, *Document zur Geschichte des schwarzen Todes, Archives für die gesamte Medizin* 2 (1841): 26–59.

Percy, George. *Observations Gathered out of "A Discourse of the Plantation of the Southern Colony in Virginia by the English, 1606" Written by the Honorable Gentleman, Master George Percy.* Edited by David B. Quinn. Charlottesville: University Press of Virginia, 1967.

———. "A True Relation of the Proceedings and Occurrences of Moment which have happened in Virginia from the Time Sir Thomas Gates was shipwrecked upon the Bermudas, anno 1609, until my departure out of the Country which was in anno Domini 1612." In *The Jamestown Adventure: Accounts of the Virginia Colony, 1605–1614*, edited by Ed Southern, 21–36. Winston-Salem, NC: John Blair, 2004.

Procopius. *The Wars of Justinian.* Translated by H. B. Dewing and revised and modernized with a new introduction by Anthony Kaldellis. Indianapolis: Hackett, 2014.

Ragueneau, Paul. "Relation of 1648–1649." *Jesuit Relations* 34: 122–37.

Rāzī, Abū Bakr Muhammad ibn Zakarīyā. *A Treatise on the Small-pox and Measles.* Translated by William A. Greenhill. London: C. and J. Adlard, 1848.

Rush, Benjamin. "The Yellow Fever: Some Family Letters (1793)." In *Selected Writings of Benjamin Rush*, edited by Dagobert D. Runes, 404–15. New York: Philosophical Library, 1947.

Sagard, Gabriel. *Histoire du Canada et voyages que les Frères mineurs recollects y ont faicts pour la conversion desl infidèles depuis l'an 1615 . . . avec un dictionnaire del la langue huronne.* 4 volumes with consecutive pagination. Paris: Edwin Tross, 1866.

Shepherd, Robert. "Narrative of Robert Shepherd." In *When I Was a Slave: Memoirs from the Slave Narrative Collection*, edited by Norman R. Yetman, 117–22. Mineola, NY: Dover, 2002.

Smith, John. *The Complete Works of Captain John Smith, 1580–1631.* Edited by Philip L. Barbour. Chapel Hill: University of North Carolina Press, 1986.

Thwaites, Reuben Gold, ed. *The Jesuit Relations and Allied Documents: Travels and Explorations of the Jesuit Missionaries in New France 1610–1791.* 73 vols. Cleveland: Burrows Brothers, 1896–1901.

Van den Bogaert, Harmen M. *A Journey into Mohawk and Oneida Country, 1634–1635.* Translated and edited by Charles T. Gehring and William A. Starna. Syracuse: Syracuse University Press, 1988.

Wyatt, Francis. "Letter of Sir Francis Wyatt, Governor of Virginia, 1621–1626." *William and Mary Quarterly*, ser. 2, 6 (1926): 117.

Yetman, Norman, ed. *When I Was a Slave: Memoirs from the Slave Narrative Collection.* Mineola, NY: Dover, 2002.

Secondary Sources

Alchon, Susan Austin. *A Pest in the Land: New World Epidemics in a Global Perspective*. Albuquerque: University of New Mexico Press, 2003.

Allison, Marvin J., Daniel Mendoza, and Alejandro Pezzia. "Documentation of a Case of Tuberculosis in Pre-Columbian America." *American Review of Respiratory Diseases* 107 (1973): 985–91.

Anderson, Fred. *Crucible of War*. New York: Vintage Books, 2000.

Angel, J. Lawrence, Jennifer Olsen Kelley, Michael Parrington, and Stephanie Pinter. "Life Stresses of the Free Black Community as Represented by the First African Baptist Church, Philadelphia, 1823–1841." *American Journal of Physical Anthropology* 74, no. 2 (1987): 213–30.

Antoine, Daniel. "The Archaeology of 'Plague.'" *Medical History Supplement No. 27* (2008): 101–14.

Armitage, Phillip, Barbara West, and Ken Steedman. "New Evidence of the Black Rat in Roman London." *London Archaeologist* 4 (1984): 375–83.

Arriaza, Bernardo T. *Beyond Death: The Chinchorro Mummies of Ancient Chile*. Washington, DC: Smithsonian Institution Press, 1995.

Ashburn, Frank D. *The Ranks of Death: A Medical History of the Conquest of America*. New York: Howard-McCann, 1947.

Askew, Susan. "Neoheroka Fort." *ECU Report* 26 (Feb. 1995).

Balicki, Joseph F. "Wharves, Privies, and the Pewterer: Two Colonial Period Sites on the Shawmut Peninsula, Boston." *Historical Archaeology* 32 (1998): 99–120.

Barker, David J. P. *Mothers, Babies, and Disease in Later Life*. London: BMJ, 1994.

———. "Fetal Origins of Coronary Heart Disease." *British Medical Journal* 311 (1995): 171–74.

Barrett, Autumn R., and Michael L. Blakey. "Life Histories of Enslaved Africans in Colonial New York: A Bioarchaeological Study of the New York African Burial Ground." In *Social Bioarchaeology*, edited by Sabrina C. Agarwal and Bonnie A. Glencross, 212–51 London: Blackwell, 2011.

Berlin, Ira, and Leslie M. Harris. *Slavery in New York*. New York: New Press, 2005.

Biagini, Phillipe, Catherine Thèves, Patricia Balaresque, Annie Géraut, Catherine Cannet, et al. "Variola Virus in a 300-Year-Old Siberian Mummy." *New England Journal of Medicine* 367 (2012): 2057–59 doi: 10.1056.

Bianucci, Raffaella, Lila Rahalison, Emma Rabino Massa, Alberto Peluso, Ezio Ferroglio, et al. "Technical Note: A Rapid Diagnostic Test Detects Plague in Ancient Human Remains: An Example of the Interaction between Archeological and Biological Approaches (Southeastern France, 16th–18th Centuries)." *American Journal of Physical Anthropology* 136 (2008): 361–67.

Bianucci, Raffaella, Lila Rahalison, Alberto Peluso, Emma Rabino Massa, Michel Signoli, et al. "Plague Immunodetection in Remains of Religious Exhumed from Burial Sites in Central France." *Journal of Archaeological Science* 36 (2009): 616–21.

Blakey, Michael L., Lesley M. Rankin-Hill, Alan Goodman, and Fatimah Jackson. "Discussion." In *The New York African Burial Ground Skeletal Biology Final Report*, vol. 1, edited by Michael L. Blakey and Lesley M. Rankin-Hill, 541–56. Report to the United States General Services Administration, Northeastern and Caribbean Region [available online], 2004.

Blakey, Michael L., Mark Mack, Autumn R. Barrett, S. S. Mahoney, and Alan H. Goodman. "Childhood Health and Dental Development." In *The New York African Burial Ground Skeletal Biology Final Report Volume 1*, edited by Michael L. Blakey and Lesley M. Rankin-Hill, 306–31. Report to the United States General Services Administration, Northeastern and Caribbean Region [available online], 2004.

Borneman, Walter R. *The French and Indian War*. New York: Harper, 2006.

Bos, Kirsten I., Verena J. Schuenemann, G. Brian Golding, Hernán A. Burbano, Nicholas Waglechner, et al. "A Draft Genome of *Yersinia pestis* from Victims of the Black Death." *Nature* 478 (2011): 506–10.

Braun, Mark, Della C. Cook, and Susan Pfeiffer. "DNA from *Mycobacterium tuberculosis* Complex Identified in North American, Pre-Columbian Human Skeletal Remains." *Journal of Archaeological Science* 25 (1998): 271–77.

Braund, Kathryn F. *Deerskins and Duffels*. 2nd ed. Lincoln: University of Nebraska Press, 2008.

Breen, Timothy H., and Timothy Hall. *Colonial America in an Atlantic World*. New York: Pearson and Longman, 2004.

Breen, Timothy H., and Stephen Innes. *Myne Owne Ground: Race and Freedom on Virginia's Eastern Shore, 1640–1676*. New York: Oxford University Press, 2005.

Brosch, Roland, Stephen. V. Gordon, Magali Marmiesse, Priscille Brodin, Carmen Buchrieser, et al. "A New Evolutionary Scenario for the *Mycobacterium tuberculosis* Complex." *Proceedings of the National Academy of Sciences, USA* 99 (2002): 3684–89.

Buikstra, Jane E., ed. *Prehistoric Tuberculosis in the Americas*. Evanston, IL: Northwestern University Archeological Program, 1981.

———. "Diseases of the Pre-Columbian Americas." In *The Cambridge World History of Human Disease*, edited by Kenneth F. Kiple, 305–17. Cambridge: Cambridge University Press, 1993.

———. "Introduction." In *Prehistoric Tuberculosis in the Americas*, edited by Jane E. Buikstra, 1–23. Evanston, IL: Northwestern University Archeological Program, 1981.

Burnet, Frank M., and David O. White. *Natural History of Infectious Disease*, 4th ed. Cambridge: Cambridge University Press, 1972.

Bushnell, George E. *A Study in the Epidemiology of Tuberculosis*. New York: William Wood, 1920.

Byrne, Joseph P. *The Black Death*. Westport, CT: Greenwood Press, 2004.

Cantor, Norman F. *In the Wake of the Plague: The Black Death and the World It Made*. New York: Free Press, 2001.

Carmichael, Ann G. "Universal and Particular: The Language of Plague, 1348–1500. *Medical History Supplement No. 27* (2008): 17–52.

Carnes-McNaughton, Linda F., and Terry M. Harper. "The Parity of Privies: Summary Research on Privies in North Carolina." *Historical Archaeology* 34 (2000): 97–110.

Carney, Judith A. *Black Rice: The African Origins of Rice Cultivation in the Americas*. Cambridge, MA: Harvard University Press, 2001.

Carpenter, Stanley J., and Walter J. LaCasse. *Mosquitoes of North America (North of Mexico)*. Berkeley: University of California Press, 1955.

Carpenter, Stanley J., Woodrow W. Middlekauff, and Roy W. Chamberlain. "The Mosquitoes of the Southern United States East of Oklahoma and Texas." *American Midland Naturalist Monograph Series* No. 3. South Bend, IN: Notre Dame University Press, 1946.

Carrigan, Jo Ann. "Yellow Fever: Scourge of the South." In *Disease and Distinctiveness in the American South*, edited by Todd L. Savitt and James Harvey Young, 55–78. Knoxville: University of Tennessee Press, 1988.

Carson, Cary, Norman F. Barka, William M. Kelso, Garry Wheeler Stone, and Dell Upton. "Impermanent Architecture in the Southern American Colonies." *Winterthur Portfolio* 16, no. 2/3, (1981): 140–96.

Carter, Henry Rose. *Yellow Fever: An Epidemiological and Historical Study of the Place of Origin*, Baltimore: Williams and Wilkins, 1931.

Centurion-Lara, Arturo, Christina Castro, Raphael Castillo, Jeanne M. Shaffer, Wesley C. Van Voorhis, et al. "The Flanking Region Sequences of the 15-k-Da Lipoprotein Gene Differentiate Pathogenic Treponemes." *Journal of Infectious Diseases* 177 (1998): 1036–40.

Chapman, Jefferson, and Patty Jo Watson. "The Archaic Period and the Flotation Revolution." In *Foraging and Farming in the Eastern Woodlands*, edited by C. Margaret Scarry, 27–38. Gainesville: University Press of Florida, 1993.

Cliff, Andrew, Peter Haggett, and Matthew Smallman-Raynor. *Measles: An Historical Geography of a Major Human Viral Disease from Global Expansion to Local Retreat, 1840–1990*. Oxford: Blackwell Reference, 1933.

Cockburn, Aiden. *The Evolution and Eradication of Infectious Diseases*. Baltimore: Johns Hopkins University Press, 1963.

Coclanis, Peter A. *The Shadow of a Dream: Economic Life and Death in the South Carolina Low Country, 1670–1920*. Oxford: Oxford University Press, 1989.

Cohen, Mark N., and George J. Armelagos. *Paleopathology at the Origins of Agriculture*. Orlando: Academic Press, 1984.

Cohen, Mark N., and Gillian Crane-Kramer. *Ancient Health: Skeletal Indicators of Agricultural and Economic Intensification.* Gainesville: University Press of Florida, 2007.

Cohn, Samuel K. *The Black Death Transformed: Disease and Culture in Early Renaissance Europe.* London: Arnold, 2002.

———. "Epidemiology of the Black Death and Successive Waves of Plague. *Medical History Supplement No. 27* (2008): 74–100.

Coimbra, Carlos E. A. "Human Settlements, Demographic Pattern, and Epidemiology in Lowland Amazonia: The Case of Chagas's Disease." *American Anthropologist* 90 (1988): 82–97.

Condran, Gretchen A. "Changing Patterns of Epidemic Disease in New York City." In *Hives of Sickness: Public Health and Epidemics in New York City*, edited by David Rosner, 27–41. New Brunswick, NJ: Rutgers University Press, 1995.

Cook, Noble David. *Born to Die: Disease and New World Conquest, 1492–1650.* Cambridge: Cambridge University Press, 1998.

———. *Demographic Collapse, Indian Peru, 1520–1620.* New York: Cambridge University Press, 1981.

Cook, Noble David, and W. George Lovell, eds. *Secret Judgments of God: Native Peoples and Old World Disease in Colonial Spanish America.* Norman: University of Oklahoma Press, 1992.

Corruccini, Robert S., Jerome S. Handler, F. J. Mutaw, and Frederick W. Lange. "Osteology of a Slave Burial Population from Barbados, West Indies." *American Journal of Physical Anthropology* 59 (1982): 443–59.

Covey, Herbert C., and Dwight Eisnach. *What the Slaves Ate: Recollections of African American Foods and Foodways from the Slave Narratives.* Santa Barbara, CA: Greenwood Press, 2009.

Cowan, C. Wesley, and Patty Jo Watson. *The Origins of Agriculture: An International Perspective.* Washington, DC: Smithsonian Institution Press, 1992.

Cowdrey, Albert E. *This Land, This South: An Environmental History.* Revised ed. Lexington: University Press of Kentucky, 1996.

Crist, Thomas A. "Babies in the Privy: Prostitution, Infanticide, and Abortion in New York City's Five Points District." *Historical Archaeology* 39 (2005): 19–46.

Cronon, William. *Changes in the Land: Indians, Colonists, and the Ecology of New England.* New York: Farrar, Strauss, and Giroux, 1983.

Crosby, Alfred W. *America's Forgotten Pandemic: The Influenza of 1918.* 2nd ed. Cambridge: Cambridge University Press, 2003.

———. *The Columbian Exchange: Biological and Cultural Consequences of 1492.* Westport, CT: Greenwood, 1972.

———. "Conquistador y Pestilencia: The First New World Pandemic and the Fall of the Great Indian Empires." *Hispanic American Historical Review* 157 (1967): 321–37.

————. *Ecological Imperialism*. Cambridge: Cambridge University Press, 1986.

————. *Epidemic and Peace, 1918*. Westport, CT: Greenwood, 1976.

————. "Influenza." In *The Cambridge Historical Dictionary of Disease*, edited by Kenneth F. Kiple, 178–81. Cambridge: Cambridge University Press, 2003.

————. "Smallpox." In *The Cambridge World History of Human Disease*, edited by Kenneth F. Kiple, 1008–13. Cambridge: Cambridge University Press, 1993.

————. "Virgin Soil Epidemics as a Factor in the Aboriginal Depopulation of America." *William and Mary Quarterly* 33 (1976): 284–93.

Cummins, Stevenson L. *Primitive Tuberculosis*. London: John Bale Medical Publications, 1939.

Deetz, James F. *Flowerdew Hundred: The Archaeology of a Virginia Plantation, 1619–1864*. Charlottesville: University Press of Virginia, 1993.

Desowitz, Robert S. *New Guinea Tapeworms and Jewish Grandmothers: Tales of Parasites and People*. New York: W. W. Norton, 1987.

DeWitte, Sharon, and G. Hughes-Morey. "Stature and Frailty during the Black Death: The Effect of Stature on Risks of Epidemic Mortality in London, A.D. 1348–1350." *Journal of Archaeological Science* 39 (2012): 1412–19.

DeWitte, Sharon, and Philip Slavin. "Between Famine and Death: Physiological Stress and Dairy Deficiency in England on the Eve of the Black Death: New Evidence from Paleoepidemiology and Manorial Accounts." *Journal of Interdisciplinary History* 44 (2013): 37–61.

Diamond, Jared. *Guns, Germs, and Steel: The Fates of Human Societies*. New York: W. W. Norton, 1999.

Dirks, Robert. "Famine and Disease." In *The Cambridge World History of Human Disease*, edited by Kenneth F. Kiple, 157–63. Cambridge: Cambridge University Press, 1993.

Dixon, Cyril W. *Smallpox*. London: J. and A. Churchill, 1962.

Dobyns, Henry F. "Disease Transfer at Contact." *Annual Review of Anthropology* 22 (1993): 273–91.

————. "Estimating Aboriginal American Population: An Appraisal of Techniques with a New Hemispheric Estimate." *Current Anthropology* 7 (1966): 395–449.

————. *Their Number Become Thinned: Native American Population Dynamics in Eastern North America*. Knoxville: University of Tennessee Press, 1983.

Donoghue, Helen D. "Insights into Ancient Leprosy and Tuberculosis Using Metagenomics." *Trends in Microbiology* 21 (2013): 448–50.

Drancourt, Michael, G. Aboudharam, Michel Signoli, Olivier Dutour, and Didier Raoult. "Detection of 400-Year-Old *Yersinia pestis* DNA in Human Dental Pulp: An Approach to the Diagnosis of Ancient Septicemia." *Proceedings of the National Academy of Science* 95 (1998): 12637–40.

Drancourt, Michael, Michel Signoli, La Vu Dang, Bruno Bizot, Véronique Roux, et al. "*Yersinia pestis Orientalis* in Remains of Ancient Plague Victims." *Emerging Infectious Diseases* 13 (2007): 332–33.

Dubisch, Jill. "Low Country Fevers: Cultural Adaptations to Malaria in Antebellum South Carolina." *Social Science and Medicine* 21 (1985): 641–49.

Dubos, Rene, and Jean Dubos. *The White Plague*. New Brunswick, NJ: Rutgers University Press, 1996.

Duffy, John. *Epidemics in Colonial America*. Baton Rouge: Louisiana University Press, 1953.

———. *A History of Public Health in New York City 1625–1866*. New York: Russell Sage Foundation, 1968.

Dutour, Olivier, György Pálfi, Jacques Berato, and Jean-Pierre Brun, eds. *L'Origine de la syphilis en Europe: Avant ou après 1493?* Paris: Editions Errance, 1994.

Eccles, William J. "The Fur Trade in the Colonial Northeast." In *Handbook of North American Indians*. Vol. 4, *History of Indian–White Relations*, edited by Wilcolm Washburn, 324–34. Washington, DC: Smithsonian Institution Press, 1988.

Edelson, Samuel M. *Plantation Enterprise in Colonial South Carolina*. Cambridge, MA: Harvard University Press, 2006.

Ellison, Peter T. "Evolutionary Perspectives on the Fetal Origins Hypothesis." *American Journal of Human Biology* 17 (2005): 113–18.

Erickson, Clark. "Agricultural Landscapes as World Heritage: Raised Field Agriculture in Bolivia and Peru." In *Managing Change: Sustainable Approaches to the Conservation of the Built Environment*, edited by Jeanne-Marie Teutonico and Frank Matero, 181–204. Los Angeles: Getty Conservation Institute, 2003.

———. "The Lake Titicaca Basin: A Precolumbian Built Landscape." In *Imperfect Balance: Landscape Transformation in the Precolumbian Americas*, edited by David Lentz, 311–56. New York: Columbia University Press, 2000.

Eshed, Vered, Avi Gopher, Ron Pinhasi, and Israel Hershkovitz. "Paleopathology and the Origin of Agriculture in the Levant." *American Journal of Physical Anthropology* 143 (2010): 121–33.

Ethridge, Robbie. "Introduction: Mapping the Mississippian Shatter Zone." In *Mapping the Mississippian Shatter Zone*, edited by Robbie Ethridge and Sheri M. Shuck-Hall, 1–62. Lincoln: University of Nebraska Press, 2009.

Ewald, Paul W. *The Evolution of Infectious Disease*. New York: Oxford University Press, 1994.

Fisher, Charles L., Karl J. Reinhard, Matthew Kirk, and Justin DiVirgilio. "Privies and Parasites: The Archaeology of Health Conditions in Albany, New York." *Historical Archaeology* 41 (2007): 172–97.

Forattini, Oswaldo Paulo. "Chagas' Disease and Human Behavior." In *Demography and Vector-Borne Diseases*, edited by Michael W. Service, 107–20. Boca Raton, FL: CRC Press, 1989.

Foster, Kenneth R., Mary F. Jenkins, and Anna Coxe Toogood. "The Philadelphia Yellow Fever Epidemic of 1793." *Scientific American*, August 1998, 91.

Frank, Steven A., and Paul Schmid-Hempel. "Mechanisms of Pathogenesis and the Evolution of Parasite Virulence." *Journal of Evolutionary Biology* 21 (2008): 396–404.

Fraser, Claire M., Steven J. Norris, George M. Weinstock, Owen White, Granger G. Stutton, et al. "Complete Genome Sequence of *Treponema pallidum*, the Syphilis Spirochete." *Science* 281 (1998): 375–88.

Freeman, Scott, and Jon C. Herron. *Evolutionary Analysis*. 4th ed. Saddle River, NJ: Pearson, 2007.

Fritz, Curtis L., David T. Dennis, Margaret A. Tipple, Grant L. Campbell, Charles R. McCance, et al. "Surveillance for Pneumonic Plague in the United States during an International Emergency: A Model for Control of Imported Infectious Diseases." *Emerging Infectious Diseases* 2 (1996): 30–36.

Gallay, Alan. *The Indian Slave Trade*. New Haven, CT: Yale University Press, 2002.

———, ed. *Indian Slavery in Colonial America*. Lincoln: University of Nebraska Press, 2009.

Gates, Louis Henry, and William L. Andrews, eds. "The Life, History and Unparalleled Sufferings of John Jea, the African Preacher." In *Pioneers of the Black Atlantic: Five Slave Narratives from the Enlightenment, 1772–1815*. Washington, DC: Civitas, 1998.

Giacanni, Lorenzo, and Sheila A. Lukehart. "The Endemic Treponematoses." *Clinical Microbiology Reviews* 27 (2014): 89–115.

Gilbert, M. Thomas P., Jon Cuccui, William White, Niels Lynnerup, Richard W. Titball, et al. "Absence of *Yersinia pestis*-Specific DNA in Human Teeth from Five European Excavations of Putative Plague Victims." *Microbiology* 150 (2004): 341–54.

Gottfried, Robert S. *The Black Death: Natural and Human Disaster in Medieval Europe*. New York: Free Press, 1983.

Grainger, Ian, Duncan Hawkins, Lynne Cowal, and Richard Mikulski. *The Black Death Cemetery, East Smithfield, London*. MoLAS Monograph 43. London: Museum of London Archaeology Service, 2008.

Gregg, Charles T. *Plague! The Shocking Story of a Dread Disease in America Today*. New York: Charles Scribner's Sons, 1978.

Grinde, Donald. "Native American Slavery in the Southern Colonies." *Indian Historian* 10, no. 2 (1977): 38–42.

Haensch, Stephanie, Raffaella Bianucci, Michel Signoli, Minoarisoa Rajerison, Michael Schultz, et al. "Distinct Clones of *Yersinia pestis* Caused the Black Death." *PLOS Pathogens* 6, no. 10 (2010): e1001134, www.plospathogens.org.

Harden, Victoria A. "Epidemic Typhus." In *The Cambridge Historical Dictionary of Disease*, edited by Kenneth F. Kiple, 352–55. Cambridge: Cambridge University Press, 2003.

Hardy, Anne. "Scarlet Fever." In *The Cambridge Historical Dictionary of Disease*, edited Kenneth F. Kiple, 288–90. Cambridge: Cambridge University Press, 2003.

Harper, Kristin N., Paolo S. Ocampo, Bret M. Steiner, Robert W. George, Michael S. Silverman, et al. "On the Origin of the Treponematoses: A Phylogenetic Approach." *PlOS Neglected Tropical Diseases* 2 (2008): e 148.

Harper, Kristin N., Molly K. Zuckerman, Megan L. Harper, J. D. Kingston, George J. Armelagos. "The Origin and Antiquity of Syphilis Revisited: An Appraisal of Old World Pre-Columbian Evidence for Treponemal Infection." *Yearbook of Physical Anthropology* 53 (2011): 99–133.

Hays, J. N. *The Burdens of Disease: Epidemics and Human Response in Western History*. New Brunswick, NJ: Rutgers University Press, 1998.

Heck, Dana B., and Joseph F. Balicki. "Katherine Naylor's "House of Office": A Seventeenth-Century Privy." *Historical Archaeology* 32, no. 3 (1998): 24–37.

Henige, David. *Numbers from Nowhere: The American Indian Contact Population Debate*. Norman: University of Oklahoma Press, 1998.

Henneberg, Maciej, and Renata J. Henneberg. "Treponematosis in an Ancient Greek Colony of Metaponto, Southern Italy, 580–250 BCE." In *L'Origine de la syphilis en Europe: Avant ou après 1493?* edited by Olivier Dutour, György Pálfi, Jacques Berato, and Jean-Pierre Brun, 92–98. Paris: Editions Errance, 1994.

Higgins, Rosanne L., and Joyce E. Sirianni. "An Assessment of Health and Mortality of Nineteenth Century Rochester, New York, Using Historic Records and the Highland Park Skeletal Collection." In *Bodies of Evidence: Reconstructing History through Skeletal Analysis*, edited by Anne L. Grauer, 121–36. New York: Wiley-Liss, 1995.

Hoehling, Adolph A. *The Great Epidemic*. Boston: Little, Brown, 1961.

Hoffer, Peter C. *The Brave New World: A History of Early America*. 2nd ed. Baltimore: Johns Hopkins University Press, 2006.

Hopkins, Donald R. *Princes and Peasants: Smallpox in History*. Chicago: University of Chicago Press, 1983.

Horn, James, William Kelso, Douglas Owsley, and Beverly Straube. *Jane: Starvation, Cannibalism, and Endurance at Jamestown*. Williamsburg: Colonial Williamsburg and Preservation Virginia, 2013.

Hrdlička, Aleš. *Tuberculosis among Certain Indian Tribes of the United States*. Washington, DC: U.S. Government Printing Office, 1909.

Hufthammer, Anne K., and Lars Walløe. "Rats Cannot Have Been Intermediate Hosts for *Yersinia pestis* during Medieval Plague Epidemics in Northern Europe." *Journal of Archaeological Science* 40 (2013): 1752–59.

Hulton, Paul. *America 1585: The Complete Drawings of John White*. Chapel Hill: University of North Carolina Press, 1984.

Humphreys, Margaret H. *Malaria: Poverty, Race, and Public Health in the United States.* Baltimore: Johns Hopkins University Press, 2001.

———. "A Stranger in Our Camps: Typhus in American History." *Bulletin of the History of Medicine* 80 (2006): 269–90.

———. *Yellow Fever and the South.* Baltimore: Johns Hopkins University Press, 1992.

Hutchinson, Dale L. *Tatham Mound and the Bioarchaeology of Spanish Contact: Disease and Depopulation in Gulf Coast Florida.* Ripley P. Bullen Series, University of Florida Press, Gainesville, 2006.

———. "Treponematosis in Regional and Chronological Perspective from Central Gulf Coast Florida." *American Journal of Physical Anthropology* 92 (1993): 249–61.

Hutchinson, Dale L., and Lorraine V. Aragon. "Collective Burials and Community Memories: Interpreting the Placement of the Dead in the Mid-Atlantic and Southeastern United States with Reference to Ethnographic Cases from Indonesia." In *The Space and Place of Death,* edited by Helaine Silverman and David Small, 26–54. Arlington, VA: Archaeological Papers of the American Anthropological Association No. 11, 2002.

Hutchinson, Dale L., and Jeffrey M. Mitchem. "Correlates of Contact: Epidemic Disease in Archaeological Context." *Historical Archaeology* 35 (2001): 58–72.

Hutchinson, Dale L., and Rebecca Richman. "Regional, Social, and Evolutionary Perspectives on Treponemal Infection in the Southeastern United States." *American Journal of Physical Anthropology* 129 (2006): 544–58.

Hutchinson, Dale L., Clark Spencer Larsen, Matthew A. Williamson, Victoria D. Green-Clow, and Mary L. Powell. "Temporal and Spatial Variation in the Pattern of Treponematosis in La Florida." In *North American Treponematosis: A Natural History,* edited by Mary Lucas Powell and Della C. Cook, 92–116. Gainesville: University Press of Florida, 2006.

Jackes, Mary K. "The Mortality of Ontario Archaeological Populations." *Canadian Journal of Anthropology* 5, no. 2 (1986): 33–48.

———. "Osteological Evidence for Smallpox: A Possible Case from Seventeenth Century Ontario." *American Journal of Physical Anthropology* 60 (1983): 75–81.

Jankrift, Kay P. "The Language of Plague and Its Regional Perspectives: The Case of Medieval Germany." *Medical History Supplement* 27 (2008): 53–58.

Jellife, E.F.P. "Low Birth-Weight and Malarial Infection of the Placenta." *Bulletin of the World Health Organization* 33 (1968): 69–78.

Karlen, Arno. *Man and Microbes: Disease and Plagues in History and Modern Times.* New York: G. P. Putnam's Sons, 1995.

Karlsson, Gunnar. "Plague without Rats: The Case of Fifteenth-Century Iceland." *Journal of Medieval History* 22 (1996): 263–84.

Keller, Andreas, Angela Graefen, Marcus Ball, Mark Matzas, Valesca Boisguerin, et al. "New Insights into the Tyrolean Iceman's Origin and Phenotype as Inferred by Whole-Genome Sequencing." *Nature Communications* 3 (2012): Article number: 698, doi:10.1038/ncomms1701, 9 pages.

Kelley, Jennifer Olsen, and J. Lawrence Angel. "Life Stresses of Slavery." *American Journal of Physical Anthropology* 74 (1987): 199–211.

Kelso, William M. *Jamestown: The Buried Truth.* Charlottesville: University of Virginia Press, 2006.

———. *Kingsmill Plantations, 1619–1800: Archaeology of Country Life in Colonial Virginia.* New York: Academic Press, 1984.

Kelton, Paul. *Epidemics and Enslavement: Biological Catastrophe in the Native Southeast, 1492–1715.* Lincoln: University of Nebraska Press, 2007.

Kidd, Kenneth K. "The Excavation and Identification of a Huron Ossuary." *American Antiquity* 18 (1953): 359–79.

King, Julia A. "Living and Dying in the 17th Century Chesapeake: Previous Research." In *Living and Dying on the 17th Century Patuxent Frontier*, edited by Julia A. King and Douglas H. Ubelaker, 5–14. Crownsville: Maryland Historic Trust, 1996.

King, Julia A., and Douglas H. Ubelaker. "Living and Dying at Patuxent Point." In *Living and Dying on the 17th Century Patuxent Frontier*, edited by Julia A. King and Douglas H. Ubelaker, 105–17. Crownsville: Maryland Historic Trust, 1996.

Kiple, Kenneth F. *The Cambridge Historical Dictionary of Disease.* Cambridge: Cambridge University Press, 2003.

Kiple, Kenneth F., and Stephen V. Beck, eds. *Biological Consequences of the European Expansion, 1450–1800.* Aldershot, UK: Ashgate, 1997.

Kiple, Kenneth F., and Virginia Himmelsteib King. *Another Dimension to the Black Diaspora: Diet, Disease, and Racism.* Cambridge: Cambridge University Press, 1981.

Kiple, Kenneth F., and Virginia H. Kiple. "Slave Child Mortality: Some Nutritional Answers to a Perennial Puzzle." *Journal of Social History* 10 (1977): 284–309.

Kolman, Connie J., Arturo Centurion-Lara, Sheila A. Lukehart, Douglas W. Owsley, and Noreen Tuross. "Identification of *Treponema pallidum* subspecies pallidum in a 200-Year-Old Skeletal Specimen." *Journal of Infectious Diseases* 180 (1999): 2060–63.

Kovacik, Charles F. "Health Conditions and Town Growth in Colonial and Antebellum South Carolina." *Social Science and Medicine* 12 (1978): 131–36.

Kuhlemann, Ute. "Between Reproduction, Invention and Propaganda: Theodor De Bry's Engravings after John White's Watercolours." In *A New World: England's First View of America*, by Kim Sloan, 79–92. Chapel Hill: University of North Carolina Press, 2007.

Kupperman, Karen. *Roanoke: The Abandoned Colony.* Lanham, MD: Rowman and Littlefield, 2007.

Kurlansky, Mark. *Cod: A Biography of the Fish That Changed the World.* New York: Norton, 1997.

Kuzawa, Christopher W. "Developmental Origins of Life History: Growth, Productivity, and Reproduction." *American Journal of Human Biology* 19 (2007): 654–61.

Larsen, Clark Spencer. "Biological Changes in Human Populations with Agriculture." *Annual Review of Anthropology* 24 (1995): 185–213.

Lauber, Almond Wheeler. *Indian Slavery in Colonial Times within the Present Limits of the United States.* Williamston, MA: Corner House, 1913 [Reprint 1979].

Li, Yu, Darin S. Carroll, Shea N. Gardner, Matthew C. Walsh, Elizabeth A. Vitalis, et al. "On the Origin of Smallpox: Correlating Variola Phylogenetics with Historical Smallpox Records." *Proceedings of the National Academy of Science* 104, (2007): 15787–92.

Liston, Maria A., and Brenda J. Baker. "Reconstructing the Massacre at Fort William Henry, New York." *International Journal of Osteoarchaeology* 6 (1996): 28–41.

Littman, Robert J. "The Plague of Athens: Epidemiology and Paleopathology." *Mt. Sinai Journal of Medicine* 76 (2009): 456–67.

Livingstone, Frank B. "Anthropological Implications of Sickle-Cell Gene Distribution in West Africa." *American Anthropologist* 60 (1958): 533–62.

Mann, Robert W., Douglas W. Owsley, and Paul A. Shackel. "A Reconstruction of 19th-Century Surgical Techniques: Bones in Dr. Thompson's Privy." *Historical Archaeology* 25 (1991): 106–12.

Marcus, Alan I. "The South's Native Foreigners: Hookworm as a Factor in Southern Distinctiveness." In *Disease and Distinctiveness in the American South*, edited by Todd L. Savitt and James Harvey Young, 78–99. Knoxville: University of Tennessee Press, 1988.

Marten, Joel W. "Southeastern Indians and the English Trade in Skins and Slaves." In *The Forgotten Centuries: Indians and Europeans in the American South, 1521–1704*, edited by Charles Hudson and Carmen Chaves Tesser, 304–24. Athens: University of Georgia Press, 1994.

Mascie-Taylor, C. G. Nicholas. "The Biological Anthropology of Disease." In *The Anthropology of Disease*, edited by C. G. Nicholas Mascie-Taylor, 1–72. Oxford: Oxford University Press, 1993.

McDade, Thomas W. "Life History Theory and the Immune System: Steps toward a Human Ecological Immunity." *Yearbook of Physical Anthropology* (2003): 100–125.

McNeill, William H. *Plagues and Peoples.* Garden City, NY: Anchor Books, 1976.

Meade, Melinda S., and Michael Emch. *Medical Geography.* 3rd ed. New York: Guilford, 2010.

Merrell, James H. *The Indian's New World: Catawbas and Their Neighbors from European Contact through the Era of Removal*. New York: W. W. Norton, 1989.

Michelson, Edward H. "Adam's Rib Awry? Women and Schistosomiasis." *Social Science Research and Medicine* 37 (1993): 493–501.

Mielke, James H., Lyle W. Konigsberg, and John H. Relethford. *Human Biological Variation*. 2nd ed. Oxford: Oxford University Press, 2011.

Milanich, Jerald T. "The Devil in the Details: What Are Brazilian War Clubs and Pacific Seashells Doing in 400-Year-Old Engravings of Florida Indians?" *Archaeology* 58, no. 3 (2005): 26–31.

Millet, Nicholas B., Gerald D. Hart, Theodore A. Reyman, Michael R. Zimmerman, and Peter K. Lewin. "ROM I: Mummification for the Common People." In *Mummies, Disease, and Ancient Cultures*, 2nd ed., edited by Aidan Cockburn, Eve Cockburn, and Theodore A. Reyman, 91–105. Cambridge: Cambridge University Press, 1998.

Morse, Dan. *Ancient Disease in the Midwest*. 2nd ed. Illinois State Museum Reports of Investigations No. 15. Springfield: Illinois State Museum, 1978.

———. "Prehistoric Tuberculosis in America." *American Review of Respiratory Diseases* 83 (1961): 489–504.

———. "Tuberculosis." In *Diseases in Antiquity*, edited by Donald R. Brothwell and A. T. Sandison, 249–71. Springfield, IL: C. C. Thomas, 1967.

Mulligan, Connie J., Steven J. Norris, and Sheila A. Lukehart. "Molecular Studies in *Treponema pallidum* Evolution: Toward Clarity?" *PlOS Neglected Tropical Diseases* 2 (2008): e 184, doi: 10.1371.

Nicklisch, Nicole, Frank Maixner, Robert Gansimeier, Susanne Frederick, Veit Dresely, et al. "Rib Lesions in Skeletons from Early Neolithic Sites in Central Germany: On the Trail of Tuberculosis at the Onset of Agriculture." *American Journal of Physical Anthropology* 149 (2012): 391–404.

Nikiforuk, Andrew. *The Fourth Horseman: A Short History of Epidemics, Plagues, Famine, and Other Scourges*. New York: Viking, 1991.

Null, Christopher, Michael L. Blakey, Leslie M. Rankin-Hill, and Selwyn H. H. Carrington. "Osteological Indicators of Infectious Disease and Nutritional Inadequacy." In *The New York African Burial Ground Skeletal Biology Final Report*, vol. 1, edited by Michael L. Blakey and Lesley M. Rankin-Hill, 351–402. Report to the United States General Services Administration, Northeastern and Caribbean Region, 2004 [available online].

Nutton, Vivian. "Introduction: Pestilential Complexities: Understanding Medieval Plague." *Medical History Supplement* 27 (2008): 1–16.

Ostfeld, Richard S. "The Ecology of Lyme-Disease Risk." *American Scientist* 85 (1997): 338–46.

———. *Lyme Disease: The Ecology of a Complex System*. Oxford: Oxford University Press, 2011.

Owsley, Douglas, and Karin Bruwelheide. *Written in Bone.* Minneapolis: LeanTo Press, 2009.

Pálfi, György, Jacques Berato, and Olivier Dutour. "Paléopathologie de la série de Costebelle, Hyères [France], Var (3e–;5e siècles après J.-C.)." In *L'Origine de la syphilis en Europe: Avant ou après 1493?* edited by Olivier Dutour, György Pálfi, Jacques Berato, and Jean-Pierre Brun, 125–32. Paris: Editions Errance, 1998.

Papathanasiou, Anastasia. "Health Status of the Neolithic Population of Alepotrypa Cave, Greece." *American Journal of Physical Anthropology* 126 (2005): 377–90.

Patterson, K. David. "Yellow Fever Epidemics and Mortality in the United States, 1693–1905." *Social Science and Medicine* 34 (1992): 855–65.

———. "Bacillary Dysentery." In *The Cambridge Historical Dictionary of Disease,* edited by Kenneth F. Kiple, 43–44. Cambridge: Cambridge University Press, 2003.

Pavlovsky, Evgeny N., ed. *Natural Foci of Human Infections.* Urbana: University of Illinois Press, 1963.

———. *Natural Nidality of Transmissible Diseases (with Special Reference to the Landscape Epidemiology of Zooanthroponoses).* Urbana: University of Illinois Press, 1966.

Pechenkina, Ekaterina A., Robert A. Benfer Jr., and Wang Zhijun. "Diet and Health Changes at the End of the Chinese Neolithic: The Yangshao/Longshan Transition in Shaanxi Province." *American Journal of Physical Anthropology* 117 (2002): 15–36.

Pelto, Perti. *The Snowmobile Revolution: Technology and Social Change in the Arctic.* Menlo Park, CA: Cummings, 1973.

Peters, Wallace, and Herbert M. Gilles. *Tropical Medicine and Parasitology.* 4th ed. London: Mosby, 1999.

Pollitzer, Robert. *Plague.* Monograph Series 22. Geneva: World Health Organization, 1954.

Porcher, Richard Dwight, Jr., and William Robert Judd. *The Market Preparation of Carolina Rice: An Illustrated History of Innovations in the Lowcountry Rice Kingdom.* Columbia: University of South Carolina Press, 2014.

Powell, Mary L. "Endemic Treponematosis and Tuberculosis in the Prehistoric Southeastern United States: Biological Costs of Chronic Endemic Disease." In *Human Paleopathology: Current Syntheses and Future Options,* edited by Donald J. Ortner and Arthur C. Aufderheide, 173–80. Washington, DC: Smithsonian Institution Press, 1991.

Powell, Mary L., and Della C. Cook, eds. *The Myth of Syphilis: The Natural History of Treponematosis in North America.* Gainesville: University Press of Florida, 2005.

Pusch, Carsten M., Lila Rahalison, Nikolaus Blin, J. N. Graeme, and Alfred Czarnetzki. "Yersinial F1 Antigen and the Cause of Black Death." *Lancet Infectious Disease* 4 (2004): 484–85.

Quinn, David B., ed. *The Roanoke Voyages, 1584–1590*. New York: Dover, 1991.

Rackham, James. "*Rattus rattus*: The Introduction of the Black Rat into Britain." *Antiquity* 53 (1979): 112–20.

Raff, Jennifer, Della C. Cook, and Frederika Kaestle. "Tuberculosis in the New World: A Study of Ribs from the Schild Mississippian Population, West-Central Illinois. *Memórias do Instituto Oswaldo Cruz* 101, supp. 2 (2006): 25–27.

Ramenofsky, Ann. "Diseases of the Americas, 1492–1700." In *The Cambridge World History of Human Disease*, edited by Kenneth F. Kiple, 317–28. Cambridge: Cambridge University Press, 1993.

———. *Vectors of Death: The Archaeology of European Contact*. Albuquerque: University of New Mexico Press, 1987.

Rankin-Hill, Lesley M. *A Biohistory of 19th Century Afro-Americans: The Burial Remains of a Philadelphia Cemetery*. Westport, CT: Bergin and Garvey, 1997.

Rankin-Hill, Lesley M., Michael L. Blakey, Jean E. Howson, Sherrill D. Wilson, E. Brown, et al. "Demographic Overview of the African Burial Ground and Colonial Africans of New York." In *The New York African Burial Ground Skeletal Biology Final Report*, vol. 1, edited by Michael L. Blakey and Lesley M. Rankin-Hill, 266–304. Report to the United States General Services Administration, Northeastern and Caribbean Region [available online], 2004.

Raoult, Didier G., Gérard Aboudharam, Eric Crubézy, Georges Larrouy, Bertrand Ludes, et al. "Molecular Identification by 'Suicide PCR' of *Yersinia pestis* as the Agent of Medieval Black Death." *Proceedings of the National Academy of Sciences* 97 (2000): 12800–803.

Rathbun, Ted A. "Health and Disease at a South Carolina Plantation: 1840–1870." *American Journal of Physical Anthropology* 74 (1987): 239–53.

Rathje, William. *Rubbish! The Archaeology of Garbage*. New York: Harper-Collins, 1992.

Reinhard, Karl J., and Arthur C. Aufderheide. "Diphyllobothriasis in Pre-Columbian Chile and Peru: Adaptive Radiation of a Helminth Species to Native American Populations." Paper presented at the Eighth European Members Meeting of the Paleopathology Association, Cambridge, UK. Abstract, in *Paleopathology Newsletter* 70, supp. (1990): 18.

Roberts, Charlotte A., and Jane E. Buikstra. *The Bioarchaeology of Tuberculosis: A Global View on a Reemerging Disease*. Gainesville: University Press of Florida, 2003.

Roberts, Daniel D., and John P. McCarthy. "Descendant Community Partnering in the Archaeological and Bioanthropological Investigation of African-American Skeletal Populations: Two Interrelated Case Studies from Philadelphia." In *Bodies of Evidence: Reconstructing History through Skeletal Analysis*, edited by Anne L. Grauer, 19–36. New York: Wiley-Liss, 1995.

Rothhammer, Francisco, Marvin J. Allison, Lautaro Nuñez, Vivien Standen, and Bernardo Arriaza. "Chagas' Disease in Pre-Columbian South America." *American Journal of Physical Anthropology* 68 (1985): 495–98.

Ruiz, Alfonso. "Plague in the Americas." *Emerging Infectious Diseases* 7, supp. 3 (2001): 539–40.

Rutman, Darrett B., and Anita H. Rutman. "Of Agues and Fevers: Malaria in the Early Chesapeake." *William and Mary Quarterly* 33, no. 1 (1976): 31–60.

Salo, Wilmar L., Arthur C. Aufderheide, Jane E. Buikstra, and Todd A. Holcomb. "Identification of *Mycobacterium tuberculosis* DNA in a Pre-Columbian Mummy." *Proceedings of the National Academy of Science* 91 (1994): 2091–94.

Sandison, A. T., and Edmund Tapp. "Disease in Ancient Egypt." In *Mummies, Disease, and Ancient Cultures*. 2nd ed., edited by Aidan Cockburn, Eve Cockburn, and Theodore A. Reyman, 38–68. Cambridge: Cambridge University Press, 1998.

Sauer, Carl O. *Sixteenth-Century North America*. Berkeley: University of California Press, 1971.

Savitt, Todd L. *Medicine and Slavery: The Diseases and Health Care of Blacks in Antebellum Virginia*. Urbana: University of Illinois Press, 1978.

Savitt, Todd L., and James Harvey Young, eds. *Disease and Distinctiveness in the American South*. Knoxville: University of Tennessee Press, 1988.

Schmid, Boris V., Ulf Buntgen, W. Ryan Easterday, Christian Ginzler, Lars Walløe, et al. "Climate-Driven Introduction of the Black Death and Successive Plague Reintroductions into Europe." *Proceedings of the National Academy of Sciences* 112 (2015): 3020–25.

Schmid-Hempel, Paul, and Steven A. Frank. "Pathogenesis, Virulence, and Infective Dose." *PLOS Pathogens* 3 (2007): 1372–73.

Schmidt, Danny W., and David M. Givens, prods./dirs. *Jane: Starvation, Cannibalism, and Endurance at Jamestown*. Williamsburg: Colonial Williamsburg Foundation and Preservation Virginia, 2013.

Scott, Susan, and Christopher J. Duncan. *Biology of Plagues: Evidence from Historical Populations*. Cambridge: Cambridge University Press, 2001.

Scrimshaw, Nevin S. "Interactions of Malnutrition and Infection: Advances in Understanding." In *Protein-Calorie Malnutrition*, edited by Robert E. Olson, 353–67. New York: Academic Press, 1975.

Shimkin, Demitri B. "Models for the Downfall: Some Ecological and Culture-Historical Considerations." In *The Classic Maya Collapse,* edited by T. Patrick Culbert, 269–99. Albuquerque: University of New Mexico Press, 1973.

Silver, Timothy. *A New Face on the Countryside: Indians, Colonists, and Slaves in South Atlantic Forests, 1500–1800*. Cambridge: Cambridge University Press, 1990.

Šmajs, David, Steven J. Norris, and George M. Weinstock. "Genetic Diversity in *Treponema pallidum*: Implications for Pathogenesis, Evolution and Molecular

Diagnostics of Syphilis and Yaws." *Infection, Genetics, and Evolution* 12 (2012): 191–202.

Smith, Bruce D. *The Emergence of Agriculture.* New York: W. H. Freeman, 1998.

Smith, Marvin T. *Archaeology of Aboriginal Culture Change in the Interior Southeast.* Gainesville: University Press of Florida, 1987.

Snow, Dean R. "Disease and Population Decline in the Northeast." In *Disease and Demography in the Americas,* edited by John W. Verano and Douglas H. Ubelaker, 177–86. Washington, DC: Smithsonian Institution Press, 1992.

Snyder, Christina. *Slavery in Indian Country: The Changing Face of Captivity in Colonial America.* Cambridge, MA: Harvard University Press, 2010.

Stannard, David E. *American Holocaust: The Conquest of the New World.* Oxford: Oxford University Press, 1992.

Stanwood, Owen. "Captives and Slaves: Indian Labor, Cultural Conversion, and the Plantation Revolution in Virginia." *Virginia Magazine of History and Biography* 114 (2006): 435–63.

Starbuck, David R. *The Great Warpath: British Military Sites from Albany to Crown Point.* Hanover, NH: University Press of New England, 1999.

———. *Massacre at Fort William Henry.* Hanover, NH: University Press of New England, 2002.

Stearns, Steven C. "Issues in Evolutionary Medicine." *American Journal of Human Biology* 17 (2005): 131–40.

Steckel, Richard H. "Birth Weights and Infant Mortality among American Slaves." *Explorations in Economic History* 23 (1986): 173–98.

———. "A Dreadful Childhood: The Excess Mortality of American Slaves." *Social Science History* 10 (1986): 427–65.

———. "A Peculiar Population: The Nutrition, Health, and Mortality of American Slaves from Childhood to Maturity." *Journal of Economic History* 46 (1986): 721–41.

———. "Women, Work, and Health under Plantation Slavery in the United States." In *More Than Chattel: Black Women and Slavery in the Americas,* edited by David Barry Gaspar and Darlene Clark Hine, 43–60. Bloomington: Indiana University Press, 1996.

Stenseth, Nils C., Noelle I. Samia, Hildegunn Viljugrein, Kyrre L. Kausrud, Mike Begon, et al. "Plague Dynamics Are Driven by Climate Variation." *Proceedings of the National Academy of Sciences* 103 (2006):13110–15.

Stevens, Sarah C., and Margaret T. Ordoñez. "Fashionable and Work Shoes from a Nineteenth-Century Boston Privy." *Historical Archaeology* 39 (2005): 9–25.

Sutter, Richard. "Dental Pathologies among Inmates of the Monroe County Poorhouse." In *Bodies of Evidence: Reconstructing History through Skeletal Analysis,* edited by Anne L. Grauer, 185–96. New York: Wiley-Liss, 1995.

Taubenberger, Jeffery K., and Ann H. Reid. "Archaeovirology: Characterization of the 1918 'Spanish' Influenza Pandemic Virus." In *Emerging Pathogens:*

Archaeology, Ecology, and Evolution of Infectious Disease, edited by Charles Greenblatt and Mark Spigelman, 189–202. Oxford: Oxford University Press, 2003.

Taubenberger, Jeffery K., Ann H. Reid, Amy E. Krafft, Karen E. Bijwaard, and Thomas G. Fanning. "Initial Genetic Characterization of the 1918 'Spanish' Influenza Virus." *Science* 275 (1997): 1793–96.

Taylor, Alan. *American Colonies: The Settling of North America*. Viking Penguin Books: New York, 2001.

Tholler, Max. "The Virus." In *Yellow Fever*, edited by George K. Strode, 43–136. New York: McGraw-Hill, 1951.

Thompson, Angela. "To Save the Children: Smallpox Inoculation, Vaccination, and Public Health in Guanajuato, Mexico, 1797–1840." *Americas* 49 (1993): 431–55.

Thornton, Russell. *American Indian Holocaust and Survival: A Population History since 1492*. Norman: University of Oklahoma Press, 1987.

Trigger, Bruce G. *The Children of Aataentsic: A History of the Huron People to 1660*. Reprinted with a new preface from the 1976 edition. Montreal: McGill-Queen's University Press, 1987.

———. "Early Iroquoian Contacts with Europeans." In *The Handbook of North American Indians*, vol. 15, *Northeast*, edited by Bruce G. Trigger, 344–56. Washington, DC: Smithsonian Institution Press, 1978.

———. *Natives and Newcomers: Canada's "Heroic" Reconsidered*. Montreal: McGill-Queen's University Press, 1986.

Truls, Jensen, Andrew E. Cockburn, Paul E. Kaiser, and Donald R. Barnard. "Human Blood-Feeding Rates among Sympatric Sibling Species of *Anopheles quadrimaculatus* in Northern Florida." *American Journal of Tropical Medicine and Hygiene* 54 (1996): 523–24.

Tuchman, Barbara W. *A Distant Mirror: The Calamitous 14th Century*. New York: Alfred A. Knopf, 1984.

Tumpey, Terrence M., Christopher F. Basler, Patricia V. Aguilar, Hui Zeng, Alicia Solórzano, et al. "Characterization of the Reconstructed 1918 Spanish Influenza Pandemic Virus." *Science* 310 (2005): 77–80.

Ubelaker, Douglas H. "North American Indian Population Size, A.D. 1500–1985." *American Journal of Physical Anthropology* 77 (1988): 289–94.

Ubelaker, Douglas H., Erica B. Jones, and Diane B. Landers, eds. *Human Remains from Voegtly Cemetery, Pittsburgh, Pennsylvania*. Smithsonian Contributions to Anthropology, No. 46. Washington, DC: Smithsonian Institution Press, 2003.

Usner, Daniel H., Jr. "Economic Relations in the Southeast until 1783." In *Handbook of North American Indians*, vol. 4, *History of Indian–White Relations*, 391–95, edited by Wilcolm Washburn. Washington, DC: Smithsonian Institution Press, 1988.

Verano, John W., and Douglas H. Ubelaker, eds. *Disease and Demography in the Americas*. Washington, DC: Smithsonian Institution Press, 1992.

Walker, Sally M. *Written in Bone: Buried Bodies of Jamestown and Colonial Maryland*. Minneapolis: Carolrhoda Books, 2009.

Walløe, Lars. "Medieval and Modern Bubonic Plague: Some Clinical Continuities." *Medical History Supplement* 27 (2008): 59–73.

Walter, John, and Roger Schofield. "Famine, Disease and Crisis Mortality in Early Modern Society." In *Famine, Disease and the Social Order in Early Modern Society*, edited by John Walter and Roger Schofield, 1–73. Cambridge: Cambridge University Press, 1989.

Ward, Vincent, dir. *The Navigator: A Medieval Odyssey*. Australian Film Commission, 1988.

Warren, Andrew J. "Landmarks in the Conquest of Yellow Fever." In *Yellow Fever*, edited by George K. Strode, 43–136. New York: McGraw-Hill, 1951.

Webster, Robert G. "Influenza." In *Emerging Viruses*, edited by Stephen S. Morse, 37–45. Oxford: Oxford University Press, 1993.

Webster, Robert G., and Elizabeth Jane Walker. "Influenza: The World Is Teetering on the Edge of a Pandemic That Could Kill a Large Fraction of the Human Population." *American Scientist* 91 (2003): 122–29.

Weiss, Robin A. "Virulence and Pathogenesis." *Trends in Microbiology* 10, no. 7 (2002): 314–17.

Wheaton, Thomas R., Amy Friedlander, and Patrick H. Garrow. *Vaughan and Curriboo Plantations: Studies in Afro-American Archaeology*. Contract report administered by the National Park Service (C-5950-79) and prepared by Soil Systems, Inc., Marietta, Georgia (Project No. 476-91219), 1983.

Wheelis, Mark. "Biological Warfare at the 1346 Siege of Caffa." *Emerging Infectious Diseases* 8 (2002): 971–75.

White, Richard. *The Middle Ground: Indians, Empires, and Republics in the Great Lakes Region, 1650–1815*. Cambridge: Cambridge University Press, 1991.

Wiechmann, Ingrid, and Gisela Grupe. "Detection of *Yersinia pestis* DNA in Two Early Medieval Skeletal Finds from Aschheim (Upper Bavaria, 6th Century A.D.)." *American Journal of Physical Anthropology* 126 (2005): 48–55.

Wiley, Andrea S., and John S. Allen. *Medical Anthropology: A Biocultural Approach*. Oxford: Oxford University Press, 2009.

Williams, Cicely D. "Kwashiorkor: A Nutritional Disease of Children Associated with a Maize Diet." *Lancet* 2 (1935): 1151–52.

Wills, Christopher. *Yellow Fever, Black Goddess: The Coevolution of People and Plagues*. Reading, MA: Addison-Wesley, 1996.

Winslow, Charles-Edward Amory. *The Conquest of Epidemic Disease*. Madison: University of Wisconsin Press, 1980.

Wood, James W., Rebecca J. Ferrell, and Sharon N. Dewitte-Avina. "The Temporal Dynamics of the Fourteenth-Century Black Death: New Evidence from Ecclesiastical Records." *Human Biology* 75 (2003): 427–48.

Wood, Peter H. *Black Majority: Negroes in Colonial South Carolina from 1670 through the Stono Rebellion.* New York: W. W. Norton, 1974.

———. "The Impact of Smallpox on the Native Population of the 18th Century South." *New York State Journal of Medicine* 87 (1987): 30–36.

World Health Organization (WHO). Annex Table 2A, Under-Five Mortality Rates, 2003.

———. "Childhood Stunting: Challenges and Opportunities Report." WHO/NMH/NHD/GRS/14.1, www.who.int, 2014.

Wray, Charles F., Martha L. Sempowski, and Lorraine P. Saunders. *Tram and Cameron: Two Early Contact Period Seneca Sites.* Charles F. Wray Series in Seneca Archaeology, Vol. 2. Rochester, NY: Rochester Museum and Science Center, 1991.

Wray, Charles F., Martha L. Sempowski, Lorraine P. Saunders, and Gian Carlo Cervone. *The Adams and Culbertson Sites.* Charles F. Wray Series in Seneca Archaeology, Vol. 1. Rochester, NY: Rochester Museum and Science Center, 1987.

Young, Martin D., Don E. Eyles, Robert W. Burgess, and Geoffrey M. Jeffery . "Experimental Testing of the Immunity of Negroes to *Plasmodium vivax.*" *Journal of Parasitology* 41 (1955): 315–18.

Zimmerman, Michael R. "Alaskan and Aleutian Mummies." In *Mummies, Disease, and Ancient Cultures,* 2nd ed., edited by Aidan Cockburn, Eve Cockburn, and Theodore A. Reyman, 138–53. Cambridge: Cambridge University Press, 1998.

Zink, Albert R., Erika Molnár, Nasim Motamedi, György Pálfi, Antónia Marcsik, et al. "Molecular History of Tuberculosis from Ancient Mummies and Skeletons." *International Journal of Osteoarchaeology* 17 (2007): 380–91.

Zinsser, Hans. *Rats, Lice, and History.* New York: Little, Brown, 1934.

INDEX

Page numbers in *italics* indicate figures, maps, and tables.

tive peoples in, 61–63; in munitions, 68; in New France, 61. *See also* Deerskin trading; Fur trading; Slave trade, Indian

Translations of representations of past, 8–9

Transmission of disease: cholera, *17*, 175; common cold, 15; connection between water and, 165; influenza, 57; malaria, *16*, 38, 117, 118; measles, 55; mosquitoes and, 118–19, 121, 132, 165–66; overview of, 14–15; plague, 23–26; smallpox, 55; virulence and, 38, 218n2

Transovarial infections, 72

Trauma and wounds, 95–97

Treatise on the Smallpox and Measles (Rhazes), 88

Treponemal diseases, 29–30

Treponema pallidum, 30, 33

Tuberculosis (TB): diagnosis of, 34–35; in New York, 178; Ohio hospital for, *36*; in precolumbian America, 37; thoracic vertebra with lesions from, *35*

Tuscarora War, 77–78

Typhoid fever, 109–11

Typhus, 88, 94–95, 177

Urban disease vectors, 165–66

Urbanism, history of, and disease, 19–23, 26

Vaccination, 90–92, *91*

Variolation, 88–90, 161

Vectors: biological, 16, *16*; definition of, 15–16; fleas as, 24; insects as, 165; mechanical, 16, *17*; mosquitoes as, 118–19, 121, 132, 165–66; ticks as, 71–74; urban disease, 165–66

Venereal syphilis, 29, 30

Victim of Syphilis (Durer), 32

Vietnam, plague in, 25–26

Virginia: early settlements in, 128–29; labor shifts in, 136; stratification in, 129; Tidewater area of, 104–5, *106*, 107–11, 118; tobacco in, 111, 129

Virgin soil epidemics, 28, 37

Virulence: definition of, 28; evolution toward decrease in, 37–38; mode of transmission and, 38, 218n2

Voegtly Cemetery, Pittsburgh, 179–80

War. *See* Conflicts in Americas

Washington, George, 84, 95

Wasting, 138

Water supply: at Jamestown, 108–9; for New York, 158–59; for Philadelphia, 168; transmission of disease and, 165

Westos, 68

White, John: *Fireflies and Gadfly, 7; The Manner of Their Fishing, 6*; paintings of, 3–4; *Pefe porco, 4*; Roanoke colony and, 104; *The Towne of Pomeiooc, 5; The Towne of Secoton, 7*

Williams, Cicely D., 211–12n24

Wills, Christopher, 185

Winthrop, John, 50

Wood, Peter, 114

World War I and influenza, 183, 184, 185

Wren, Christopher, 154

Wyatt, Francis, 109

Xenopsylla cheopis (Oriental rat flea), 24

Yamasee War, 78–80

Yaughan plantation, 143

Yaws, 29, 30

Yellow fever, 164–69

Yersinia pestis, 23, 24, 25

Zoonosis, definition of,

Dale L. Hutchinson is professor of anthropology at the University of North Carolina at Chapel Hill whose teaching and research are focused on the health and nutrition of present and past populations, disease ecology, forensic anthropology, and mortuary archaeology. He is also affiliated at the same institution with the Research Laboratories of Archaeology and the Institute of Arts and Humanities, and is a Fellow of the American Association for the Advancement of Science.